*Ruffles*

and

*Flourishes*

## *Within These Pages*

*Within These Pages*

# *Author's Notes*

When Napoleon Bonaparte was sent into exile and sailed for the Isle of Elba, he asked aloud, "Whatever shall we do in that remote spot? Well, we shall write our memoirs. Work is the scythe of time."

I felt exactly like Napoleon on January 20, 1969, when I went into exile in the upstairs study of my home in Washington. I donned my old blue bathrobe and fuzzy slippers and set out to relive the best years of my life equipped with a manual typewriter of questionable ancestry and a massage chair. I had the foresight to take into exile with me a secretary-researchist, Cynthia Wilson, who had worked with me in the White House. Cynthia had a superb electric typewriter, a straight-backed chair and a salary from me. These factors were a constant glaring reminder that I must *write.*

There were many others who kept me going:

Ken McCormick and Margaret Cousins, at Doubleday, sent encouraging notes. Maggie Cousins, my editor, became an instant soulmate. A Texan by birth, she understands the language of bluebonnets and the Pedernales River. Who can resist an editor who writes, a few days after you start the book, "I hope your fingers are bleeding from beating the typewriter. I am braiding some new thongs into my whip. It has been a week Monday since you finished packing. Where is the manuscript?"

Frances Lewine of the AP, Isabelle Shelton of *The Washington Star* and other newspaper friends paused in the midst of covering the New People long enough to comb their files for a missing quote or date.

Down in Texas, Tom Johnson and Helene Lindow at the Lyndon Johnson Library-to-be answered my telephone inquiries and requests promptly. On Memorial Day, when I needed to check the population of Johnson City, Tom even dispatched Jessie Hunter, curator of the LBJ Boyhood Home, out to the city limits to read the sign: "Population, 854."

Dozens of newspaper friends and former White House staff members, former Vice President Hubert Humphrey and others, such as the Johnson Cabinet, let me pick their brains.

Ervin Duggan, a frequent partner-in-crime in speechwriting, gave up several Monday evenings to read the drafts and help structure my memory, over fried chicken and hot biscuits.

Ruth Jackson, my good-humored housekeeper, fried the chicken and produced other delicacies and kept the stereo playing appropriate background music: the theme song from *Gone With the Wind*, during the Whistlestop chapter, Western music when I wrote about the ranch.

My friend and lawyer, Carol Agger Fortas, guided me through the contract; my banker, Leo Bernstein, kept me solvent.

My husband patiently provided me a dozen green leather scrapbooks of every menu, press clipping and guest list from those five years. As I faced exile with the emotions of saying goodbye to the White House and the desire to write about it, I warned him: "I'm probably going to be very difficult to live with during the next few months."

"So what's new?" he said with a grin.

And, of course, I must thank the former President and Mrs. Johnson, who must have wondered what in thunder I was writing, but who did me the honor of never asking.

When I wrote LBJ for permission to use some of the unpublished pictures taken at the White House, he not only sent them along promptly, but also threw in a few more for laughs, including one I had never seen. In this picture, I am barely visible riding in an antique carriage. What is *highly* visible are the rear ends of the two old gray mares. Thank you, Mr. President!

LIZ CARPENTER

*Washington, The Bahamas, Majorca*
*January 21–July 28, 1969*

# *Cast of Characters*

Liz Carpenter—The Heroine, beautiful, svelte press secretary to the First Lady, advice-giver to Presidents, tireless match-maker, wife of one, mother of two.

Les Carpenter—Keeper of the Hearth, husband of the Heroine, father of two, member of the Fourth Estate.

Lyndon B. Johnson—Hereafter referred to as The President, LBJ, one-time Vice President, You-Know-Who, The Boss, Mrs. Johnson's husband, The Long Arm.

Mrs. Lyndon B. Johnson—Hereafter referred to as the First Lady, Mrs. Johnson, Mrs. J., Lady Bird, LBJ's wife, the Gentle Hand.

Hubert H. Humphrey—Vice President, the Good Humor Man, one-time neighborhood druggist with a prescription for everything.

Lynda Johnson Robb—Older daughter of the President, White House bride number two, wife of Marine Captain Charles Spittal Robb, mother of Baby Lucinda.

Luci Johnson Nugent—Once known as Lucy Johnson, first White House bride in fifty years, wife of Patrick John Nugent, mother of Little Lyn.

Little Lyn—Confidant and adviser to the President, favorite of White House telephone operators.

Yuki—Top dog in the White House, rags-to-riches canine with tree-climbing and singing talents.

Him and Her—Two beagles, recognizable by oversized ears.

Blanco—Shy white collie with schizophrenic personality.

W. Marvin Watson—Special Assistant to the President, holder of the purse strings, also referred to as "The Miser" and, later, Mr. Postmaster General.

Jack Valenti—Appointments Secretary to the President, Jack-of-All-Trades, now president of Motion Picture Association of America.

Bess Abell—White House Social Secretary, the Iron Butterfly, guardian of invitation lists.

Press Secretary to the President:

No. 1: Pierre Salinger

No. 2: George Reedy

No. 3: Bill Moyers

No. 4: George Christian

Dr. Eric Goldman—Intellectual in brief residence, pen pal of Robert Lowell.

Eartha Kitt—Luncheon guest.

Joan Crawford—Dinner guest.

Traphes Bryant—Dog-sitter.

James W. Symington—Ambassador of song and skit.

Richard M. Nixon—LBJ's replacement, thereafter referred to as The President.

Bit Parts:

George Hamilton, a gentleman caller.

George C. Wallace, the only subject was roses.

Lassie, television's best friend, but not Blanco's.

The Shah of Iran, among the palace set, a good host.

Mr. and Mrs. Henry Ford II, safe at any speed.
Herb Alpert, who had brass.
Adele Simpson, a life-saver.
Mary Lasker, who put azaleas within the reach of everyone.
Princess Margaret, who came with her own photographer.
Laurance Rockefeller, who gave General Sherman a cleaning.
Senator Barry Goldwater, not conservative about conservation.
Duke Ellington, with us in concert.
Mrs. Vincent Astor, topped, for once, on Park Avenue.
Carol Channing, a star.
Joe Garagiola, a character.
John Lindsay, a mayor.
Gregory Peck, a dream-boat.
Robert Merrill, who discovered *It Ain't Necessarily So.*

And innumerable Kings, Queens, Prime Ministers and Presidents, both at home and abroad.

Plus a cast of thousands, including the National Security Council, speechwriters, Secret Service, chefs, calligraphers, secretaries, gardeners, the press, a Pakistani camel driver and the American people.

# *Over My Shoulder*

At the end of each day, when I left the White House, I had my own private ritual. I simply had to look back over my shoulder. The house was always beautiful—in autumn, framed through the great elms or, in spring, alive with fountains splashing above a circle of red tulips and grape hyacinths. Even after midnight, when the house fell silent, the Marine Band had gone home, and the cleaning women were coming in, I could sense its strength.

There have been thirty-seven Presidents of the United States, thirty-three First Ladies and innumerable Presidential sons and daughters. There have been thousands of White House staff members and a dozen or more press secretaries. Every four or eight years, the American political system moves them on, and the house fills up again. But until it has happened to you, and suddenly you are outside the fence like any tourist, you are unaware what it was really like to "do time" in the White House.

My time was with the Johnsons, but I suspect that some things don't vary too much from Administration to Administration: the tingling that comes with the first gripping notes of

*Ruffles and Flourishes,* followed by *Hail to the Chief,* those stirring drum rolls and trumpet calls which belong to the President; the satisfaction of a program launched and realized; the pride of country embodied in the man and woman who live there; and the parade of ideas, events and people through the corridors in this first of all houses of America. After you have shared these things, you are never quite the same again.

Many stories can be written about any Administration in the White House—about great decisions of truly earth-shaking significance, and the events which lie behind them. I leave that task to the historians, whose stock in trade is somber analysis. Rather than trying to tell all of the story, I have chosen to share the events that unfolded for me, in a house that is not only a center of the nation's political life, but also the home of a family.

Now I have left my work at the White House. I wrote this book because, once again, I had to look back over my shoulder.

# *The Ecstasy and the Agony*

I was sitting at my desk in the White House, minding *everybody's* business and thoroughly enjoying it, when three sharp buzzes jolted me—a phone call from the 36th President of the United States.

"Liz, if you don't learn to keep your mouth shut"—I could hear the rising fury of a great nation in his voice—"I'm going to give you to the Johnson City Foundation."

"Well, I don't want that to happen, Mr. President," I said, trying to sound nonchalant. "It's a nice place to visit, but I wouldn't want to live there."

I couldn't remember what I had done. Had I enraged some friendly country or precinct? Had I toppled the stock market? How many times had I been through this before?

No doubt it was something in the newspapers again. If only he would stop reading them, life would be a lot simpler. Duller, perhaps, but simpler.

Being a "spokesman" at the White House—or anywhere for that matter—necessarily precludes the admonition to "keep your mouth shut," a requirement of modern communication he seldom accepted. By virtue of your job, you are obliged to speak.

You are the bridge between those two separate worlds: the First Family and the press, the participants and the critics, the hunted and the hounds.

There are some jobs in the United States government which are not nearly as dangerous as being a "spokesman"—2,990,513 jobs, to be exact. Most of the people on the federal payroll join Uncle Sam and spend twenty-five calm, secure years never tempted by controversy nor threatened by the President of the United States. They take *all* their sick leave and vacations with regularity and retire at age sixty-five, none the worse for wear.

Not yours truly. Show me the eye of a bureaucratic storm, and I head right into it.

Working hours? In the LBJ White House, we applied the slogan of the United States Postal Service—neither rain, nor hail, nor sleet, nor the President cutting off the lights could stay us from our appointed rounds.

We came to work early, and if we didn't, we might as well have, because Lyndon Graham Bell himself was on the phone, bolting us out of bed with some gentle wakener, like: "Have you read page three of *The Washington Post*?"

I wasn't the only one who became familiar with the dawn's early light. This Paul Revere of the Capital City would wake up Dean Rusk, Bob McNamara, Henry H. Fowler and all the members of his sleepy staff without apology or shame. History tells us that LBJ got into this habit as a child when he was roused by his father in the early hours each day with the admonition: "Son, every boy in town is out of bed and has an hour's start on you!" Because of this mass insomnia epidemic in the 1920s in Johnson City, the nation collected a lot more for its money from the White House personnel of the Johnson Administration.

The LBJ phone calls would catch people in the most intimate circumstances—shaving, bathing, pulling a new girdle over the kneebones, and well, other ways which somehow won't fit into family literature. Suffice it to say that my husband more than once shouted into the night, "I don't care if he *is* President of the United States! Does he have to butt into *everything?*"

I like Lyndon Johnson. There were days when I could have gladly told him to take a running dive into the Pedernales River—but there was no time I wouldn't have followed him.

We both have roots in rural Texas—I was born in Salado—and that says a lot.

"You're the only one around here," he told me once, in a rare moment of open admiration, "who understands Salado and Johnson City."

He meant this quite literally. Once CBS came down to the LBJ Ranch to film a documentary about President Johnson on the range. With a rancher's pride, he was determined to show his best cattle on camera.

"*Life* magazine came down here the other day, and they didn't know a bull from a milk cow," he said in disgust. "Now if they insist on making this picture, the least we can do is get some of the better cattle on camera. So herd 'em up here."

I found myself behind a lazy bunch of white-faced Herefords, tenderly shooing them toward the CBS cameras. Suddenly, the ranch foreman looked across a two-thousand-pound bull at me and said, "Isn't it wonderful, Liz, to occupy such a high policy position in Washington!"

Not all of my time was spent as a part-time ranch hand. I had left Texas for Washington in 1942—with stars in my eyes and a journalism degree in my suitcase.

I arrived just in time to see the last of the New Deal and, as a cub reporter, record the ups and downs of FDR's jaunty cigarette holder and of wartime Washington.

I stayed to hear the press conferences of Harry S Truman,

who knew how to turn off a questioner with a crisp, "No comment."

I covered General Eisenhower through eight years of relative calm and what we in the press chidingly called glittering "General-ities."

In 1960, I took leave of my reporting job and, some people said, my senses, to help Jack Kennedy and Lyndon B. Johnson get elected.

Actually I enjoyed the change of assignment—answering the questions instead of asking them. My newspaper friends were intrigued with my new role.

"How does it feel, Liz," they asked, "to be walking on one side of the street after walking on the other?"

I thought this frame of reference rather unfortunate—to compare government service to an ancient and dishonorable profession.

My job as Executive Assistant to the Vice President kept me traveling for three years. Then, from December 1963 to January 20, 1969, I watched from the front row as a member of the White House staff.

My title seemed to be clear enough—Press Secretary and Staff Director to the First Lady. But when people asked me to clarify it, I just said, "I help her help him." And that covered everything.

The White House sits—no, pulsates—at 1600 Pennsylvania Avenue in downtown Washington. It is conveniently located within a stone's throw of everyone. And almost everyone does.

There are 18 acres, 132 rooms, a swimming pool, a bomb shelter, but no place to hide. The glare of the world's spotlight never dims.

My years with Lyndon Baines Johnson were anything but placid. They were eventful, frustrating, exhausting, exhilarating, hilarious—in short, the best years of my life. An old friend who served in the Roosevelt Administration warned me, "When you've worked in the White House, the rest of your life is like playing poker for match sticks."

He was right.

The scene of my crime was primarily the East Wing, which housed the First Lady's press office and my St. Francis of Assisi prayer (that's the one where you are big about everything and see love in the midst of turmoil). It had been hastily framed and installed during Luci's engagement. Nearby was the social office, which had a refrigerator and a shower. Social secretaries are expected to work like plowhorses all day and look like butterflies at night. Thus, the shower. There was also the office of the military aides, who appeared sheepishly misplaced when hurriedly ordered to zip up an evening gown as we rushed to our duties in the East Room.

"We're an Army in a goddam boutique," Sergeant Major Bill Gulley said in disgust one day.

The East Wing also housed the family correspondence section which cranked out five thousand letters a week to pen pals who wanted to get out of Vietnam, find out how many teeth Patrick Lyndon Nugent now had, and whether a pink dogwood would grow in Arizona.

The Secret Service had a cubbyhole down the hall and their work was so secret that we didn't even know whether they were working or not. They liked it that way.

There is also a tremendous room where the calligraphers turn their talents to writing invitations in delicate banknote script. A good calligrapher is very hard to find. Many calligraphers are so good at making a fast buck—literally—that they go into counterfeiting and live happily every after. Ours were honest, but I often considered how easy it would be to pay off the national debt, if they just didn't have so many invitations to address, and we had really put our mind to it.

The tour office was also in the East Wing, and through these portals pass ten thousand visitors (Mrs. Johnson would never let us call them tourists) each day to see the ground floor and first floor of the house.

"Does the President *live* here?" they would often ask, which shows how attentively they listened to the guides.

And last, and least, it often seemed, was the payroll office.

I arrived at the White House each day at 8 A.M. My driver picked me up at home at 7:30 and drove me in a shiny black government Mercury, my favorite fringe benefit. When I go to heaven, I've reserved the same car and driver. Richard M. Nixon has pressed him into other service in the interim.

There was always a thrill of anticipation in coming into the White House, because you never knew what kind of challenge the day would hold. I could hear the phones ringing down the hall. My office suite had twelve overworked telephone lines and, even at that early hour, half of them would be lighted up—with an inquisitive reporter on every line.

"How many beagles now in residence? What sex?" This, in the clipped accent of a Manchester *Guardian* reporter long-distance from England.

"Is Lynda meeting George Hamilton to attend the Hollywood premiere? Is it true the President can't stand him?"

"What are the First Lady's plans for Easter? Even off-the-record? What is she doing today? When will we have the text of her Radcliffe speech?" This barrage of questions twice a day from AP and UPI.

"What does it cost the taxpayers to paint the White House —and by the way, when did it become the White House?" That from the history-minded *New York Times*.

*The Washington Star*—checking another rumor that Luci and Pat are expecting. "Are they? If not, why not?"

A tourist—a lady with a Southern accent—calls a complaint

that the azaleas on Pennsylvania Avenue are dying. "Mrs. Johnson should see that they are watered."

Walt Rostow's office wants me at the meeting in the Situation Room at 3 P.M. to discuss the forthcoming visit of the King of Saudi Arabia.

The President's chief speechwriter is on the phone. "Will you gather your Humor Group together and send over a draft for the Gridiron speech? By tomorrow at noon?"

An advance man is calling from a small town in western Minnesota. He has checked out all the landing strips for Mrs. Johnson's next trip. None is large enough to take even an Electra, much less a jet. We'll have to land in South Dakota and take a bus back to Montevideo, Minnesota, for the ceremony there. An extra two hours is involved but we can shorten it by box lunches on the bus.

Two brisk rings—the First Lady's signal. Could I join her on the second floor to go over the plans for next week's trip?

I start out the door. One more call. *Life* magazine has been holding on the fourth line for ten minutes. How about letting them photograph the next State dinner, all of it, from buying the groceries to the moment the President lifts his glass to toast the guest of honor? "No," the *Life* editor argues, "we won't get in the way. We'll even pay for the extra lighting in the dining room." I'll need the President's permission, but I promise to try.

Finally, I am out of the office and on my way to Mrs. Johnson's room, weaving through groups of chattering tourists in the hall. At last I reach the private elevator and ride gratefully up to the peace and quiet of the second floor family quarters.

When I step off the elevator, I hear Mrs. Johnson singing in her room, humming when she loses the words, picking up again when they come to her. This happy sound—something as simple as a woman singing about her daily chores—always came as a surprise to me in this house of history and pressures. The President, spending the morning in the Mansion for a session of memo-reading, is in the next room at his paper work, comfortable with the sound of her voice nearby.

Mrs. Johnson is petite and pretty in a bright red dressing gown—a gift from the President. (He heaps gifts on her, and she always says quite truthfully, "Lyndon indulges me in much more expensive things than I would allow myself.")

Sunshine fills the room. From her window she can look out, past the enormous magnolias planted by Andrew Jackson, past the Washington Monument to the Jefferson Memorial. (It was a view she adored. Shortly after moving in, she pleaded with a maid who was drawing the long heavy curtains at sunset, "Please, don't ever close the light out until the very last ray is gone.")

She looks up and greets me.

"Hello, Miss Liz. I'm getting jittery when I look at the calendar. I've signed up for four speeches for this trip next week. Are you all tied up or can we spend the next hour or so on them?" she says.

Before I can answer, the door opens and the President strides in. I have known him twenty-seven years, but I always have the same reaction that most people have upon seeing him for the first time: He's much taller than his pictures suggest—and better looking. He begins reading over his wife's shoulder, our itinerary for the trip.

She smiles up at him. "Any suggestions?"

"No," he says, "it looks all right. You might want to get the two Senators over here and ask them questions. I'll try to find time to call the governor for you. I doubt if he's very interested in educating poor people. But he might as well know we are."

The phone interrupts and I pick it up. It's the switchboard operator. "Secretary Rusk is trying to reach the President." He takes the phone from me, "Tell the Secretary I'll be in my office in two minutes and talk from there." With that, he says, "I've got to be going," and heads for the Oval Office and another day filled with burdens.

"Poor blessed man," Mrs. Johnson said, "he hardly slept at all last night. He was on the phone to the Situation Room from 2 A.M. on."

Thus began a typical day at the White House, for him, for her and for one press secretary.

For LBJ and all of us who served him, there were 1887 action-crowded days and 45,288 hours, day and night.

"Full of peaks and depths. Rugged and exciting," as Mrs. Johnson put it.

For me, those days meant being perpetually on a precipice—spine-tingling, thrilling, never sure what would happen next. My duties were "elastic," as Mrs. Johnson once explained, and I sometimes felt in a two-way stretch—working as I did for both him and her.

My job kept me matching wits with swarms of my old colleagues in the press who were interested in everything from Chiefs of State to chefs of kitchen, from the Presidential daughters to the Presidential dogs.

Stately, glistening white, the great House fans out with East and West Wings filled with offices. They are tied to it physically, professionally and emotionally. There labor the advisers and aides, the speechwriters and secretaries, the expert and not-so-expert, clerks and calligraphers, the President's pilot and his cook, not to mention the President himself.

Nerve center of the West Wing is the Situation Room whose electronic fingers reach out to every spot on the globe.

Lights burn there around the clock. The hotline hookup through the Pentagon ties the Soviet Union to this House. Once, during the Kennedy Administration, a man with a hoe, while weeding the Rose Garden, cut the electronic cable in two and for a few nervous hours, the lines in the President's office were out of service.

This simple pastoral error in tilling the soil is all the more surprising in view of the highly sensitive wiring of the House. Hundreds of complicated devices to detect possible bombs alert the Secret Service. On one occasion, a White House secretary who had undergone medical tests with radioactive materials for a thyroid condition set off the alarm system. In moments, she found herself surrounded by suspicious agents and a White House policeman with his pistol removed from its holster.

The division of duties between West and East Wing is simply this: the West Wing serves the President; the East Wing serves the President and the First Lady. Offices and people are located according to their tasks. In the West Wing is the President's Oval Office, where each President has left his mark. During LBJ's time, the office had three television sets and a telephone with forty-two buttons. A reminder of President Eisenhower can be found near the door to the garden—a series of small holes in the floor, made by his cleated golf shoes. The historic marks have been carefully preserved. Nearby the President's office are the suites of his special assistants and his press secretary, crowding the West Wing. The Presidential aides jockeyed for space, and space was at a premium. In fact, every time one of the President's assistants deigned to come over to our side of the House, I was always afraid he wanted to confiscate some of our larger offices.

In the most prominent location in the West Wing is the press lounge, more spacious than gracious. In the basement is the Staff Mess, where top staff lunch, and a one-chair barbershop—

a convenience for those Presidents fortunate enough to have hair.

It wasn't an uncommon sight to see the President in the barber chair, giving orders to a retinue of aides, while Steve Martini clipped away. LBJ did some of his best thinking in the barber chair, and he didn't like to waste the time when he could be getting on with a speech, or a decision.

The White House is the end point for several thousand telephone and telegraph lines—and, at any one time, for thousands of urgent problems. The House—and the office of the Presidency—are the focus of the hopes, fears and frustrations of millions of people. That's what Harry S Truman meant when he said, "The buck stops here."

But no one can work there without losing part of her heart to it. And occasionally her hide. I loved it, every minute of my five years.

I wasn't the President's favorite employee. I wasn't his *least* favorite either. And I was far from his most intimate adviser.

Well, not *very* far from her.

My usual method of operation with the President was to write memos filled with candid suggestions—more than anyone could say grace over. At the day's end, I would slip quietly into his empty room and leave my memos conspicuously on the President's bedside table—then, stay out of range until an answer came by phone or note. Such things as "No! LBJ" or "Okay, good idea!" could squelch or set a whole trip or project in motion. Sometimes the directions were more explicit. Sometimes there was no answer at all.

I tried to tell him what I thought he ought to know—ignoring the delicacies. In answer to one of my more fiery suggestions about his handling of the press, LBJ scribbled across the memo, "For the present this is all right, but I *do* reserve the right to act in accordance with both *my* decisions and *my* better judgment." *Just because he was President!*

Actually, I think he liked the nerve of some of my memos. My style contrasted with that of the more timid types who didn't write memos and who would stand motionless, or just nod agreement, under the pressure of Johnson's powerful personality.

"Liz would charge hell with a bucket of water," he told a columnist friend who is something of a hell-charger.

Lyndon Johnson understood Washington with a Westerner's disdain for status symbols. So did I. When I first came to the White House, I listened to the Ivy League aides place-drop such fancy addresses as Martha's Vineyard—all the time thinking it was some woman's wine factory!

Both the Johnsons reflected the land that nurtured them. She had been reared in the rich plantation country of deep East Texas, and she was gentle and serene as the cypress trees there—quiet, deep-rooted, protected. The President was as strong and open as the weather-worn hills of West Texas. His was the land of wide skies and white caliche, limestone clay soil and men of uncomplaining determination.

Unashamed, Lyndon Johnson wore his heart on his sleeve. Once when Lynda was elected to the honorary society at the University of Texas—by earning three A's in her freshman year—he stopped by Austin to see her on his return from a speech in California. He carried two big boxes of clothes—slacks, casual dresses and evening gowns. While the delighted Lynda modeled them, he watched—and then, with all the feeling that fathers so seldom put into words, he exclaimed, "I love you so much!"

He brought the same open, exuberant and sentimental spirit to his official duties. He felt poverty right to the pit of his stomach, and he could make others feel it, too.

One hot July day, I stood in the back of the East Room and thrilled as I heard him tell the press and the world, "When I was a boy in Texas, there was so much poverty around us, we didn't know it had a name."

I watched him give it a name and a program. I sat in the Red Room of the White House with the First Lady, Sargent Shriver and a group of advisers when they hammered out the War on Poverty—weapon after weapon: the Job Corps, Head Start, all of the hopeful gambles aimed to lift people off the dole. Time and again, I heard the First Lady ask, "Will it work?" The answer usually was, "It's worth trying." From these meetings came the giant effort which helped lift 13,000,000 people out of poverty in five short years.

If you are a child of the depression like me—if you saw the parade of men who were out of work in the early 1930s, if you remember hearing a jobless man knock at your door and ask to rake leaves, or sweep the steps, or do anything—just for a meal, or a bit of change—you can realize what it meant to me to live through those exciting White House days.

That meeting in the Red Room—one of many which launched the War on Poverty—was a high point of my five years at the White House.

The low points sometimes came when I had to do the talking—when I had to face five hundred news-hungry reporters knowing that a mistake could be heard round the world—or worse, could be read by the President. Although I had often repeated, as blithely as the next journalist, the old line, "Washington is the only asylum run by its own inmates," no amount of preparation, no journalism school, no reporting experience could have prepared me for such events as the resignation of a temperamental French chef, the life and times of Presidential beagles, plus the day Eartha Kitt came to lunch and stayed too long. Even the most stable reporters became unglued and demanding, for example, when Luci Johnson announced her plans to marry. For eight months reporters attacked me with shrill questions on everything from the design of the bride's blue garter to the recipe for her wedding cake. The Perils of Pauline were pale compared to my cliff-hanging life with Luci and her press following.

The White House wedding bells began to ring and the whole country wanted to get into the act. When a Boston labor organizer discovered that Luci's dress would bear no union label, Dave Dubinsky, the passionate, longtime leader of the garment workers' union and devoted friend of LBJ, called the President and cried.

The President rang me and roared, "If there is a mistake that hasn't been made in this wedding, it's because you haven't thought of it!"

We made peace with the union.

By the time the last bit of rice had been thrown, and Luci and Pat Nugent were safely off to a honeymoon in Nassau, I was almost a stretcher case. I was ready to board the first plane to Bermuda, swearing never to answer another question except, "What do you want to drink?"

Just as we were leaving for the airport, the phone rang. It was the President, and he was purring. "Liz, the whole thing couldn't have been more perfect. It was just great. You took more hell than anyone. But then, you should have, because you're in the Hell Department."

I melted, tore up my letter of reisgnation and recuperated in Bermuda.

It is the Hell Department. What else? When your job is to keep reporters happy and the First Family unscathed, you learn to walk between raindrops.

# *Up from Texas*

It was simply a matter of love at first sight.

Below the plane window, the city lay there in the night, twinkling like a necklace of diamonds along the black ribbon of the Potomac. That great sweeping, white marble, magnificent city of monuments and circles!

World War II had put lines on the face of Washington. But the excitement and majesty were there.

On the drive in from the airport, I circled half-round the Lincoln Memorial and found it irresistible. So I stopped the car and raced up the steps to the top. The Lincoln Memorial is a temple, even more beautiful in the shadowed blue lights of the war. I defy anyone to stand there without a prayer. To this day I cannot, and it is twenty-seven years later.

What does it hold, this Washington that I loved? Beauty, intrigue, the in-the-know luncheons, the breathless waiting through a tight vote on Capitol Hill, the bartering in the cloakrooms of Congress, the over-the-shrimp-bowl gossip at five.

If you are young, and a reporter—and I was—there is no escape. The mood is there. The city is yours. And you become a part of it. It is the power and the glory. Listening post of

American politics. Trumpets for a Head of State. Revolving door for the free world!

Speaker Sam Rayburn, who ran the House of Representatives like a Puritan father—and got results—once said to Lady Bird Johnson as they admired the handsome white Capitol dome, "Lady Bird, how do you like *my* building?"

"Arrogant?" she philosophized when she told me about it later. "How can you say a man is arrogant who gave forty years of his life to that building?"

This sense of possessiveness makes Washington intensely personal. It became mine, as a cub reporter, fresh from Journalism School at the University of Texas and remained so for five Presidents, one husband and two children.

Wartime Washington was expensive. And a girl reporter's salary of $25 a week didn't go far. I wired home for help with the threat, IF YOU DON'T SEND MONEY, I'LL HAVE TO SELL MY BODY TO THE SMITHSONIAN.

My down-to-earth brother, George, wired back, SELL IT BY THE POUND. But he sent the money.

That's my family—easygoing, happy-hearted, Protestant stock. My mother, who inherited a library of classics brought to Texas by wagon from Tennessee before 1836, blessed us all with a gift of poetry and wit and inner calm. (My inner calm was the first to go!) My father, blunt, optimistic, an Al Smith Democrat, worked hard to help his five children "amount to sumpthin'." Always for the underdog, he had few prejudices, but one of them was Oklahoma. I never knew why.

"Never trust a man from Oklahoma," he admonished me. With that, he wiped out a whole state. My mother followed it up with, "Never marry a German." She wiped out a whole country.

My early childhood had been spent in Bell County, Texas—one of those rocky rural Central Texas counties the depression hit hard. You can still run against Herbert Hoover there and win. About the only event which broke the monotony were the infrequent meetings of the Children of the Confederacy.

Years later when I campaigned with the Johnsons in the black ghetto areas, I wondered how the militants would react if they knew a "Child of the Confederacy" was among them. But I was less than six at the time I signed up, and it was the respectable thing to do if you had any ancestors in the Army of the Gray. I did—in abundance.

The small towns of Salado and Belton seemed listless then, but I am ever in their debt. The Homeplace built and occupied by my forebears for six generations cast a spell upon all those it had touched. For me, it is still like the rose petals in a lovely old earthenware jar. Every corner is fragrant with memories. Dozens of cousins on pallets in the summertime, reading the worn old books in *The Little Colonel* series, the cool dignity of the old parlor where my mother and father were married. Cleaning out the spring so the watercress could grow free. Cutting down your own cedar tree in the back pasture for Christmas. Feeding baby lambs in spring with a bottle. My uncle saddling up the tamest mare so I could ride to Norwood's Store for the mail!

The enchantment came later. At the time, I felt an emptiness as I watched the cars speed down the highway on to Austin, the state capital, home of the University of Texas, and I knew new horizons lay beyond.

When the oldest son, my brother Tommy, was college age, my mother packed us all up and we moved to Austin so she could put her children through "The University." I adored my college years and got involved in everything political and journalistic. I became the first girl vice president of the student body, and fell in love all before graduation.

But the object of my affection, Leslie Carpenter, was headed for the U. S. Navy and letters from my brother, Tommy, now in Washington convinced me that Washington was what I wanted. And perhaps that is why my parents dug down deep when I got my degree from college, furnished the $250 to send me to Washington to seek my future. So, Washington it was.

To a young girl fresh from Texas, the National Press Building looked lively but frightening. Like a magnet, it pulled me. I put on my best clothes, took my scrapbook of clippings, and timidly began knocking on its doors for a job.

Opportunity came in the form of a dynamic blond newswoman from Michigan who looked like Brunhild and was known as "The Duchess." Esther Van Wagoner Tufty hired me as assistant everything—reporter, secretary, bartender. Her news bureau gave me a press pass that took me everywhere. I began to meet the city and know its temperaments.

Washington mirrors the personality of its Presidents. The papers in the incoming and outgoing boxes move in rhythm with the President's pace. I saw it best when—after the long war years of rationing and restrictions—Dwight Eisenhower came in. The people were sick of government and regulations and the Democrats. They wanted out on the golf course, and Ike led the way.

With Kennedy, the whole town became hyperthyroid—action, movement, youth—up and down perhaps, but movement. With Johnson, we matured and we were on the phone, getting the necessary bills to Congress, getting most of them through.

Those early years of pounding the pavement on Capitol Hill served me well. For one thing, I learned the power of those magic words, "White House calling."

I was writing a tender little column called "Southern Accents in Washington" with my Texas friend, Jean Begeman. We were sharing an office with a conglomeration of people washed into Washington by the war.

Across from my desk sat one Mr. George Whitehouse, salesman for an efficiency supply company, a firm which sold paper clips and file cabinets to the mushrooming government agencies.

"That's the third time it's happened to me today," Mr. Whitehouse said one morning, hanging up the phone in wonder.

"What happened?" I asked.

"I called the War Production Board to try to sell them some supplies. I opened the conversation by saying, 'Whitehouse calling.' First thing I knew the operator had switched me to the head of the agency, and I was talking directly to Administrator Donald Nelson himself."

Later, I realized Mr. Whitehouse should never have left Washington after the war. He could have made the most of his name for years.

Thrilling as Washington was, it didn't compare with the excitement that accompanied letters and phone calls from Les, soon to finish sea duty and be stationed in the Philadelphia Naval District. I don't remember that he really ever asked me to marry him. We both just assumed we would. For me, I knew that if I didn't marry him, I would always feel I'd missed the boat. So, on June 17, 1944, we married in a chapel of Washington's National Cathedral with a hundred friends present, mostly Texans-in-Washington. Two of those friends were my Congressman from home and his wife, Representative and Mrs. Lyndon B. Johnson. I didn't know them well then, but it was a characteristic gesture, as I later discovered. To him, we were a couple of young people from his home district who happened to be two thousand miles away from our parents in the middle of the war. He didn't want us to be alone at that big moment. And so he came, offering congratulations to us, cheering us on our way—to Philadelphia where Les was stationed and where we lived for a year and a half. I stayed in our tiny apartment for all of two weeks before I finished cooking all the recipes in the *Better Homes and Gardens Cookbook.* I couldn't stand the day-long solitude or making apple crisp one more time; so I got a job with the United Press, covering everything from the Securities and Exchange Commission to a Philadelphia streetcar strike.

When the war ended, and Les had completed his Navy duty in 1945, Washington beckoned us back. For us, there was simply no other place. He quickly landed a reporting job with the Bascom Timmons News Bureau, later founding his own news bureau.

Children we wanted, and children we got. In 1946, I was headed for the obstetrician. Two in three years. A son Scott, and a daughter Christy—gorgeous if I say so myself. Deep brown eyes like their father. Long and lean like their father. In fact, everything like their father. He got the by-line, and I did all the work.

However, raising children while working for a dozen newspapers is no way to grow old gracefully. Rapidly, but not gracefully.

I was covering Capitol Hill at the time, and while I had expected Congress to acknowledge my condition and go home in time for these youngsters to be born "sine die" or some such thing, it was still filibustering when I was seven, eight, then nine months pregnant. My brother Tommy came to town while I was still out on my beat, unattractively oversized. He took one look at me and said, "For God's sake, go home. You look like you're with the Communist *Daily Worker*."

There is something in the modern superwoman that wants to do everything at once—bear children, talk to Congressmen, and even dictate news stories from her hospital bed. I don't know why I thought I personally had to break the news of every new postmaster or upstream dam in the Southwest or phone in a show biz story to *Variety,* but that is the kind of female I am.

Our children seemed to thrive on it. They grew up from toddlers through their teens knowing how to answer long distance phone calls and get the information right.

It wasn't unusual to come home after they were asleep and find a message in childlike handwriting, "Jerry Jones of the Arkansaw Gazzette (sic) wants you to check wire serrvices (sic) story that Brooks Haze (sic) will be named to State Deptment job."

They are bright, sharp kids and some of the credit must go to what the psychologists call "healthy neglect." The mixture of being mom, reporter and organization woman builds maternal character—I guess. The year I was president of the Women's National Press Club, Les and I were invited to our first White House dinner. President Eisenhower was host, and I was thrilled to the top of my long white gloves.

Les confessed later that he had made only one known faux pas during dinner. Being a Southern-born boy, when they passed the hollandaise sauce, he thought it was cream gravy. So he put it on his filet mignon. He realized his mistake when he caught a horrified gleam in the eye of his dinner partner. "I'm funny about food," Les said recovering. "I always have liked hollandaise sauce on my meat." After the dinner, the ladies gathered in the adjoining room. One Republican lady with a diamond tiara, Mrs. Laura Gross, stated for all to hear: "It's been twenty-four years since I've been in the White House—twenty-four long, horrible years." The evening was sparkling champagne all the way, and I came home with stars in my eyes.

Came morning—Christy had a raging fever and volcanic

stomach. It was *my* turn to be Den Mother for Scott's cub scout troop. When I hurried down with the bedsheets to the washing machine, I found the basement floor was flooded by most of the Potomac. Our pet dachshund, Mitzi, had done her share by breaking training. Meanwhile, the troop of cub scouts had arrived at the front door with their orange juice cans, and twine, to "do crafts."

Well, it does build character!

As the children have grown older (they are now in college), I have asked them if they thought this childhood left them scarred. They assure me it hadn't, but they feel it left me scarred in the brain—for I am chronically absent-minded about vital family statistics. They love to recount the time "that Mommy took Christy to a Book Fair and asked for a book for a twelve-year-old child."

Christy kept tugging at my dress. "But Mommy, I'm only ten!"

Or the time we had our dog at the vet's for three weeks, and I dashed by to pick her up on my way home from work. She had lost so much weight and looked so small that I reproached myself all the way home for leaving that poor affectionate dog with a coldhearted vet. I kept apologizing to her with endearing words. "Oh, Mitzi, I am so sorry. Please forgive me, Mitzi. Never again, Mitzi." She didn't even give me a nod.

At home, the kids came tumbling out of the house to greet Mitzi, took one look at this shrunken shell of a dog, and shrieked, "Mommy, that's not Mitzi."

I dashed to the phone to call the vet. Sure enough, the "rather overweight dachshund" was still there. The vet had given me the wrong dog, and I had taken it.

The children forgave me for not knowing my own dog.

"That's Mommy for you," one of them told the other. But some of my dog-loving friends remain chilly to this day.

There was also the matter of remembering gifts for special occasions. It is very frustrating and downright irritating to be married to a man who has never once—not once—forgotten to produce beautiful packages for me on birthdays, anniversaries, Mother's Day, St. Valentine's—even, occasionally, Groundhog Day. This is particularly annoying when you remember *his* special days ten minutes before the stores close on Saturday night. That's how we ended up with Jesus in our garden instead of St. Francis of Assisi. An enthusiastic weekend gardener, my husband had been wanting St. Francis for some time. He had just the spot for the bird-loving saint at the foot of the ivy-covered bird bath. And I wanted to give it to him on Father's Day. Wouldn't you think that the merchants of Washington would stock St. Francis? After a mad dash to two or three florist shops, and only a few minutes to spare, I located hundreds of garden-sized saints at a department store. I bought one. I had barely gotten into the car when my daughter spied it and screamed in disdain, "Mommy, that's not St. Francis. That's Jesus."

For one brief moment, I considered going back. But somehow I just couldn't exchange Jesus. My hymn-singing Protestant conscience wouldn't let me turn Him in. So, Jesus has been in our garden at the foot of the bird bath for ten years now.

Working and raising a family has another side effect. Those who try it develop raging guilt complexes. At least, I did. So I was forever trying to make the most of the time I was home. As a result, I generally overdid it.

I never missed a PTA meeting. I programed too much and, instead of just taking it easy like any run-of-the-mill mother, I tried to be supermother when I was there.

Christmas was always my downfall. I'm overly sentimental anyway, and I felt my city-bred offspring needed some old-fashioned James Whitcomb Riley Christmases like I used to have. So we would have Christmas *projects*. One year it was making Yule logs for everyone from Mamie Eisenhower and Perle Mesta to the postman. We soaked old logs in kerosene, tied boughs of cedar on the logs, sprayed frosted tips, decorated with pine cones, and a red bow. And wrote a poem to go with it! I was in seventh heaven. The children grimly went through the paces.

Another Christmas, we made pound cakes because I felt that the smells of Christmas were important. We must have made seventy-five, and I burned up twenty. On Christmas Eve, I drove the children around to friends and neighbors to deliver something "from our pantry to yours." The kids groaned, particularly when I made them carry sleigh bells. And Christy, who was born more sophisticated than Greta Garbo, was vocal about her contempt. "How corny can you get, Mother?" she would complain as she reluctantly delivered cakes.

Scott was more sympathetic. He liked projects, too. In fact, he decided that he would like to have a newspaper route, delivering *The Washington Evening Star*. If you have never shared a delivery route with your son, you have missed one of the most poignant periods of a mother-son relationship, or, at least, I think it was poignant.

Weekdays, the *Star* is a respectable, easy to handle *afternoon* paper. Scott could handle the whole thing at a decent hour—5 P.M. But Sundays, it was delivered by early morning—"Before 7 A.M." was the request. And the newspaper was so heavy that no one except the Marquis de Sade could make a small boy crawl out into the cold morning and carry those pounds and pounds of newspapers alone.

So every Sunday it was Mom at the wheel of the car, and

Scott would trudge to the front doors with the *Sunday Star* in hand. By daylight, we met the neighborhood, who were often in pajamas. You find out a lot about your neighborhood between 6 and 7 A.M. In ours, the early risers were the Catholics and the retired Army generals. The Catholics were on their way to church, and the Army generals—accustomed to a lifetime of early reveille—were furiously pacing the front walk waiting for the paper.

Ruefully, I reflected that all week long I was writing for newspapers, and Sunday I was carrying them house to house. But it gave me a new respect for the industry. It is the last one on earth, I daresay, that depends on a small boy to reach the consumer with the end product.

After a winter of this, and when Scott had banked all he needed to reach his goal of $100, he came home one afternoon and said happily, "Well, I resigned today from my paper route."

"Why?" I asked, trying to hide my delight.

"I just told the manager the job was too hard on my mother."

I felt as though I had been sprung from prison. But I managed to keep control and say, "Well, I really enjoyed it, son. I'll miss those Sunday mornings."

To be a working mother, you need three vital ingredients: a husband who wants you to be a working mother, good help and saintly neighbors.

I was blessed with all three. Les always encouraged me to share "the real world, his world." Fortunately, I had two great ample-bosomed Negro women from North Carolina to help me through all twenty years of raising kids. First Gladys Francis, and then Ruth Jackson. Both possessed the love and affection of Mammy in *Gone With the Wind,* and I paid them the wages of an NAACP organizer. It worked well. I love them dearly, and my children were blessed with their high standards, warm hearts and home cooking. We enjoyed soul food long before it was fashionable.

My neighbors—Ruth Shook and Jean Douglas—enjoyed my various careers—and were great about hurried phone calls in an emergency. As Christy bluntly put it, "They would always come get us if we puked at school." Ruth Shook is one of the few women in the world who is a superb career homemaker. I bless her. I envy her. I admire anyone who can unleash her creativity on her own home instead of the country at large. I can't. Saturdays and Sundays, *yes!* But not seven days a week. Occasionally, there were moments when I felt that I let those in my family down. But then there are those moments of reward. My daughter returns from a series of saccharine-flavored wedding showers for a friend. She has met a whole roomful of my friends—women my age who stayed home and raised their families in a normal way.

"I'm never going to another one!" she storms. "You just wouldn't believe the conversation! Every little detail about Johnny's girlfriend, a tuna casserole, their little ailments. The least they could do is to take some graduate courses so they can converse intelligently!"

I breathed a sigh of relief. If I had a guilt complex, she wiped it out.

When the 1960 political conventions rolled around, we took the children with us. First to Los Angeles, where our longtime friend and Senator, Lyndon Johnson, surprised everyone by accepting the Vice Presidential spot on the ticket with John F. Kennedy. It was a surprise because as majority leader, Johnson had been number one Democrat in a position of power. He'd made a hard last-minute try to get the nomination as President, and found that delegate strength does not rest with U. S. Senators, but with Governors. First ballot results—Kennedy, 806 votes, Johnson, 409.

After Los Angeles, we went on to Chicago to cover the Republican National Convention and see them produce the Nixon-Lodge ticket.

I was sitting in the Conrad Hilton Hotel beauty shop trying to recover from two weeks of smoke-filled rooms when a call came from the LBJ Ranch. It was Mrs. Johnson.

"Lyndon asked me to call you, Liz, and see if you could take off from your newspapers until after the election. We'd like you to share the great adventure of our lives."

My heart leaped, but I asked for time to think about it. For three days I thought of nothing else, day or night. One fear kept plaguing me as I wrestled to a decision—my fear of flying. You see, I just hate to fly. Hardships I can bear, but get me more than two feet off the ground and my palms perspire, my blood pressure rises, and I search frantically for the emergency exits. I hate myself for it, but I am that way. And I knew very well that in political campaigns you fly—and fly and fly.

Everyone in the family thought I should accept. It was too great an opportunity to miss, but they were sympathetic about my cowardice.

Finally, our son, Scott, philosophical at age fourteen, cinched the decision.

"Just look at it this way, Mom," he said. "There never has been a bird that crash-landed. And you'll be flying with Lady Bird."

With a child like that, how could I say no?

Somehow the Lord and Lyndon Johnson gave me courage. We flew. I survived. We won. And by this time, I was a willing captive of politics. The great adventure was well underway. Already I had made one discovery. It was more dangerous to be a participant than a critic, but it was infinitely more satisfying.

# *The Long Arm*

When I joined the Johnson staff, I had known the Johnsons nearly twenty years as reporter and as friend. For all those twenty years, and ever since, I have pondered the question asked me by so many people: What is Lyndon Johnson like? What is he *really* like?

I wonder. How do you measure what a man—especially a public figure—is *really* like? We can list his public actions, the causes he has championed; we can pile up dates, statistics, quotations. That's the accountant's method.

But mostly, I think, we come to know a person through moments—some great, some small. We gain impressions from little bits of evidence—a few words, a letter, a chance remark. Then the moments—the scraps and memories—take shape and begin to form a pattern.

When I think of Lyndon Johnson, I always seem to see a Long Arm—reaching out to pick up a telephone, to grab a sheaf of papers, to shake hands, to embrace, to comfort, to persuade, sometimes even to shove—but always to include, yes, always to include.

More than any man I ever met, he was a creature of

unabashed sentiment. And he reserved the right to be impromptu about appearances, parties and remembrances.

"Women and servants like to be able to plan ahead," Mrs. Johnson often observed. But she never tried to fence him in with a routine or a schedule, or a forced commitment ahead of time. Those of us who worked with him learned to stay fluid. And we even came to accept the game of matching our capabilities to the instant happening.

Few in the press were as good-humored about this quality as Bonnie Angelo of *Time* magazine, who said with a giggle, "When I come to work in the morning, I don't know whether I'm going to spend the day in the West Wing or West Texas."

Those of us close to him collected our Johnson legends—enjoyed them and embellished them. Bill Moyers, a special assistant and later press secretary to the President, tried to joke about it once to a group of editors.

"I'm glad to be here today," Moyers told them. "At the last minute the President changed his schedule rather suddenly and I almost had to cancel. He has a way of doing that. Not too long ago, he telephoned me in my office and said, 'Bill, I'm going to Honolulu.' I said: 'Fine, Mr. President; I'll come over and talk to you about it. Where are you?' He said: 'Over Los Angeles.'"

But most reporters whose lives and wives were tied to the activities of one man, namely the President of the United States, were not amused.

Just why he had this quirk, never to divulge his plans ahead of time, was explained to me once when I was urging him to release his forthcoming plans to visit a certain city.

"I'm just not going to do it," he said firmly. "I went to see a politician once and he never showed up. I was a young fellow working in Johnson City, and I heard that Governor Dan Moody was coming to New Braunfels. So I got someone to take over my job, and I took the day off. I went there and I waited all day. He didn't come. I was deeply disappointed, and I don't want to disappoint people."

Frustrating though it was, this trait gave spice to the job. I loved it the morning it was snowing—the first snow of the season—and he looked out the White House window and said, "Let's have Congress down this afternoon."

All day we scurried around getting ready. The blanket invitation was delivered from the rostrum of the House and Senate. The reception with refreshments and music was held for more than a thousand people. Congress was charmed. LBJ was pleased. We were hysterical over the hilarious operation.

There was also the matter of Christmas. At Christmas, LBJ makes Santa Claus look like Scrooge. He wants everyone remembered.

In fact, once he even *bought* Santa Claus. It was the year he was elected to the Senate—LBJ, that is. Several of his staff and newspaper friends and their children were gathered at his home on Christmas Eve for a party. Contrary to what the cartoonist, Herblock of *The Washington Post,* would have you believe, LBJ *does* let his staff off work on Christmas. But back to Senator Johnson. He was riding along Connecticut Avenue late that evening en route to the party, and he saw Santa Claus walking along the street. He pulled over to the curb and asked, "What are you doing, Santa Claus?"

Santa had just finished up his last job with a department store and was on his way to a bar to recover from his day with all the little tykes.

"Well, how would you like to earn $25?" asked Johnson.

Never one to pass up a fast buck, Santa agreed. He hopped into the car and spent the rest of the evening at the Johnson's house dispensing presents to the children, staff and friends.

That was only one Yuletide! There was another, in the

White House, that I will never forget. We now refer to it as Our Going to the Well Christmas.

"Going to the well" is a Johnson expression borrowed from the Old West.

When you say, "He's the kind of man I would go to the well with," you are describing the kind of pioneer you would take with you from your cabin to the well when the Indians were lurking around—someone who wouldn't get rattled, someone who keeps a cool head in trouble, someone who wouldn't panic and run.

About ten days before this particular Christmas, I was waiting for the elevator to go upstairs and see Mrs. Johnson on the second floor of the White House when The Long Arm reaches out and whisks me into the elevator with him.

"Liz, I want you to think of something very original and imaginative for me to give those girls who work in my office. They work their hearts out all day, and I want them to have something they will treasure. So you just get busy and give me some suggestions." It was LBJ talking, giving orders in sixty seconds that I knew might take days to execute. Then he added, "By this afternoon."

So I thought of a well—a small gold well—that his secretaries could wear on a charm bracelet. I dispatched Oghda O'Gulian, my adventure-loving secretary, to the jewelers to see what she could find. Because it *was,* after all, the President of the United States, she found a jeweler who could produce a dozen wells before Christmas, complete with a tiny Presidential seal on the base. The President was delighted. But before this order was filled, I got a frantic call to "make it another forty wells." Christmas came and went, and the "well-wearing" secretaries were thrilled with the gift from the President. But before New Year's, there was another frantic call. He needed fifty more, in a hurry, because he remembered some others he wanted to go to the well with. Before February, he had ordered 152 wells. My secretary had lost five pounds running back and forth to fetch the wells. The jeweler had become so fascinated with the President that he remains his undying admirer. Weeks after the well episode, there came an autographed picture from the President to my secretary and on it was inscribed: *To Oghda O'Gulian who went to the well FOR me.*

I told this story one night at a party of Johnson friends when we were sitting around telling our favorite Johnson stories. It is a pastime—like the mood of the Texas campfire—where one storyteller tries to top the other—and often does.

Just as I reached the pinnacle of the well story, an old LBJ friend, Frank Ikard, spoke up: "That's nothing," he said. "You should hear about the time he admired my son's tieclasp." As he described it, and the buying operation that followed, I noticed that every Johnson friend in the room was wearing *that* tieclasp.

On one memorable day, President Johnson decided that women were being discriminated against in getting high level government jobs. Again, I was waiting at the elevator—my apparent Waterloo—when the doors opened. He stepped out, and I found myself propelled along by his Long Arm toward his office. I was taking three steps to his one, as we headed past the Rose Garden. He was talking as fast as he was walking.

"Anna Rosenberg Hoffman tells me that we need more women in government," he said, accepting it as a fact, and embracing it as his cause, because of his great respect for this longtime friend and top management expert. "Call Esther Peterson and both of you be at the Cabinet meeting at ten o'clock in the morning, and we'll do something about it."

Translated from Johnsonian into English, this meant I should locate Esther Peterson at the Department of Labor where she headed the Commission on the Status of Women, and be prepared with facts and figures worthy of an audience with the Cabinet.

We were there. We had worked all night on our presentation. And we assured the Cabinet that all brains didn't come in male packages.

Then Johnson took over. "I'm sure there are plenty of high level positions available for qualified women in your departments. And I am sure there are many women already on your payrolls who have been waiting for promotions for a long time. So, go back to your departments and see what you can do. Then, report back to me next Friday how many you have placed."

Those were the magic words—"report back to me." The program began to move. All over the government, personnel officers who had been ignoring their women employees for years suddenly had a wolflike gleam in their eyes. The hunt was on.

The President joined the talent search for women. For instance, I was lying in bed on a Saturday evening enjoying Mrs. Johnson's favorite TV show, *Gunsmoke* with Matt Dillon. (He was on the screen; not in the bed.) Just as Miss Kitty was about to step in and stop a gunfight in the Long Branch Saloon, the phone rang, and it was You-Know-Who.

"Liz, are you watching television?" he said.

"Yes sir."

"There is a terrific woman on television," he continued.

"Not Miss Kitty!" I panicked, privately wondering how she would perform as U. S. Treasurer, a post that LBJ wanted to fill with a woman.

"This woman is on a panel show," he continued, as I breathed a sigh of relief, "and she knows a lot about handling money. She has been supporting her children, as a lady banker since her husband died. I haven't the remotest idea whether she is a Democrat or a Republican, and I don't care. But find out who she is and see if she will do."

I switched channels, got the name and began tracing. Alas, although we brought her to Washington for an interview, we discovered that the federal government couldn't afford her.

These were the kind of unending orders that accompanied his enthusiasm. He was determined to get more women in government. Everytime there was a vacancy, I was asked to supply some women's names. The problem about luring women into government is that though people talk a lot about it, there are few women who can put aside family obligations, or leave a more lucrative business position. But I didn't want to pour cold water on the President's enthusiasm. We searched, and we found, quite a few—more than 150 new appointees and eight hundred promotions within a few months. We followed every lead, no matter how fruitless. One of the great finds was Betty Furness who gave government a conscience about consumer problems. Another was Katie Louchheim, a veteran of party ranks who held various trusted posts at the Department of State.

Drew Pearson gave me a suggestion one day. It would be wonderful if the President would honor Agnes Meyer, widow of the publisher of *The Washington Post,* and quite an outstanding welfare expert herself. He said that Mrs. Meyer, who was now an elderly woman, would be a worthy delegate to the forthcoming inauguration of the President of Venezuela.

"Great," the President said. "Find her and ask her."

I called on my friends, the white House switchboard operators, to find Mrs. Meyer. We had been told she was cruising on a yacht, the *Panda,* in the Caribbean.

The White House switchboard operators are plugged in all over the world. They are terrific at tracking down their prey.

In tracking down Mrs. Meyer, they outdid themselves. They didn't locate one yacht in the Caribbean called the *Panda.* They located two. Talking on a ship-to-shore radio through two languages, English and Spanish, we spent several hours trying to make "the real *Panda* stand up." Finally, we found the one we were looking for. Alas, Mrs. Meyer said she wouldn't be able to accept the invitation. Later, Drew Pearson told me "You know the reason Agnes didn't accept? You caught her away from home without her favorite jewels."

One summer, LBJ had his own personal program to elevate women in government. He brought up from Texas two young family friends to study shorthand and typing and work part-time at the White House. La Fay Davis was the daughter of his cook at the LBJ Ranch; Susan Stephenson was the daughter of friends in Johnson City. The girls had just graduated from high school in Stonewall and Johnson City.

"It will help them all their lives if they can say they worked in the White House," LBJ said. So they lived on the third floor of the White House. He put Ashton Gonella, whose office as personal secretary to Mrs. Johnson was also on the third floor, in charge of the girls. With LBJ paying the bills out of his own pocket, he enrolled them in business school and dispatched Ashton to buy them some clothes which would "make them look more like Washington."

Making people around him "make the most of themselves" was a Johnson credo. I was his failure. He tried over and over to get me to lose weight, even offering to diet along with me. I belligerently replied that it wasn't I who was overweight. "Everyone else is underweight," I would insist.

All staff members left the White House with many notes sent through the years on the occasion of a birthday, an anniversary, an illness. My favorite, because it contains his own hurried scrawl, came when I had an emergency appendectomy. Even before the note arrived with the largest bouquet I had ever seen, he had called my husband several times to find out how I was doing. He even asked if I had plenty of hospital insurance. Fortunately, I did.

The letter is choice:

THE WHITE HOUSE
WASHINGTON

October 9, 1968

Dear Liz:

Your own appendix has done what I could never do -- taken you by surprise. As long as the doctors haven't cut out the secret seat of your sense of humor, it's good riddance. I've never had much patience with useless hangers-on.

Don't take off too much time convalescing; we don't want you to get in the habit of lying around lazy. We need you back on your feet: jolly, spreading joy and making trouble.

I send you these flowers with much good cheer. Get well -- now! And just one friendly tip: Don't go showing your scar to just any old reporter not even in confidence or off the record -.

Sincerely,

Lyndon B. Johnson

Honorable Elizabeth Carpenter
Georgetown University Hospital
Washington, D. C.

It wasn't just the staff—but everyone—that LBJ wanted to help. He liked to be needed. In the summer of 1964, Bobby Kennedy needed him.

I received a call one day from former Governor Averell Harriman, asking me and my husband to dinner. I knew the governor, who had become an ambassador and at this time was working in the Department of State, but I did not know him well. I was rather surprised at the call. He said he had something he wanted to discuss with me. So a date was set—August 5. That night I found myself—to my surprise—seated beside him. A memo in my files, which I sent to the President the next day, tells the story:

THE WHITE HOUSE

MEMORANDUM August 6, 1964

To: The President
From: Liz

Governor Harriman went to some rather elaborate lengths to give me what I interpret as a message for you.

(1) That you are going to carry New York State by one million votes, including such GOP strongholds as Westchester County.

(2) That Bobby can carry it by 500,000 and is the only person sure of beating Keating (except Harriman).

(3) That a decision is going to be made *this weekend* on whether Bobby will run.

(4) That Harriman wants you very much to give a nod to Bobby to run in the New York race.

(5) That Mayor Wagner doesn't like "any other stars in the orbit," but that he will accept the President's wishes.

(6) That Harriman is willing to do anything he can to help elect you.

P.S. Harriman told me he had recently been sailing with Ethel Kennedy. I gather this represents her thinking.

The rest of the story is political history. Bobby Kennedy ran. Three times he asked the President to come help him in New York. Three times the President went to New York State to campaign with him. When the votes came in, both had won. But it was obvious who made the difference in the victory. The President carried every county in the State and led the ticket by 2,700,000 votes. Bobby Kennedy won by 650,000.

I had learned long before that these acts of kindness sprang from the man himself. I found this out when I went to work for him as Vice President, and he called me into his inner office one day and closed the door so the secretaries in the outer office couldn't hear.

"Geraldine Williams is going to get married to Bob Novak," he said. "And I want you to plan the wedding reception. We'll have it out at the Elms. Make it just as nice as though it were for Lynda or Luci."

Geraldine was a very young secretary from Texas; Bob Novak, a sophisticated Washington newsman subsequently the Novak of the Evans and Novak political column. LBJ dictated a letter to her parents in Hillsboro to make them feel more at ease about the man their daughter had decided to marry. It was a moving letter and went right to the questions that any parents of modest means, living in a small Texas town, might have about the city-slicker they had never met whom their daughter had chosen to marry.

The reception was beautiful and expensive. It must have been a tremendous thrill for the bride, although the groom is not of a temperament that is easily thrilled. He later became one of Johnson's most acid critics.

During the Vice Presidential years, I was LBJ's Executive Assistant. At least that's what the title was. My duties, in addition to producing wedding receptions, included being a baby-sitter for a camel driver and LBJ's fellow traveler on round-the-world missions.

The camel driver experience started innocently enough shortly after we landed in Karachi, Pakistan. The motorcade into town is ten miles long, and ten miles of cheering Pakistanis had turned out to welcome the Vice President of the United States.

Suddenly we ground to a halt, and I saw that tall familiar figure open the door and start handshaking through the crowd of natives to a cluster of men with camels on a hillside. He plunged into the group of camel drivers, shaking hands and dispensing greetings including a pat for the camels.

Next day, to my amazement, the local paper reported that LBJ had invited a camel driver, Bashir Ahmed, to the ranch.

"Today all the city people are talking about the simple approach of Lyndon Johnson, the American Vice President, who went out to meet the common people of Pakistan," wrote Ibrahim Jalis, the most widely read columnist in Pakistan. "Even before he went to call on President Ayub Khan, he took the hand of a poor camel-cart driver, Bashir Ahmed. Everywhere people are saying the American Vice President invited Bashir to come to America. My, Bashir is certainly lucky! Now Bashir will go by jet comet and stay in the world's biggest hotels. He'll stay in the Waldorf Astoria Hotel in New York. The listeners feel sorry we couldn't be in Bashir's shoes."

The column continued, in its interesting if awkward translation, "If Lyndon Johnson, like his predecessors, had gotten off at the airport with a stiff neck and gone straight to the President's house and talked only with cabinet ministers, and then gone back to America and had not talked to the people of Karachi, then, who is Lyndon Johnson and when did he come and when did he go? Lyndon Johnson's manner of meeting with common people was characteristic of him. But if it represents also a happy turn in American foreign policy, that would be no mistake."

The columnist then quoted an old saying: "Don't conquer a country, don't conquer a government. If you wish to conquer, conquer the hearts of the people."

It was a generous report all because of one handshake. But we were not to forget it. By the time we were back in Washington, the wire-service stories out of Pakistan made me wonder if Bashir Ahmed, the camel driver, was holding press conferences every day. He would be pleased to accept the Vice President's invitation, but he had no money.

"I don't want that man to be disappointed," LBJ said. "See if you can't work out something."

Actually, it wasn't very hard. People-to-People, a private organization headed by former President Eisenhower, stepped forth and bought the round-trip ticket. And we began to make plans. Most of our available information came through the press, rather than the State Department, which was getting increasingly nervous about the fact that the camel driver was getting more publicity than the President of Pakistan. Indeed, it looked as if the camel driver were going to visit the United States before President Ayub Khan could.

LBJ had gotten along very well with then-President Ayub Khan. Both are strong leaders, and they know the necessity of keeping a wary eye on the adversaries. During our visit, the Pakistani President had told Johnson: "Go back home and tell your young President that the Rusisans will be testing him in the next few months. They'll try a lot of things just to see how tough he is."

LBJ brought the message back and President Kennedy replied, "I want to meet that man. See if you can get him over here soon."

With these two incentives, LBJ went to work and moved

up President Ayub Khan's visit from the fall to July. This way he would have come and gone before our camel driver friend got here.

Within a few weeks, Operation Camel Driver was occupying most of my time. But the Vice President was getting alarmed at the tone of some of the news stories, which began making fun of Bashir Ahmed. Some reporters predicted a three-ring circus. Columnists made snide accusations that Bashir didn't know how to eat. (Camel drivers, being short of silverware, quite sensibly eat with their fingers.)

LBJ was indignant that the press would ridicule a humble man who was his guest. I was getting worried, too. My phone was busy with mischief-making reporters who wanted to be part of the "Camel Driver Followers" when LBJ met the camel driver in New York and escorted him to the LBJ Ranch in Texas. *Life* magazine stepped in with a grandiose plan to hire a plane. The magazine would pick up the entire check and fly the camel driver and the Vice President to Texas. Of course, two other passengers would be *Life* photographers snapping pictures all the way. We replied with a firm *no.*

I suggested that we talk to the heads of AP and UPI in New York and see if we couldn't persuade them to handle the story in a more human manner. The Vice President told me to arrange the meeting, and he and I met for two hours with the two top gentlemen of the wire services. Call it managed news if you like; it was well worth it!

The Vice President was marvelous. He outlined what our friendship means in Southeast Asia. To him, it was more than a colorful humorous story. He gave a down-to-earth evaluation of the importance of good relations with Pakistan, where there are important strategic air bases. As I listened, I knew why he had always been able to push through bill after bill on Capitol Hill with only a one-margin vote. The AP and UPI apparently understood his point. By the time we reached Texas with Bashir, the fun-and-games reporters had been called off.

Bashir Ahmed got a better press than the Vice President usually enjoyed. This smiling, dark-faced man saw Johnson City with LBJ, saw Kansas City with former President Truman, and met President Kennedy in Washington, and then-Mayor Bob Wagner in New York City.

I had enlisted help from the unenthusiastic State Department and had been lent two excellent aides: Tony Merrill and Saeed Khan, an interpreter who had served as Queen Elizabeth's interpreter on her visit to Pakistan. (Saeed Khan performed so ably in the camel driver operation that he has since served as Protocol Officer at four world's fairs—in Seattle, New York, Montreal and HemisFair in San Antonio.)

The news and TV stories of the smiling, visiting camel driver blanketed Asia. Our American Embassy in Karachi cabled: BASHIR IS THE TALK OF THE TEAHOUSES. Thousands of letters poured in from all over the U.S.—interestingly enough, most from the South. They sent pencils and paper for Bashir to take home to schools in Pakistan. And the Ford Motor Company gave him a truck. Originally, the gift was a red truck, but we were advised that red is the Communist symbol in Pakistan. Ford quickly switched it to green.

We had solved the eating problem by letting Bashir dine alone when he wished. As a Moslem, he needed to face Mecca four times a day for prayers, and I somehow couldn't see the Vice President joining him in facing Mecca—although, of course, you can never tell about LBJ.

When we dined together, we had a menu that made it possible for all of us to eat with our fingers, such as fried chicken, stuffed celery, deviled eggs, potato chips. On one such occasion during a visit to Dallas, I looked around the table and saw the presidents of four banks and Neiman-Marcus all eating with their fingers to make the camel driver feel at home.

Mrs. Johnson was marvelous. She served as tour guide for Bashir through the White House, the Capitol, to the Lincoln Memorial and to the Moslem Mosque in Washington.

Through the interpreter, Mrs. Johnson and Bashir exchanged civilities at rapid rate. She quoted Jefferson. He quoted from the Koran. As one reporter put it, "Their train of journalists were as busy as reporters at a tennis match."

We sent Bashir back to Pakistan by way of Mecca in Saudi Arabia. By visiting the birthplace of Muhammad, the holy city of Islam, Bashir would return to his home with new status in his neighborhood.

Operation Camel Driver had been a success from everyone's standpoint. As President Kennedy said, "I don't know how Lyndon does it. If I had done that, there would have been camel dung all over the White House lawn."

Asia was newly aware that, in the Vice President of the United States, they had a friend who understood the average man. I was newly aware how an irresponsible press could have made the whole operation a disaster. We were lucky this time.

The accolades came in from all sides, but one especially significant one came from Lyle Wilson, chief of the UPI bureau in Washington. He wrote:

October 24, 1961

Dear Lyndon:

"I would have bet almost anything against your dime when I heard your camel driver was coming to the United States, that you had a bear by the tail and would be embarrassed in a big way before it was all over and perhaps, be mauled to boot. I am aware, of course, that you suggested to the UPI and AP brass in New York that the funny writers and ridicule slingers should not be set on your boy.

Well, my friend, as it turned out, you need not have done that. Your Pakistani visitor was a gentleman in his own right. Moreover, he was gracefully articulate. I hope his fellow countrymen will get some idea of how warmly he was received and appreciated here.

However that may be, his visit was good for our fellow citizens. Here was a poor man, unlearned, unaccustomed to indoor plumbing and all of that who was able to demonstrate to us by his conduct and his observations that such a man is a high-class article, a good and desirable citizen of whatever state he may claim.

I doubt if one of ours, complete with the usual education and experience of creature comforts, freedom and all such could make as good an impression in any foreign country as Bashir made in the United States. His visit was a tremendous success for which I congratulate you and your guest.

Sincerely,
Lyle C. Wilson.

Having a close view of LBJ as Vice President gave me a key to the bigness of the man. After all, he had vied with John F. Kennedy for the prize at the Democratic National Convention. He lost. And many of his supporters and political allies never forgave him for accepting Kennedy's invitation to take the second spot. Wasn't he more powerful as Senate Majority Leader where he led that body—drove it, really, at times—harder than anyone in history? Wasn't he taking the number two spot in the executive while giving up his number one spot in the legislative? But, LBJ reasoned, Kennedy was big enough to ask him and he, the older man, should be big enough to accept. Together they had received 1296 of the 1521 delegate votes. Together they could pull the country forward.

The office of Vice President has been called many things—most of them unprintable in family literature. John Nance Garner called it as worthless as a bucket of warm spit. Hubert Humphrey said it was like the car rental agency, Avis: "I'm number two and I have to try harder." But Johnson settled down in the Senate to try to be the best Vice President in history. That was not easy. On one side, he had Senate Leader Mike Mansfield, whom LBJ had groomed and recommended to Kennedy as his successor as Senate leader. Already the suspicious voices of lesser men were busy: "Don't let the Great Johnson run you." "He'll make you a puppet." So, Mansfield, unable to resist these suspicions, drew a shell around himself, cutting himself off from the man who had picked him for power in the first place. If LBJ ever resented this, he never showed it. But more and more, he found himself having to seek support and help in other directions than the Democratic leader of the Senate.

Aside from Mansfield's new frosty attitude, President Kennedy couldn't always keep his swashbuckling Irish mafia in line. They were newcomers to town and wanted to show their vigor on Capitol Hill without any help from "the Great Johnson"—that is, until they got in a jam, and they would have to turn to him to move in and rescue a close vote.

His assignments now originated at the White House, rather than from the people. "The difference between being Senator and Vice President," Mrs. Johnson once summed it up succinctly, "is the difference between power derived and power assigned."

Jack Kennedy understood and did his best to help out. He invited the Johnsons to everything, public and private, at the White House. If his staff people forgot (and this occasionally happened), he had their scalps and was quickly on the phone to Social Secretary Tish Baldridge telling her to make amends.

Actually, Johnson was much closer to Jack and Jacqueline Kennedy than the public ever knew. There was the kind of relationship that permitted the three of them to dine comfortably on a particularly troubled day. "You're the only one who will really understand," Mrs. Kennedy told him.

It was Jackie who personally selected LBJ to make the speech at a dinner honoring French Cultural Minister André Malraux.

President Kennedy assigned the Vice President to "show the American flag" abroad in Africa, Southeast Asia, the Dominican Republic, Jamaica, Scandinavia, the Benelux Countries, Berlin and the Middle East.

Senegal was the first foreign assignment. LBJ was to head the U.S. delegation to the celebration of this new African Nation's independence. Flying over the Atlantic, I studied my briefing book so I would be very familiar with the names. And they were *familiar* names. The President's name was pronounced Singwhore. Another official was Mama Du Dia. Actually, we had a strange name on our own roster. One of the American delegates had the most romantic name in the world: Romeo Champagne.

The delegate from the Soviet Union was Mr. Malik, and before we arrived he was getting major attention in the press. The Vice President was determined that the Russians wouldn't outshine us, so he buoyantly explored the marketplaces of Dakar, meeting the people on the street and letting them know the U.S. was their friend. In the hot, smelly heat, we drove out of the city to Kayar, a small fishing village. While the American

Ambassador, a gentleman of the old school of diplomacy, remained in the air-conditioned car, LBJ walked up and down the dusty streets, shaking hands and making friends.

We trailed along behind him among the natives, the dead chickens and human excrement that is everywhere. Indoor plumbing had not come to Kayar! Suddenly I heard Dr. Willis Hurst, our delegation physician, gasp, "My God, he's shaking hands with a leper!"

LBJ couldn't have cared less. "If they"—he nodded toward the State Department people—"think they are going to meet me at an airport and put me in an air-conditioned Cadillac and drive me past hundreds of people who want to shake hands with the United States of America embodied in me, well, they've got another think coming."

Obviously, this personal diplomacy was popular. After we had spent two hours in Kayar, the wonderful old tribal chieftain came up panting, his white robes whipping against his legs as he ran to say one more goodbye to the Vice President. His tribal tongue had to be translated from Woluf to French to English. But the message was loud and clear. "You go back and tell your President that you are the first important man from any country to visit my village."

When he traveled, LBJ always wanted to bring home a personal gift to everyone on his staff and in his family who hadn't gone along. Sometimes he'd forget to give this order until midnight. In Lebanon, this was the case, and Bess Abell and I found ourselves trying to buy two pictures off the wall of the Phoenicia Hotel where we were staying. When we removed them to take a look, the back indicated: *Made in Japan.*

In an Istanbul bazaar, he had spied some Turkish slippers, brightly colored and embroidered. They were perfect, he thought, for ladies to wear as house slippers. So he dispatched his personal secretary, Juanita Roberts, to the bazaar with instructions to select one hundred pairs in various sizes. The Turks simply toss all slippers, pairs separated, into one big barrel so it was a long, tedious job sorting them out. That was the day Juanita lost her 20–20 vision.

The Vice President loved to share the gracious hospitality he was offered in his travels with his staff. Aside from being a working convenience, he knew that we would be thrilled to stay in the marble halls and palaces. He was right. Some of the thrills were unexpected.

In Iran, Bess Abell and I shared a suite in the Shah's guest palace in the heart of Tehran. Our drawing room was the size of a football field with ancient Persian carpets and tapestries. The bedroom was tremendous, silver ornaments everywhere, and a beautiful tiled floor. Mirrors made of tiny mosaics in the Persian fashion adorned the paneling of the room. It was truly fit for an Empress. There was only one catch which somehow made the sublime ridiculous. Bess and I discovered we had to share our bathroom with thirty-five Secret Service agents who must have been housed in nearby closets and crevices of this guest palace. There was no lock on the bathroom door, and we quickly revived the old custom of singing in the bathtub. Even though SS agents are early risers, it is a long wait while thirty-five men shave.

Traveling abroad with LBJ was as rigorous as campaigning with him in the United States. Surprisingly, he got one of his most helpful campaign hints from Richard M. Nixon. In 1960, Nixon had suffered a knee injury, and LBJ went to visit him at Bethesda Naval Hospital.

"One thing I learned in campaigning," Nixon confided, "was to change shirts frequently. Your staff won't want you to take time for it. But it freshens you up immediately. So I carry several shirts in a brief case to have handy. It rests you in those long hot grueling days."

That fall, we carried a shirt supply along. But one day in Houston, LBJ had run out of them. It was sweltering and he had thrown so much enthusiasm into his speeches that he was wringing wet. Just before our motorcade was leaving the downtown hotel for the auditorium where he would make his next speech, he spied me and said, "See if you can't get me a shirt before the next stop—size 17½–37."

I darted into a nearby department store hoping that the motorcade was long enough to enable me to catch a ride in the last car. Fortunately, I had an understanding clerk.

When I shouted, "I need a white shirt, size 17½–37 for the Vice President of the United States," she didn't blink an eye. She pulled out a shirt, and I thrust $10 in her hand, not waiting for the change, and was out the door just in time to thumb a ride on the "caboose" of the motorcade.

Campaign rides were never routine, and LBJ was full of surprises. Once in Pittsburgh, he was campaigning in the steel mill district during the middle of a threatened steel strike against steel boss Roger Blough. At his side was labor leader David MacDonald. All along the route, they were leaping out and shaking hands and finally when they reached the union hall, The Long Arm went out. He had an idea how to avert the strike, and he said, "Let's get Roger Blough on the phone."

In fifteen minutes they were closer to a compromise.

Man-to-man government; man-to-man diplomacy. Those were Lyndon Johnson's specialties. But that sentiment was always there. Sam Rayburn was his political father, and his last illness hung over the Vice President like a dark cloud. Doctors had told us death was imminent, but you are never quite prepared. LBJ's press secretary, George Reedy, and I were with the Vice President one November morning en route to the airport where we were joining President Kennedy to fly to Seattle, Washington, to campaign for that Democratic stalwart, Senator Warren Magnuson.

"I'm going to enjoy this trip," LBJ said to George and me. "There won't be a lot of speaking to do and I am with two of my favorite people."

The phone in the limousine rang. He picked it up, listened, muttered a few words, and then placed it down with an air of finality.

"The Speaker is dead," he said and then added, "and I'm not sure I want to live in this town any more."

We turned the car around. On our way back to the Johnson's home to make plans to go to Bonham, Texas, for the funeral, he was full of memories about Mr. Sam. "He was always where I could reach him and get his counsel, and now he is gone."

We flew to Bonham that day, and The Long Arm was out in comfort to the Speaker's sisters and nieces and nephews, and to all the friends of Mr. Rayburn who came to pay their respects in that comfortable old white frame house that sits on the black waxy soil of Texas's old fourth district. It was a house that was right for the man. Kitchen matches on the mantel. Lots of rocking chairs. Patchwork quilts, the work of loving women in the family. And lots of pictures of kinfolks.

Sam Rayburn's friends of seventy-nine years came, and the Vice President met them every one. "We feel a little closer to Mr. Rayburn having Lyndon come," one man told me.

It is a digression, but Sam Rayburn must have a place in any book I write. He was made of the sturdiest fabric. Once after his oldest sister, Miss Lucinda Rayburn, died, he showed me a delicate lavaliere she had worn, which he now carried on his watch chain. "That belonged to Miss Lu," he said simply. Then he added with deep pride, "She wore it when she walked into the State Dining Room on the arm of three Presidents."

What a pity that neither of them lived to walk through the Great Hall of the White House on the arm of the President they had nurtured.

The funeral was set for the following afternoon, but our stay was interrupted with a call from Arizona. Venerable Senator Carl Hayden, who had served Arizona since it was a territory, was anticipating a tough political campaign the following year and had been counting on the Vice President as a drawing card at his big political dinner that night in Phoenix. The Vice President tried to beg off.

"Sam would have wanted you to do it, Lyndon," the canny old Senator said.

So we left to fly to Arizona and returned the next day for the funeral. The Vice President made a magnificent speech for Hayden. We had returned to our Arizona hotel and gone to sleep when the phone woke me. Mrs. Johnson's brother, Tony Taylor, had just had a serious heart attack and been taken to the hospital in Santa Fe. I went next door to the Johnsons' room to give them the news. LBJ was on the phone immediately and for the next two hours, while we packed, he was talking to doctors, checking with the pilot to change our plans, calling his heart specialist in Atlanta. He was in charge. Listening to him as we packed, Mrs. Johnson said what she so often repeated: "Lyndon is a good man to have in an emergency."

We flew back to Bonham by way of Santa Fe, leaving Mrs. Johnson to be with her brother.

At the Baptist Church, the President and Vice President of the United States listened to the lengthy funeral service performed by the Primitive Baptist Minister—Brother Ball.

When it was over, President Kennedy, a man pressed by

many burdens, was anxious to return to Washington. "I see no reason to go to the cemetery," he said to the Vice President.

"I'm going," Johnson said, looking him straight in the eye.

And so, they both went—two men who had served under that strong and compassionate gavel—and saw the Speaker laid to rest.

I remember, too—Dallas on November 22—when, under the most terrible circumstances, Lyndon Johnson became President. And through the shock and horror everyone shared, The Long Arm went out via the plane's radiotelephone, summoning the Cabinet and the Congressional leaders to a meeting at the White House that very night. And then, the painful call to comfort the mother of President Kennedy.

With the shades of Air Force One drawn, and only the sound of an occasional sob, soft footsteps and whispers, the words of Mrs. Johnson kept coming back to me. "Lyndon's a good man to have in an emergency."

Even on that tragic day, the country was never without a President. That was more than six years ago. Since that time I have seen problems arise day after day, and a remarkable number conquered in years that produced more problems than solutions.

Shortly before the Johnsons left the White House, Mrs. Johnson was asked what her feelings had been that day when she had moved in—as mistress of that house.

"An overwhelming sympathy for the family that had been struck," she said, "and a sympathy beyond expression for my husband. I don't suppose in all history there ever was another President who saw the man he had served assassinated in front of his own eyes, and in his own state. It was a wound, and it was very hard.

"I realized," she said, "that my sympathy must go on through the years with an increasing understanding—that the world must go on, and we must go on with the world."

If President Johnson was The Long Arm, Lady Bird Johnson was The Gentle Hand. Her soft, Southern voice, her quick sympathy, an air of quietude that seems to accompany her express this innate gentleness.

Mrs. Johnson has the talent for making every house she lives in intensely hers, and her family's. Even the museum-like qualities of the White House yielded. Lincoln's bedroom came to life with Luci's long white wedding veil stretched lengthwise across it, for it was the only place in the house spacious enough to accommodate it.

The two cozy sitting rooms on the second floor with their fabric-paneled walls—the Queen's Sitting Room and the Lincoln Sitting Room—were favorite spots of Mrs. Johnson for a small meeting or an interview. Tea tables would be set, usually with spiced tea in the winter, for the occasion.

"I like these rooms," she would always explain to her visitors, "because they each have only *one* door." Thus, there would be no crosstrail of interruptions.

For larger meetings, she used the Treaty Room, which had served as the Cabinet meeting place in earlier White House days. It was an incongruous sight to be planning beautification projects on a green felt Cabinet table, surrounded by somewhat atrocious bric-a-brac of the Victorian period with gilt mirrors, heart-back chairs and a large crystal chandelier ordered by President Grant.

But most of the activity on the second floor revolved around the living room area of the West Hall and the family dining room adjoining it. They were crossroads for the President's Tuesday luncheons with the Secretaries of State and Defense. But even the solemnity of the business did not offset the feeling that the Johnsons lived there. Family momentos made it homelike—their own books, her favorite needlepoint pillows, lots of picture albums of Johnson milestones. As Lyn, their grandson, grew, his baby pictures dominated the big, round table and were always the conversation pieces.

With each move—and there had been many in the life of the Johnsons—she had promptly set about to create an "oasis of peace." It was seldom that—more a springboard for ideas.

"Lyndon is the catalyst, and I am the amalgam," she often explained. It was a truth. But she had a talent for decorating and making wherever they lived really seem like home.

People often compared her to Mrs. Roosevelt because both were widely traveled and openly interested in national life. While she admired Mrs. Roosevelt greatly, she was very different. Mrs. Roosevelt was an instigator, an innovator, willing to air a cause even without her husband's endorsement. Mrs. Johnson was an implementer and translator of her husband and his purposes. She is a WIFE in capital letters.

After a year in the White House, Nan Robertson of *The New York Times,* whom Mrs. Johnson liked tremendously, asked the First Lady if she considered herself a private person.

"Yes, I do," she replied promptly. "I do prefer to spend my life with personal interests and friends. I am, however, propelled by a genuine concern in my husband's life into learning about the things he is trying to do and the people who implement them. This past year has increased the dimensions of my mind and heart. I became better acquainted with our national parks and what they offer in beauty, serenity and pleasure to the people. I learned a great deal from my visit to the Kentucky mountains where people and government are trying to face a changing economy and offer training and jobs to young people.

"But," she summed it up, "the net of it is that I am a private person extended into public life somewhat because of the opportunities and impelling call of my husband's jobs through the years. The aspect of the role one doesn't forget is that it all hinges upon the man you've married. My needs are groomed into helping him."

"Helping him!" That was her mission and her love. Ironically, it was without ambition for him. Had he remained a rancher, she would have been content to find horizons reading poetry in a hammock.

But "helping him" meant speech lessons to enable her to face an audience better prepared. It meant being more thoughtful in choosing clothes, colors and styles that pleased him and that served the public purpose. It meant taking an endless round of constituents around town when he was in the Congress and growing with his job as it grew. She never let this effort become a duty or a chore.

More and more, he leaned on her judgment. Some of the Johnson critics liked to make snide remarks when the President would enter a room and impulsively kiss her in front of everyone.

"Frankly, I love it," she told a friend who asked her own reaction.

She adored his intense masculinity. Her life had been spent in the company of "head men." Her father, who stood over six feet tall like the President, was known in his country as "Mister Boss." Perhaps it was in contrast to their own strength that it seems so, but I think she is the most feminine woman I have ever known, reveling in womanly things—home, children, the beauty of the world around her. She brought these qualities to the White House and in doing so, somehow made the word *politics* seem nicer than it had ever seemed before.

Once I came upon a letter the President had written her when he was a young Congressman and she was back home on a long visit. I was struck with the fact that their marriage still retained the same lighthearted and refreshing flavor it had had from the beginning. I asked him for a copy.

LYNDON B. JOHNSON
10TH DISTRICT TEXAS

COMMITTEE ON
NAVAL AFFAIRS

CONGRESS OF THE UNITED STATES
HOUSE OF REPRESENTATIVES
WASHINGTON, D. C.

May the seventh
1 9 4 3

Dearest Lady Bird,

I'm writing a letter to Mother for Mother's Day and I wish you would be a good girl and go down and buy her a suitable present. You know what she would like a lot better than I, so just use your own judgment.

If you don't start writing me more often I am going to have you drafted into the WAACS. Then you'll <u>have</u> to write your next of kin at least twice <u>a month</u>.

Had dinner with Bill Douglas last night and he was his usual entertaining self. He wished that you could have been there, but not half as much as

Your Congressman

Lyndon B. Johnson.

Mrs. Lyndon B. Johnson,
2519 Harris Blvd.,
Austin, Texas.

That's the kind of people the Johnsons are. I guess I'm glad when people ask me that question.

# *Men Who Make Advances*

Until I got into politics, I thought the term—"advance man" —was just a jazzy expression for a fast wolf. Now that I've been in politics, I know that I was absolutely right. The term actually means someone, either male or female, who goes before the VIP and makes all the plans—*lays* all the plans, if you will—for the public figure's forthcoming appearance. Advance men are a hardworking, rollicking breed with a pioneer spirit and a talent for staging a spectacular arrival ceremony.

In ancient days, Roman emperors would order a slave to run ahead of them repeating over and over, "You are mortal, you are mortal." This was to remind the Emperor to remain humble. This ancient custom is not the job of an advance man.

Today, an advance man's job is to produce a crowd and a show that will get nationwide attention for the visiting dignitary. Much depends upon his ingenuity and ability to get along with the local people and leave them happy about all the work they've done and bills they've paid for the visit. He must listen to innumerable ideas among bickering party factions advising what the President or First Lady should do during their forthcoming visit, formulate his own plan, and make the local people think they agreed to it. Usually an advance man arrives in the town a week or so before the designated visit, works out the motorcade route and begins all the arrangements aimed to attract attention for his boss.

Success of an advance man is measured in only one way: how big was the crowd? So, in the business of producing instant people, finding them and keeping them in place for the candidate, it is amazing the things an advance man finds himself doing.

I had a friend, Henry Diamond, who was an advance man for Nelson Rockefeller's ill-fated campaign for President. He spent the entire spring of 1968 cornering the helium balloon market, and to this day, he is convinced that the reason for the failure of his boss to get in the White House was the guy who, at a Virginia airport, released the strings of balloons ten minutes too early. Governor Rockefeller arrived and all he saw of the balloons was a speck about 10,000 feet upward drifting away, just like his delegate strength.

I once knew an advance man who solved the crowd problem by calling fire trucks to come to a hotel entrance just as the candidate arrived. A good advance man is hard to find. When you do find one, you try to keep him on the road for you.

Once we lost an advance man in Samoa for three weeks. It was during our planning operation for the President's trip to Asia and the summit meetings in Manila. We sent Chuck Lipsen, one of our top advance men and one who relishes the role of the bon vivant, to the Paradise of the Pacific, Samoa, to make arrangements for the two hours that the President's plane would land, refuel and head toward Australia. The census shows that 20,000 people live happily in this Garden of Eden. The men wear lava-lavas (a sarong) and the women wear pula-tesis. They chew sugar cane and smile and laugh 99 percent of each day. They loved LBJ because he put educational TV into their school system.

Our advance man's task was to get to know the natives through their chiefs (a hospitable group) and to be sure that when Air Force One landed, all 20,000 people were at the airport cheering madly. Never was an advance man so unnecessary. Whenever any plane lands (which is only four times a week)—for that matter, whenever a butterfly lands—there is nothing else to do on Samoa except go and greet it. So the happy, hospitable Samoans greet everything that flies in.

Meanwhile, back at the White House, Bill Moyers, who was masterminding the trip, and I were in the Situation Room for one last telephone check on all advance posts before the Presidential plane started out next day.

We talked to Wellington, Melbourne, Kuala Lumpur, Bangkok, Manila and Seoul, but the calls to Pago Pago, Samoa, were unanswered. No sound or sign of the advance man. We kept working on the two-way radio connection, but without any luck. Where was Chuck Lipsen? Had he been devoured by cannibals? Was he suffering from jungle rot? How can you get lost on an island that is only fifty-three square miles, where lovely native girls with lotus blossoms behind their ears and sharks' teeth around their necks are romping playfully throughout the woods?

We finally roused Marcia Maddox and Joe Laitin, our advance team in Hawaii, the nearest point to Samoa. They were instructed to get on the next plane and search through jungle and palm trees until they found that advance man, dead or alive.

They landed after a five-hour flight. Naturally most everyone on the island was on hand to greet the plane.

"Everywhere we looked were friendly natives in gay, bright loincloths," Marcia recounted. "Our eyes finally fell upon a vaguely familiar profile of a figure wearing the native dress.

His arms were thrown around a voluptuous-looking native girl who was a dead ringer for Dorothy Lamour or Miss Lotus Blossom of 1966. Joe and I reached out to shake hands. 'Bob Hope we presume.'

"He was very surprised to see anyone from the mainland. He sheepishly explained that the job of a good advance man is to get acquainted with the local people, and he had been working at it," she recalled.

"These natives are the friendliest people in the world," the advance man said gleefully. "Each night a different chief asks me to attend his fia-fia. The appropriate dress for a fia-fia is a lava-lava. The menu is kava-kava. Any good fia-fia lasts all night. Everyone in the tribe sits around and partakes of this mildly narcotic liquid (kava-kava), which is extracted by an entire village wringing the juice out of kava-kava roots with their bare hands.

"The juice is then poured into a gourd, and the honored guest (lucky boy!) drinks it. Within ten minutes afterward, you really don't mind a bit because it has the effect of about five tranquilizers washed down with a swig of straight gin," Chuck Lipsen said. "In fact, one major tranquilizer company from the United States spent several weeks and hundreds of dollars researching its possible use for pharmaceutical houses. The trick in the midst of a kava-kava is to keep your feet clamped to the ground. In Samoa, it is very anti-social to show the soles of your feet."

Marcia and Joe were convinced the advance man had gotten the real feeling of the island. Since they were to telephone us back from Hawaii with all the details of the Samoan visit, they pressed further.

"Oh yes," said our advance man, "there are several things the President should know about, so he won't be surprised when they occur at this stop. The thirty chiefs are very protocol-minded. There is the Head Chief who has under him the Talking Chief (he's the only one who gets to talk to the Head Chief), and under the Talking Chief are about twenty-eight lesser chiefs. All of them will be at the plane door to greet the President, and escort him to a kava-kava ceremony.

"Right after the President watches the making of kava-kava and sips it from a ceremonial gourd (not showing the soles of his feet, of course), then—and this is the payoff—the children of the island chiefs, in a final tribute and salute, will all take off their lava-lavas and wave them over their heads, as a gesture of respect to the Big Chief (namely LBJ)," the advance man said.

"Wait a minute," said Joe Laitin who fortunately was well versed in the satellite transmission TV arrangements for the trip. "Do you know that this ceremony will be on coast-to-coast TV, and I don't mean Samoan TV, I mean the United States?" He could envision what would happen if several hundred Samoan youngsters were photographed in living color—stark naked and wildly waving their farewells to the President. This *did* pose a problem. Fortunately, Governor Rex Lee was able to get this final tribute changed to a song for this occasion.

As it turned out, the Secret Service stepped in and refused to let LBJ drink the kava-kava. The chiefs accepted Mrs. Johnson as a sacrificial substitute and the SS permitted it, since she was not elected to her position and was, therefore, expendable.

The First Lady was cheered wildly as she sipped from the gourd. She was the first woman—and fortunately not the last—to accept kava-kava. Later, she described it as a very bitter-tasting liquid, and she slept most of the way to New Zealand, our next stop.

She woke up just in time to view the ceremonial arrival of the Maori warriors who met the plane at the New Zealand airstrip and, in the spirit of pre-Christian tribesmen, stalked forward and cast spears before the Johnsons to greet the guests. This may be acceptable among Maori warriors, but it will never replace the handshake. No wonder LBJ was the first American President to visit the South Pacific. The others must have had stickier Secret Service men.

When we were in Australia, Mrs. J. met a kangaroo that belonged to Prime Minister Harold Holt. The kangaroo was named Fred, and he was very useful, as kangaroos go. Each morning, Fred picked up the newspaper, put it in his pouch, and delivered it to the Prime Minister. I saw this as a good story and briefed the press on the talented Fred. That night, a correspondent for *Reuters* got frantic cables from his London office. He thought a Vietnam truce must have been reached, but it turned out to be his editor wanting to know: "If the kangaroo is named Fred, how does he have a pouch?"

As a matter of fact, Fred did have a pouch—and whether Fred is a nickname for Fredericka, I don't know. But it is what I guess some would call the Australian Credibility Gap.

Being an advance man is highly educational. Sometimes you pick up the most interesting intelligence. Barbara Keehn was our "advance man" in two Asian countries to help set up dinners and receptions which the President would give as return hospitality.

She worked with the protocol chiefs of the host countries. "I hope you don't mind if we record the toasts at the President's dinner," she said. "I assume microphones don't bother the King."

"Not at all," the protocol man replied. "We always have microphones hidden in the centerpieces."

CIA, take note!

In drumming up crowds, all kinds of methods and devices are used, including inviting many bands to perform.

The largest turnout of a crowd in contemporary history took

place in Korea where three million people stood on the streets of Seoul to welcome the President. Planes had flown overhead before, skywriting the red, white and blue of the American flag. Motorcading into town required more than an hour, for the road was clogged with people.

"That was more humanity than I've ever seen," LBJ said later, "and I should know because I have been looking for it all my life."

At the time, the President simply couldn't believe his eyes. As Leonard Marks, director of United States Information Agency, overheard the conversation between the two Presidents, it went this way:

LBJ: "How many people is this?"

South Korean President Park: "Three million. I'm sorry it isn't more, but that's all the people we've got."

There were bands playing "The Yellow Rose of Texas," "San Antonio Rose," "Home on the Range" and other unlikely numbers for Korea. The ingenious advance man had taken a large supply of sheet music with him, and all of these smiling Koreans were thrilled to sing, with Oriental accents, the favorite music of the Western President.

Few, if any, welcomes for a President of the United States equaled the one in Korea. It was a tribute to the office, our flag, the American people and LBJ's policies. Korea was backing us to the hilt in Vietnam with troops. The President was anxious for the people back home, especially the anti-Vietnam group, to see this expression of support from the ally on the battlefield. He wanted Americans to know that millions of Koreans turned out to cheer the United States.

When President Johnson learned the press buses were lost behind dozens of cars and unable to witness this great welcome, he stopped the whole motorcade as it drove into Seoul. He learned about it in the following manner:

The usually unflappable George Christian, a new member of the staff trying to get a feel of the job, was riding the last press bus. He flapped on the walkie-talkie to Moyers: "Slow this thing down for God's sake. The whole story is going down the drain if these reporters can't see what's taking place up front."

In vain, Moyers tried to reach the Secret Service agent riding with the President and convince him that he must stop the car. The agent simply balked. Agents have little patience with public relations. Their mission is to deliver one body breathing and intact, with or without photographs.

It was a frantic moment because thousands of picture possibilities were being missed as the Presidential limousine sped on. Christian was screaming at Moyers. Moyers was screaming at the agent, and the motorcade rolled ahead.

Finally through the walkie-talkie could be heard the excited conversation of Moyers and Hal Pachios, a press staff man, riding ahead on a flatbed truck with photographers.

MOYERS: Hal, do you read me?

HAL: Yes, I read you, Bill.

MOYERS: Tell the President to stop the car. We're losing the press bus.

HAL: I'm on a flatbed truck with photographers moving thirty miles an hour. We are fifty feet in front of the President. How the hell do you expect me to stop the President's car?

MOYERS: You'll think of something. Why not jump off and stand in front of the President's car?

HAL: Are you crazy?

MOYERS: Hal, I order you to throw yourself in front of the President's car!

Looking as though this was the last deed he would perform for his country, Hal leaped off the flatbed truck with hands raised as in surrender and stood before the President's oncoming car.

"All I could see was this tremendous black limousine—widely publicized as the heaviest one ever built—rolling toward me. I could see the eyes of the Secret Service agent, Lem Johns, getting narrower and narrower. I had time for one prayer before it stopped three inches in front of me," he recalled.

The President stuck his head out of the car window.

"What is it, Hal?"

"Sir, we have lost the press buses. They need to catch up."

The President understood immediately. Part of his job, he knew, was to give exposure to the friends we have in Southeast Asia and get their story back to the people at home.

"I think I'd like to go see the rice fields," LBJ said, glancing past the roadsides and immediately figuring a way to stall for time. So, handshaking through hundreds of people with President Chung Hee Park of Korea trailing along, President Johnson headed for the wet and muddy rice paddies and took a close look at a native crop, quizzing the startled rice farmers who were standing there.

When the press bus caught up, he returned to the car, and we rode on at a slower pace. In a minute, there was a necessary order over the radio from the Presidential car to the President's valet.

"Come in, Paul Glynn. Come in, Paul Glynn. Please bring towel and a clean pair of shoes to the President's car at the next stop."

Crowds are vital in a visit abroad, but they are very welcome at home, too. Back in the United States, some of the places Mrs. Johnson chose to go had more jackrabbits than people.

She liked the remote spots, and we didn't worry about crowd-gathering, even though we knew that inevitably the first news story to move would be the naked wire-service report, "Mrs. Johnson was greeted by a small group of two thousand people . . ." with no mention that the total population of the county was only one thousand.

We discouraged people from coming out most of the time. Her purpose, we felt, was on-site inspection of the Head Start project, the school, the downtown project. Large cumbersome arrivals took time and emphasis away from the real mission we wanted to be covered. In election years, it was a different matter. We were then in the "people business" in a big way, and we wanted hands, faces, cheers from the airport all the way through town.

One longtime Johnson advance man, John Ben Shepperd, found an ingenious way of rounding up crowds in faraway places. He appointed everyone in town to the welcoming committee and gave them each a badge. Once when we arrived at an abandoned airfield near Alpine, Texas, John Ben's receiving line at the foot of the plane was one hundred persons long, a badge on every one.

He also had a system for inviting groups who wanted to make a presentation to the First Lady to be on hand for arrivals. This was an excellent technique because garden clubs love to present a bouquet, children's groups enjoy bringing a class project, horse raisers would even turn up with a donkey. The groups like the publicity as well as the hospitality, and it added to the color of the arrival.

We embellished this system to such an extent that in one of the First Lady's last political appearances—when she flew to Louisville, Kentucky, to campaign for Hubert Humphrey—there were thirty presentations including a Sterling silver mint julep cup, a baseball bat from the Little League team and a donkey.

Advancing abroad not only involves gathering crowds and planning trips, but also helps determine the nature of gifts, entertainment and the kind of impact the United States will have on the host countries.

When the President decided to swoop down on five Central American countries in the spring of 1968, he sent me to El Salvador to help plan his two-day stop there. Barbara Keehn went along from Bess Abell's office to plan a large reception President and Mrs. Johnson would give for the five Presidents of the Republics.

We "buena vistaed" our way into the Hotel International headquarters—complete with that handiest of all instruments—a direct telephone line to the White House.

For several days, I really cased the country, looking over places where the President could visit. Advancing is actually much more fun than the visit itself, because you have more time. There is a great sense of discovery as you go around looking over a number of possibilities, so you can choose the right one. I checked out volcanos (extinct), a Peace Corps installation and several coffee plantations, called *fincas*.

The United States ambassador in San Salvador was one of the best. He had the unlikely name of Raul H. Castro. He had been a judge in Phoenix, and he knew the name of the game. He suggested I go down to the ghetto area of El Salvador to a grammar school—the Lyndon B. Johnson School—and see if this wouldn't do for a Presidential stop. After the last earthquake, Ambassador Castro got the United States to provide several million dollars in disaster funds, and he made a point of seeing that the money was spent rebuilding fifteen schools. One of the schools was named for the President who made the disaster funds available.

I walked through the classrooms of the Lyndon B. Johnson School with the principal, a gnarled old woman of great character who probably didn't even hold a high school diploma. The place was filled with beautiful brown-eyed boys and girls—poorly dressed—but malnutrition had not yet dimmed that sparkle in their eyes. There were a number of very young teachers, and I was immediately reminded of the Mexican-American school in Cotulla, Texas, where Lyndon Johnson began his own teaching career.

I knew he would love this school and the fact that American aid was being well spent to lift some of these Latin children out of their misery.

Obviously, this was the spot for the President to visit. Now, I proceeded to the arrangements. Mrs. Johnson's inspiration had made me litter-conscious, and this schoolyard was a mass of filth, papers and junk strewn around until there was barely a place for the children to play. A glance around the yard and I knew one reason—not one single trash can. So trash cans we must have, and an anti-litter drive.

Then, there was the matter of a gift. The President loves to give gifts, and he likes appropriate ones. I asked the principal, "If the President wants to bring a gift, what does the school most need? What would the children most enjoy?"

"Piano," she said without a pause. "Piano."

"Piano?" I repeated, wondering how we could obtain one.

I hurried back to the hotel to start working on getting litter cans and a piano. Barbara Keehn was on the phone to the White House. I could hear her saying, "I want three hams, five bunches of parsley, four turkeys, and you'd better send about five of those whole filets of beef."

It never ceased to amaze me that the White House thinks nothing of ordering groceries across several international boundaries. Here was Barbara giving a grocery list at a distance of

1910 miles, to be put aboard the next plane flying in our direction. Actually, it's cheaper, safer and dinner is likely to be more elegant this way, but I'm provincial enough to be impressed at an order of multidistance parsley.

When Barbara finished, I took the phone to talk to Bess Abell, the one person I knew who could deliver anything—including a piano.

"Bess, you're a can-do woman, and you're the only person I know who can do the impossible," I said, picking up the LBJ technique. "On the next plane, we need a piano which the President can give to a school here. That's what they want in El Salvador, and I'll bet you can do it."

Bess is accustomed to unusual requests, and her voice didn't even quaver. "Tell me more about the school, so I can talk to my friends at Steinway," she said.

I emoted about ten minutes and she said, "I'll get to work on it."

Steinway does a great deal of work on pianos at the White House and Blair House. Since it is a public-spirited company, we thought Steinway might contribute at least a portion of the cost of the proposed gift.

Meanwhile, I turned my attention to the litter cans. San Salvador is filled with American firms. I had met a great many of their officials as I dashed in and out of the embassy, and I was impressed with their activities in local groups. The wives helped out at churches and craft shops. They knew the country well, and I got the impression that on weekends they did more than seek out the nearest golf course.

That evening at the embassy I cornered the local representative of Texaco. "Don't you have a lot of empty oil drums sitting around?" I asked.

He nodded. I proceeded to tell him about the Lyndon B. Johnson School and its littered yard. I asked him to contribute some old oil drums, and said I would talk the teachers and children into painting them with gay animals and flowers.

"We'll contribute the cans and the paint and brushes," he said. "Just tell me where you want them delivered."

Now, that's my kind of a gringo imperialist!

Meanwhile, I had a call from Washington. Bess was on the phone, and she was jubilant. She had the piano. Steinway had made it possible, and she had just talked the Air Force into putting it on the next flight headed for El Salvador.

"Do they know the size of it?" I asked.

"Well, I told them it was a large, bulky package," Bess said with a mischievous giggle.

I went back to the LBJ School that afternoon, bursting with all my good news. The teachers were delighted about the litter cans, and they promised to start some painting projects for the children to decorate them. This had the double advantage of making the children conscious of the litter can, a strange new object in a Latin-American ghetto.

The Texaco oil drums turned out to be the most artistic litter cans you ever saw. Every flower had a smiling face. The animals they devised for decoration had their mouths wide open to devour the trash! But the new piano called for a special ceremony, I thought, and wouldn't it be nice when the President came to present it, for a group of children to sing during the presentation? I told the Señora Principal the good news. A piano was coming!

"Can we keep it?" she asked instantly.

"Absolutely, it is yours!" I told her. "Now, you show me which teacher plays the piano so we can have some songs when the President comes."

"Oh," she said, very matter-of-factly, "there is no one here who plays the piano."

"You mean we've brought you a piano and no one can play it?" I said, trying to keep my voice from hitting high C.

"That's right," she said.

"Well then, why in the world, if no one plays the piano, did you want a piano?"

"Ah," she said, waving her finger in my face. "If you give us a piano, then the Minister of Education, he has to give us a music teacher."

That gnarled old principal with less than a high school education had just "conned" one world power out of a piano and her own government out of a teacher.

Hooray for the Señora!

She invented her own alliance for progress.

## *And We Can Never Go Back to That Town Again!*

The First Lady had sand in her shoes. And God knows you need to escape from behind that big iron fence around the White House once in awhile and get the feel of the country. So we traveled 200,000 miles to plant trees on mountaintops and in ghettos, to open schools in Appalachia, to visit the Head Start projects of a Newark slum, to walk through the fields of bluebonnets in a Texas pasture. From San Simeon perched above the surging Pacific to a mountaineer's shack in North Carolina, from Cape Kennedy to the redwood forests, we traveled by rubber raft, bus, ski lift, surrey, orchard wagon, rail and foot, and in Mrs. Johnson's least favorite vehicle of all, jet plane.

"I like to get out and see the people behind the statistics," she would say as we walked through the ghetto. "It makes Lyndon's memos and working papers come to life for me."

Or when we rode the rafts bouncing along through Mariscal Canyon, she would wax poetic, "How very pleasant a simple thing can be, a vagrant breeze, a drink of water, just the feeling you have enough strength to cope with paddling a canoe—to get out in the open and come to terms with things."

In the process of our travels, we saw a lot of good things

happening in this country. Some were self-starting in the local community. Some had been initiated with the dollars and know-how of Uncle Sam. Mrs. Johnson's visit was a most effective way to underline the success story of the Adminstration and get it into print and on TV.

My job was to engineer and organize the trips, direct the advance teams; in short, to keep the First Lady moving at a useful pace, find the happenings along the way, gather together enough press for good coverage (35 to 85 from well-placed papers, networks and magazines was the ideal number). Then I would charter the plane, dispatch the advance teams, and worry and pray that the weather would be good, the copy plentiful, the First Lady would be pleased, and, hopefully, we would serve the nation and the President.

A Lady Bird Safari was something to behold. A mayor would be standing at the airport. Beside him, his wife, with a newly lacquered coiffeur and an armful of roses, and the local welcoming committee. They were often startled to see the plane door swing open and, instead of the First Lady, a Secret Service agent descend the plane steps rapidly, followed by an overweight press secretary with a walkie-talkie, shouting orders to anyone in the vicinity. Next came a motley crew of cameramen, armed with their Nikis, tripods and sound equipment, then a battered group of newswomen carrying typewriters and notepads.

As Jane Schermerhorn of the *Detroit News* described this scene: "It's Lady Bird Johnson's traveling companions, not the places they visit, who need preservation and beautification on one of her trips."

On the ground at the airport, the advance men or women, always recognizable by the glazed and occasionally bloodshot look in the eyes, would be frantically signaling: "Press buses this way! Press buses this way!"

Last—after everyone else was off the plane—came the First

Lady, always prompting the same remarks from her viewers: "So much prettier than her pictures."

That was the routine, as town after town was invaded by the First Lady's entourage.

Many ingredients made these trips worthwhile—most of all, Mrs. Johnson's good inquiring mind, with curiosity and compassion and encouragement for whatever she was seeing. Before taking such a trip, she wanted to read everything there was to know about the area or the people and their history.

"He that would bring home the wealth of the Indies must carry the wealth of the Indies with him!" she would quote from the inscription on the front of Union Station, and dispatch me for armloads of background materials.

The press welcomed a First Lady who got out and did something. And since it also gave the reporters, columnists and commentators a welcome break with their daily Washington routine, they were enthusiastic backers of all trips. Mrs. Johnson considered herself just one more trained observer who would help them get their story. She had no airs of importance. We all rode together on the same plane and often in the same bus, sharing the same discomforts and the same glamour.

I tapped all the talent I could find in and out of government to work with my staff on the trips. Good organization was the difference between success and disaster. A telephone in the right place at the right moment for a reporter's deadline, and baggage delivered on time to each hotel room, plus champagne at the end of the day, were vital ingredients. One key to success was to pick a theme for the trip which indicated the mission and stick to it, no matter how many local Democrats wanted her to visit *their* favorite charity.

"I want to go down to see what the Teachers Corps is doing in Appalachia," Mrs. Johnson said one day. "See if you can work out something in March."

This kind of request set off a whole strategy of exploring

and planning that produced a three-day trip called "Adventure in Learning," which took the First Lady and a plane load of reporters to the schoolrooms of West Virginia, North Carolina and Tennessee.

"Appalachia lies deep in the heart of the nation. It is no less deep in the heart of the President," she said on departing the White House, and went on to prove it.

This particular trip ("Adventure in Learning") began in the East Room with a film about "Pancho," a small Mexican-American boy who had been medically salvaged by a Head Start project in California. Because of Head Start's medical staff, a serious thyroid deficiency was discovered in Pancho and corrected. Now, instead of the frightened, sleepy, puffy child, he was alert and, on this particular morning, a constant visitor to the bowl of strawberries on the buffet table of the State Dining Room.

By showing the film in the East Room, with the President and Mrs. Johnson as well as Pancho on hand, we were able to illustrate to a wide and influential audience of educators and the press just how much Head Start means. It also furnished the President an audience for one of the best speeches he ever made—one that required no notes because it came right from the heart.

The President was introduced by Sargent Shriver, director of the anti-poverty program. Shriver noted, "This is not the first time the President has seen this film. He's seen it twice before."

When the President arose, he corrected Shriver, "I've been seeing this story not twice but for thirty years, ever since I taught in a Cotulla, Texas, school. I brought my 'Pancho' home to Johnson City for the summer. His name was Juan Gonzalez, and my mother and I gave him a home. Now Juan is a successful businessman in South Texas." He continued to hammer home how much a little faith and investment could mean to the Panchos of the world.

Thus began this three-day trip, with a glowing send-off from the President. But the most interesting stop by far was in the mountains of North Carolina where people have, for generations, been landlocked in the hills. Only recently had the Teachers Corps begun to make an impact on the education of their young. We set up our press room in Asheville, North Carolina, at the former home of Thomas Wolfe, no less, because I wryly thought the ghost of this gifted man might inspire the reporters. Then our mission was to transport everyone (in three buses) for an hour and one half's drive to a tiny North Carolina mountain town—Canada Township—visit the school and also a mountaineer family, Mr. and Mrs. Eldon Mathis. This school was located eleven miles from the nearest phone and thirty miles from the nearest doctor.

Some hint of the planning as well as the mission is given in the detailed memorandum from our able advance man, Nash Castro, who had become an essential part of our trips because of his commendable ability to get things done well. Castro, lent to us by the National Park Service, had been in North Carolina three days before we got there. During this time, he converted the Thomas Wolfe home, with telephones and teletypes, into a press room. He had also become a familiar sight in Canada Township, our ultimate destination.

His memo reads:

> To: Mrs. Johnson
> From: (Advance Man) Nash Castro
>
> At 8:30, as you board the bus at the Asheville hotel entrance for Canada Township, you will be presented with a bouquet of gaily-colored leaves from the area by a 13-year-old Girl Scout. Name is Linda Suzanne

Woods. During bus ride, Dr. Ray Sizemore, head of Teachers Corps at Western Carolina College, will brief you and press on the loud speaker we have installed in the bus. As you enter Canada Township, you will move to a school bus for the drive (4 miles) to the home of Mr. and Mrs. Mathis. It is a winding dirt road. When the bus stops, you will still have to walk down a dirt road to the house, about five minutes away. The road is likely to be muddy. PLEASE WEAR A PAIR OF EXPENDABLE SHOES. Gertie Moss, principal of the school, will be your guide. Mr. and Mrs. Mathis will probably be in their front yard when you come. However, you will have to hop over a small stream and climb through a low fence to get to the yard. PLEASE WEAR A LOOSE SKIRT. The Mathises have seven children. Mr. Mathis ekes out his livelihood by working part-time in a nearby sawmill, which has been shut down because of a serious accident. Poor as they are, they keep all seven children in school which is remarkable for this area. They are thrilled you are coming. One of their children, Earl, suffered a bad burn on his right leg recently; his older sister has been suffering from a toothache but fears going to the dentist. In the center of the room is a potbellied stove. Nearby is a television set, which occasionally works in the mountains. The Mathis grow and can their own vegetables and fruits. Incidentally, Mrs. Johnson, THIS WAS BEAR COUNTRY UNTIL NOT TOO LONG AGO.

The bus trip proved to be exactly as Nash had described it, except for one thing. As we were riding along, I received a walkie-talkie message from the Secret Service man at Canada

Township School with these two alarming bits of news: a springtime outbreak of measles had occurred and half a dozen of the children were home, and the school was highly contagious. "Do you still want to come?" the SS agent asked. "Hell, yes," I replied impatiently, wondering how he thought anything short of all-out war could turn back three busloads of press converging on Canada Township at this point. What was the contagion period? Three weeks? I could envision fifty-five Washington reporters quarantined with measles. Oh, well, like Scarlett O'Hara, I'd think about that tomorrow.

The second salvo of glad tidings from the SS was this: "Are there Negro newspaper people aboard?"

"Yes."

"The people up here have never seen Negroes, and they are fearful there might be some insults."

"Well, we're going to broaden their education!"

I did take the precaution of alerting two staff people to stay close by the two Negro reporters to avert any problems. This precaution proved to be totally unnecessary.

Up, up, the bus pulled us, higher and higher into the mountains, thickly forested, but alive with rushing streams, and rich in rhododendrons. Two weeks before, on our first advance trip, we had spotted trickles of smoke from the moonshiners' stills in the region but there were none today. They knew the Feds were coming!

Finally, there was the clearing, and a tidy little schoolhouse with the schoolyard filled with children and a crowd of mountaineer parents all along the roadside, some carrying bouquets of wild flowers from the hills. They cheered as the First Lady stepped from our tour bus to meet the principal—redheaded, apple-cheeked Gertie Moss—and reboard the school bus to go visit the Mathis home. You meet some truly golden people in the hollows and one of them was Gertie Moss, who had taught there as long as she could remember, and been dipping into her own small salary for the emergencies—groceries for a family where the father had been laid off work or medicine. What would the world do without the Gertie Mosses?

Thanks to Nash's detailed memo, Mrs. Johnson was wearing her "expendable" shoes and "loose skirt" so she had no difficulty walking down the muddy mountain road, hopping the stream and climbing the fence to the Mathis home.

"It's best if I am with you," Gertie Moss explained. "There might be some folks up here who would think you are a revenuer."

The Mathis family was lined up in front of the two-room shack where they had enjoyed watching the "crazy TV" people for half an hour setting up their equipment in front of the cabin.

Clad in his best overalls, Mr. Mathis was direct and dignified. "Walk over this way," he warned. "We have to be careful of the rattlesnakes in the bean vines."

Mrs. Mathis put out her hand, "Ya'll come right in now," she welcomed Mrs. Johnson and the Secretary of Health, Education and Welfare, John Gardner, in Brooks Brothers's best.

The Mathises were proud they kept their children in school and, as Mr. Mathis said, "It ain't easy cause the rains come washing down the mountains, and you can't hardly climb to the bus stop up on the road."

"But Mrs. Moss don't have to send the man [the truant officer] for my children," Mrs. Mathis beamed proudly.

Mr. Mathis thought the four men teachers (supplied by the Teachers Corps) had helped a lot. The children's hair was cut now. They had new equipment at the school, and he and his "Mizziz" went there in the evening for programs. Maybe his older ones would not quit school at the third grade like he had. They might go down the mountain and go to the high school thirty miles away. He'd see.

Mrs. Johnson wanted to know what crops the Mathises raised. "The President and I have a garden at our place in Texas, and I love it," she said, enumerating the vegetables.

Mrs. Mathis said they raised some lettuce and beans and corn, "but the pigs beat us to the corn."

It was a common tongue, and before Mrs. Johnson left, she had put a jar of peach preserves from the LBJ Ranch into Mrs. Mathis's hands. "Nothing tastes as good as when it comes from your own garden," she said. "We asked the Home Demonstration woman to come to the ranch and show us how to preserve this."

The lesson was implied.

Before we left, a reporter asked Mr. Mathis what programs they watched on their TV set.

"*Lassie*," he said and listed a few more. Then, as an afterthought, he added, rather pleased with himself, "And we saw the President the other night. When he comes on, we don't turn him off. We leave him on jes' like it was any other program."

Mrs. Johnson thanked him and said she'd tell the President he had a fine family of friends in North Carolina.

We visited the Canada Township school, ate lunch off a tray with the youngsters, shook hands with the teachers and boarded our buses to drive seventy miles back to Asheville where there were more schools and our press room.

Canada Township would never quite be the same, nor would the reporters who learned through the eyes of the First Lady something more than they had known about rural poverty and the stumbling steps the government had begun taking to lend a hand.

Down the mountain, at Western Carolina College, Mrs.

Johnson continued the adventure in learning. She dedicated a new library and spoke to the students—the young future schoolteachers who might make the difference to all the Canada Townships of North Carolina.

There was—for all of us who had visited the Mathises and the Canada Township School—new meaning to the words when she quoted Thomas Wolfe: "To every man his chance—to every man, regardless of his birth, his shining, golden opportunity. To every man the right to live, to work, to be himself, and to become whatever thing his manhood and his vision can combine to make him. This is the promise of America."

That night a weary First Lady went to sleep in Asheville, but not before she visited the Thomas Wolfe home and read in his handwriting there, a prophecy: *"The wind is rising and the river flows."*

All night, amid the Wolfe family memorabilia in the boardinghouse which Thomas Wolfe had described in *Look Homeward, Angel,* and his other novels, the reporters pounded their typewriters. Canada Township was on the map.

After the trip, the First Lady went back to the White House and told the President that his Teacher Corps was helping bridge the education gap in Appalachia. If she told him that, he knew he could count on it.

Because Mrs. Johnson was a history buff, some of our trips took us to the homes of former Presidents. In New England, we learned to pronounce Quincy "Quinzy" and visited the home of the second and sixth Presidents of the United States—John Adams and John Quincy Adams. "The Old House" stands on a shaded street of Quincy, kept just as it was when the two Presidents lived there. Among the treasures are napkins and china which Abigail Adams had carried by wagon to Washington and used when the new White House had none of its own niceties. Then, she had brought those things home and they have served the Adams family ever since. Mrs. Johnson's visit prompted a gathering of Adamses—some eight of them, erect and straight-laced as old Boston. The small group gathered in the living room of the Old House for a glass of sherry. Outside, reporters kept their eyes and ears directed toward the window to learn what was going on inside. The one pool reporter admitted inside was Nan Robertson of *The New York Times.* As she described the scene, Mrs. Johnson was talking to Mrs. Abigail Adams Homans, eighty-eight-year-old grande dame of Back Bay Boston. Mrs. Homans, who uses a hearing aid, is patrician and sprightly. To illustrate a point to her visitor, she waved her sherry glass, hit it against a piece of furniture and littered the priceless rug with priceless broken glass.

"Hell," Mrs. Homans exclaimed, "I do hope that wasn't one of the historic ones."

Today, the Old House is minus one historic sherry glass.

Trips had many purposes. Some, we made to help America discover itself, and also hopefully to help the balance of payments by keeping tourist dollars here. Sometimes, Mrs. Johnson would invite a group of traveling foreign newsmen, serving as their guide through HemisFair, bluebonnet fields, courthouse squares of her own home state.

It paid off—in thousands of words abroad in London, Madrid, Rome, Bonn, Paris—on the wonders of things to see in the U.S.A.

If she visited a national park, the tourist numbers tripled within a week. If she took a raft ride, this became the "in" thing to do. She knew it and she was glad to help the U. S. Treasury a bit by taking along reporters to tell about the wonders of the West or the East or wherever we went.

She thoroughly enjoyed every minute of it, and, to paraphrase Edna St. Vincent Millay, "there wasn't a vehicle she wouldn't take no matter where it was going."

The more remote the spot, the better she liked it. And, incidentally, so did the press, provided there were telephones there. And that was the problem. The telephone company takes a very dim view of providing service when you are eighty miles from anywhere.

The Big Bend National Park is the most remote park in the system. The nearest town of more than 12,000 persons is 250 miles away. The park consists of 708,000 acres of jackrabbits, tarantulas, cougars, rattlesnakes, wild rugged mountains and a stream, the Rio Grande River, which floods or trickles down the canyon separating Texas from Mexico. To get there, you can jet to San Antonio, switch to a two-engine plane and fly four hundred miles to an abandoned airstrip left over from World War II. If the pilot circles and looks hard, he might see a Secret Service agent holding a stocking in the wind to show which direction the wind is blowing. That's what we did—and, to the delight of the city-bred reporters, had to buzz the airfield twice before landing to scare off a herd of antelope. *Time* magazine accused me of "advancing the antelope" and arranging to have them there.

Once on the ground under the wide open spaces of West Texas there was still an eighty-mile bus trip to the entrance of the park, and then another fifteen miles to our motel atop the Ghost Mountains. Beyond us was land, land, land—a life-size set for *Bonanza.*

"It's the part of the world that was left over when the Lord made it," Mrs. Johnson said.

She was into blue jeans and ready to go moments after we arrived. With Interior Secretary Stewart Udall as our intrepid guide, we hiked the three-mile "Lost Mine Trail." Eighty-five reporters single-file were behind the First Lady and about thirty photographers ahead, jumping in and out of the trail for another picture. Occasionally a photographer would let out a yelp when he backed into a cactus for a sharper picture angle—and caught the point.

To get a press room set up with telephone lines required stringing eighty miles of wire from Alpine, Texas. But we did it. We had to arrange a special air pickup at our antelope landing strip to get the film and photos out to meet Eastern newspaper and TV deadlines.

Just for laughs, Charlie Boatner, assistant to Secretary Udall, arranged to have a man on a donkey outside the press room. The sign he wore said, PONY EXPRESS—WIRE SERVICE COPY HERE.

I was determined that everyone would have a wilderness experience—particularly those reporters who generally just cover the society beat, the drawing rooms and political salons of Washington where the most danger you encounter is someone's verbal knife in your back.

There were plenty of hearty, hospitable West Texans willing to help provide the wilderness experience. They mixed the best Margueritas (tequila, Triple Sec and lemon juice in salt-rimmed glass) at sunset. They cooked a beaten biscuit breakfast at sunup from a chuck wagon. This was the handiwork of the Odessa Chuck Wagon Gang, an organization of businessmen who become outdoor cooks as a civic promotion. The natives hadn't seen such a motley array since Pancho Villa rode across the Rio Grande.

Nothing pleased Mrs. Johnson as much as songs around the campfire, high in the Chisos Mountains, followed by some tall tales of Texas about Indian fights, buffalo raids and gold miners. We all stretched out on serapes around the fire, watched a full moon rise over the rugged crags, and Washington was farther away than the heaven of stars.

Even such a travel sophisticate as Frances Koltun of *Mademoiselle* magazine said, "This is the happiest time I ever had in my life."

"Not in your entire life?" I questioned. I knew we had provided something special that evening, but not *that* special.

"In my entire life!" she said.

Next morning we were up at dawn, eating a hearty breakfast and boarding twenty-four rubber rafts (six to a raft) to float down the slow-moving Rio Grande. It was the strangest armada since Churchill gathered up every kind of boat and vessel for Dunkirk. The rafts of photographers went ahead, grinding away at our winding, meandering fleet.

The armada lasted seven hours, with a stop along the way at a sandbar I had named Rattlesnake Bar. First the photographers, then the First Lady and Secretary and Mrs. Udall, then the Secret Service raft, then the writing pool raft, and then the rest of the laughing, singing press corps. On either side of the Rio Grande the canyon walls rose high, filled with canyon wrens having a noisy birdlike discussion of the invasion of their river. Occasionally, there would be a clearing, and perhaps a few sleepy Mexicans had wandered up to stare at us from their side. The river would narrow, and we could almost touch Texas with one hand and Mexico with the other.

Then we began to scrape bottom. The rains had come too early that year, and the river was now running low. Most of us had to get out and wade, often hitting a deep hole and plunging downward to come up soaked. One raft was named Martini because it was always on the rocks.

Jim Blair of the *National Geographic* magazine plunged underwater but came up smiling. The three dripping cameras around his neck were none the worse for wear. Wouldn't you know that the *Geographic* provided waterproof underwater cameras for its photographers?

Nothing equaled, however, the sight of one newswoman who carried an opened red umbrella on trail and raft ride, throughout the entire trip. Another slipped off her jeans to reveal a revealing black and white bikini.

Seven hours from the moment we had boarded the rafts, we waded out, miles downstream. There stood our hospitable West Texas friends with cool Margueritas in hand and a steak supper sizzling on the fire.

I flung myself on the grass beside Mrs. Johnson and Stewart Udall. "How did you like your wilderness experience?" Mrs. Johnson teased me.

"Frankly," I said, "I like the parks where all the concessions are run by the Rockefellers."

We left Big Bend Park next morning. The following Sunday, park records show that the number of visitors had tripled. Again, Mrs. Johnson had helped her countrymen discover America, a part of America they hadn't known before.

All raft rides weren't as successful as this one. One down the Snake River in Wyoming was undertaken despite a heavy downpour, and we had to take shelter under a tarpaulin as we floated on for three more hours. Our boatman was Brent Eastman, a handsome outdoorsy type who had escorted Lynda occasionally. Naturally, the romantic-minded UPI reporter, Helen Thomas, stayed out in the rain to interview Brent while he paddled. The rest of us passed a handy bottle of whiskey "for medicinal purposes" under the tarpaulin.

The purpose of the trip was to show how nature unmolested by signs was more beautiful. Art Buchwald, the humor columnist, showed up in a Scottish golfer's outfit for the raft trip—woolen knickers, cap and visor, plaid coat and a pipe. He was drenched before the end of the ride.

"Art, what can I do to make you more comfortable?" I asked.

"Almost anything will make me more confortable," he replied.

To get even with the miserable sightseeing expedition and to help amuse our group, Art served as periodic city-boy guide. He would gaze through the rain across the vast meadows to the three magnificent snow-capped mountains in the distance and remark teasingly, "What a lovely place for a lot of billboards." Or add, "Can't you just envision a whole series of orange-topped Howard Johnson's in this setting? My, how I miss the neon lights."

Mrs. Johnson loved the outdoors and was always game for hikes and animal viewings at any hour. She was staying at the camp of Laurance and Mary Rockefeller at the JY Ranch in the Grand Tetons of Wyoming when we decided to go find some bear. This wasn't difficult because the foreman of the JY had a garbage dump where he emptied orange peels each day at 5 P.M. The bears knew it and regularly showed up for this delicacy.

"We'll be there at five," Mr. Rockefeller said, putting Mrs. Johnson and me in the back seat of his car. The Secret Service car followed. We went to the garbage dump and sat —and sat—and sat. For one solid hour we sat, and nothing happened.

"It goes against my grain," Mr. Rockefeller said finally, "to spend an entire hour contemplating a garbage dump."

So we left, our mission unaccomplished. Not until hours later did it dawn on us why we had been bearless. The Secret Service car always keeps its motor running, which frightened the bears away.

Another penalty of high office!

Mr. Rockefeller was one of our most enthusiastic fellow

travelers. He was anxious for us to take a trip up the Hudson River to his family's home at Tarrytown and to see all of the local efforts to preserve the charm and historic houses of that area whose citizenry had included Rip Van Winkle and Jay Gould.

He didn't have to ask twice.

Advancing Rockefeller trips is the best of all worlds. The family's vast array of bright young staff, as well as the accommodations, are impressive, even when you've become spoiled at the White House level. So another trip was born for the spring of 1968—amid rumors that Governor Rockefeller was running for the Presidency.

Our plan was to build the theme of the trip around "American Beginnings on the Hudson River." We decided to start at the Statue of Liberty, take a boat up the river, detouring into the Harlem River for a special conservation ceremony there, announcing a new park in Harlem.

Laurance Rockefeller serves as chairman of the State of New York Council of Parks and Outdoor Recreation. After considerable effort, he had obtained a piece of land on the Harlem River, presently a junkyard, for a state park. It would be a strategic outlet for the ghettos of Harlem. The federal government was going to kick in $455,000.

Mr. Rockefeller loves nothing better than a project where everyone has put in some money—not just the Rockefellers. This Harlem Park was clearly an ideal example. It would bring the governor of the state, who just happened to be a Rockefeller, and the mayor of New York, John Lindsay, and George Hartzog, director of the National Park Service, all together on this happy occasion. It illustrated state, federal and local participation.

But what I hadn't foreseen, and what Mr. Rockefeller hadn't foreseen, was that Mayor John Lindsay—at this particular moment of his life (with dreams of the Presidency)—had his own cold war underway with the Rockefellers.

So when I called the office of the mayor of New York and invited him to be present for an eleven o'clock ceremony on the Harlem River, I suffered one of the frostiest responses in history from his aide. Within an hour, the mayor himself had called me back at the White House.

"This Harlem ceremony is out of the question," he said, "because I cannot assure the safety of the First Lady. That boat will pass under five bridges, and I just don't have enough policemen to protect the First Lady."

Was this excuse just politics? We were not afraid, and I was pretty sure the mayor's office was trying to avoid spotlighting anything the Rockefeller family—Nelson or Laurance—had accomplished.

I did some checking around and found I was right. The city administration considered New York City the mayor's private political preserve. Harlem was the mayor's ghetto; Bedford-Stuyvesant was Bobby Kennedy's ghetto. The mayor didn't want anyone fooling around in his ghetto except him.

In fact, there was so much ghetto-jealousy in New York that once when Bobby Kennedy talked Mrs. Vincent Astor into giving $1,000,000 for a project in Bedford-Stuyvesant, the mayor became so enraged, she had to give another $1,000,000 to his ghetto in Harlem. Fortunately for Mrs. Astor, the mayor and the Senator only had one ghetto each.

Mrs. Johnson thought the whole stalemate over the Harlem ceremony was silly. She didn't see any reason the mayor should stop the presentation.

"I'm not afraid. Just invite him, and if he doesn't want to come along, he doesn't need to," she said. "We can have the ceremony anyway. It is a good project, and Mr. Rockefeller has worked hard for it."

The mayor was rocked by the news. I got the impression that if we tried to go up that river, he would personally be there to fire upon us. I began to explore the possibility of whether we could circle Manhattan and enter the Harlem River above the bridges, tiptoeing in without the mayor's knowledge. In fact, I got so carried away with the strategy of invasion that I even contemplated asking for a U. S. Marine Division as escort.

The mayor realized that we were determined. We were going to have our ceremony, if we had to have it in Grant's Tomb, a setting which might have been more cheerful under the circumstances.

He finally agreed to let Mrs. Johnson come into the city of New York as long as she stayed in the Hudson River and didn't come over to Harlem. He promised to board our Hudson River boat at 43rd Street. We would pull out into the river. The federal check would be turned over in a ceremony. And then we would come back to the dock and let him off.

We agreed to go along with this ridiculous itinerary rather than argue with the mayor any more, although it didn't make sense to be giving a check for a Harlem River park in the middle of the Hudson River. But such is politics!

Our trip started at the Statue of Liberty, and all went well. We sailed up the Hudson River to the 43rd Street Circle Line docks. First, Governor and Mrs. Rockefeller came aboard. Then, the mayor arrived, flashing his boyish smile toward everyone who wasn't named Rockefeller. Out we sailed to the middle of the Hudson River. The ceremony was performed. Mrs. Johnson and National Park Service Director George Hartzog turned the check over to Laurance Rockefeller. By sheer brute force, I managed to get mayor, governor, Mrs. Johnson and Laurance Rockefeller close enough together for one picture. Cameras flashed. The deed was done, and we set sail back to the Circle Line harbor. But sailing up the river at a rapid rate came the city of New York's red fireboat. The mayor just couldn't stand to be there any longer than necessary. He had ordered it to pull alongside. As it did, he leaped from our deck to the fireboat and was off down the river, leaving the governor startled, Mrs. Johnson amused, and Laurance Rockefeller happily holding the check. Well, boys will be boys.

All political figures we met on trips were not as difficult as handsome John Lindsay.

One of the best traveling companions we ever had was Harry S Truman. When King Paul of Greece died in 1964, the President named a special delegation to attend the funeral in Athens. Heading the delegation were Mrs. Johnson, to deliver the President's personal condolences, and former President Truman who had never visited Greece, although his Greek-Turkish loan had saved that country.

If you've got to go, King Paul knew how to go. All the royal blood of Europe came to pay respects for three days.

Each foreign delegation was met by a royal relative and escorted into Athens. We drew Prince Michael, the handsome young cousin of the new King Constantine, and he had obviously done his homework for the assignment. So when he settled in between President Truman and Mrs. Johnson on the ride from the airport, he opened the conversation with the amenities.

"I feel very close to the United States," he graciously began, "because my great-great-grandfather was aide-de-camp to General Grant."

But the mischief-making Harry Truman wasn't going to let this pass. He slapped the young man on the knee with a hearty gesture and said, "Well, son, as far as this lady and I are concerned, he was on the wrong side."

The young prince was ashen, and Mrs. Johnson tried to rescue the situation which Truman was thoroughly enjoying.

"Well, the important thing about that war," she said, "was our ability to emerge as a strong nation."

But the Prince was not the same for the rest of the visit.

President Truman also took a dim view of all the royal cousins and aunts. Some two hundred of them, many from nations which hadn't existed for fifty years, were on hand. They had dug out their old uniforms, plumes and medals for the occasion, and the only person in Athens who looked grander was the doorman of the Athens Hilton.

Mr. Truman gazed on this array of royalty briefly, taking in the red and blue uniforms, and the chests full of medals, and then exclaimed, "Never occurred to me to bring all my medals. I got a whole tubful like these back in Independence."

But despite this attitude, President Truman had a respect for the dignity of the state funeral. When the press in Athens kept trying to get him to hold a press conference, he refused. He felt it just wouldn't be proper at this time. Some of the Greek reporters prevailed on me to ask him one more time to meet with them. After all, Greece owed him a lot.

I went to President Truman and told him how eager all the press was to interview him. But he was steadfast.

"No, child," he said. "Some damn fool reporter would ask me some damn fool question, and I'd give some damn fool answer."

That's what I call good Missouri horse-sense.

In September 1967, Secretary of Agriculture Orville Freeman was anxious to advertise the bountiful life of small-town living. It was a worthy cause—illustrating through a trip, how many advantages are available to people in the small towns of this country—good schools, country theater, clean air and unlittered parks. A surprisingly large percentage of this nation lives in towns of less than 25,000 population, and my own political mind was at work. Didn't we have an election coming up next year? Wouldn't it be well to plan a trip with the First Lady—and, yes, the second lady, too—to see some of these towns?

So, "Crossroads U.S.A." was the theme and Mrs. Johnson and Mrs. Humphrey set out to see the small towns from Montivideo, Minnesota, through six Midwestern states to Hannibal, Missouri. Highlight of this trip was a twenty-mile boat ride down the Mississippi River from Quincy, Illinois, to Hannibal, where we would meet, in person, Tom Sawyer and Becky Thatcher in that famous home town of Mark Twain. Well, not exactly in person, but the town does have a young freckle-faced boy and a pretty girl with ringlets who serve as a facsimile each year for the tourists.

One reporter—Barbara Furlow of *U.S. News & World Report*—was so taken with Mark Twain Country that she wrote her own version in the Huck Finn style of *Life on the Mississippi.*

"You don't know about this trip without you have read a release by the name of Operation Crossroads, but that ain't no matter. That release was made by Mrs. Elizabeth Carpenter, and she told the truth, mainly. There was things which she stretched, but mainly she told the truth. That is nothing. I never seen anybody but lied one time or another, without it was Miss Lady Bird or Muriel. They wuz along too and the release is mostly a true release, with some stretchers as I said before."

One of the real "stretchers" turned out to be our trip down the lazy river, the Mississippi. It was supposed to be luncheon aboard and a two-hour trip downriver, well—two and one-half hours at most. Our advance man made the mistake of advancing it in a motorboat when we were riding a sizable river barge. Then Orville Freeman made an addition. He felt we shouldn't just ride joyfully down the Mississippi on our river boat. Oh, no—not when our boat could be pushing six barges holding 8500 tons of wheat.

"Don't you see the value of that?" said Secretary Freeman. "This wheat is headed for India and it will be part of the whole story, the breadbasket of the U.S.A. producing wheat for the world. All we do is let our boat push the barges and after we get to Hannibal, we wave goodbye to the golden grain and none of us is the worse for wear."

There was one thing I forgot. I forgot to have the advance man run the river again, pushing 8500 tons of wheat. When our day on the river arrived, it took, not two hours, but four, to get to Hannibal where a very weary and bedraggled Tom Sawyer and Becky Thatcher and all the weary townspeople who had waited for hours welcomed Mrs. Johnson and Mrs. Humphrey.

I had the distinct feeling that "the good life" of Smalltown U.S.A., which we had come to salute, was sometimes better when we weren't there.

# *Forgive Them Their Press Passes*

## PART I: HIS PRESS

Sooner or later all Presidents have their share of trouble with the press. Lyndon Johnson had more than his share—both sooner and later.

Partially, the problem is numbers. There is only one President and there are 930 reporters accredited to the White House. Well, actually, 928. While we were there, Arthur Krock retired and Walter Lippmann left town. I always suspected the President felt these were two of his major achievements.

The majority of people never meet the President. They get to know him through the news media. That's why Presidents have press secretaries—a task that requires the combined wisdom of Plato, Sophocles, Aristotle and Spiro T. Agnew. A press secretary is the voice of the President. Every misstep has worldwide implications. And twice each day, the President's press secretary is publicly on the rack.

Of course, there is never a shortage of advice on how to run your job. For most members of the press are armchair Presidents, armchair Secretaries of State, armchair press secretaries. And, let's face it, most Presidents are armchair reporters. Occasionally, I would wonder if we couldn't have one day when everyone switched jobs just for the hell of it. I always wondered what it would be like to have the President demanding that Sarah McClendon get us out of Vietnam, ma'am, and watch while she did it before the next press briefing.

Actually, the White House press corps is a lovable bunch—to their mothers. They wait for news from the large lounge area in the West Wing and transmit millions of words from a tiny workroom nearby.

Before LBJ, the waiting lounge had always been a nondescript room whose most prominent piece of furniture was a tremendous round, badly scratched and cracked table where reporters tossed their coats and hats in a disorderly pile. In our zeal to improve things, a decorating job was undertaken. The historic round table went out. New green leather couches were installed, along with chairs and tables arranged in conversation groups. The whole room took on a different look, if somewhat "motel modern." One veteran reporter, Eddie Folliard of *The Washington Post,* arrived the morning after it had been remodeled, took a long look in wide-eyed disbelief and said, "I'll play the piano, but I won't go upstairs."

There are at least sixty White House "regulars" on duty there all the time, plus innumerable photographers.

One of their main gripes, and they voiced it incessantly, was the unpredictability of the President. News doesn't break in neat and tidy packages, and LBJ refused to serve it up to suit the convenience of the press. He would put out a story anytime and anywhere he wanted to—in walking press conferences on the South Lawn, in hastily called conferences at a variety of locations from his office to the upstairs dining room. Occasionally, he invited a group of newsmen to go swimming with him, and they found themselves getting the news while doing the Australian crawl up and down the White House pool.

The President's idiosyncrasies so irritated the press that I frequently felt reporters let this color their appraisal of him. But there were times when I could understand their complaints.

One evening when Hal Pachios and Joe Laitin were manning the press office, the President was meeting with McGeorge Bundy about the Dominican crisis. The hungry and weary reporters wanted to go home, but Bundy insisted that they stay because he wanted the President to make an announcement of some anticipated development. The hours dragged by, and the press grew increasingly irritable. Finally, near midnight, "Mac" Bundy called Hal and said that the President had decided not to make the announcement; so the press could go home. Joe and Hal stared at each other in horror. How could they possibly face the angry mob?

"Okay, Hal," Joe said. "Let's do it this way. You get on the loud speaker and tell the press. I'll have the window open, we'll climb out and we'll both run like hell. When you hit Pennsylvania Avenue, you turn right. I'll turn left."

And that is what they did. Press aides must be fast on their feet in thought and motion.

Self-crowned king of the White House press room is Merriman Smith, who has covered five Presidents, beginning with FDR. Smitty, by virtue of seniority, is the one who concludes every press conference by saying, "Thank you, Mr. President." He's been doing it for twenty-eight years. And not once in all those twenty-eight years has one President ever said, "You're welcome."

This is not to reflect on Smitty. He is able, knowledgeable and constructive—a legend in his own time. Even his office pays homage. They practically strike up *Ruffles and Flourishes* and *Hail to the Chief,* when he arrives each day, and generally treat him with the same awe and respect with which a French flagbearer might have treated General De Gaulle.

When Joe Laitin was assistant press secretary to LBJ, he

was awakened one morning about 3 A.M. by the desk man at Smitty's bureau, United Press International. The editor wanted to check a fact that appeared in a story which had broken earlier that day.

Rather surprised by the call, Joe gave him the information but added, "Why did you have to call me at 3 A.M.? Your own man Smitty could have answered the question."

"I know," replied the UPI man, "but I wouldn't dare call Mr. Smith at this hour!"

Smitty gains such extra attention and makes so much money delivering speeches, appearing on TV and writing books that he is valuable property at UPI. His sense of humor shows up more in speeches than in his UPI copy, although there are occasions when White House stories present a real chance for humor.

Back when Eisenhower was President, Smitty found out that the squirrels in the White House grounds were digging up Ike's putting green on the South Lawn to bury nuts. President Eisenhower told the gardening staff to do something about it. Rather than risk poisoning the squirrels, which was certain to invoke the wrath of animal lovers, they caught them, put them in a bag, transported them to the suburbs and let them loose.

Smitty learned about it and wrote a feature story about this considerate technique of removing squirrels from the White House grounds. The story was read by a farmer in nearby Rockville, Maryland, who suddenly noticed that his garden had been invaded by squirrels, more squirrels than he had ever seen. His lettuce patch was being destroyed with digging. A few nights later, the Secret Service agent on duty at the White House was surprised to see a large bag suddenly flung over the fence. In it were two dozen live squirrels—a returned gift from the irate farmer.

LBJ had his animal problems, too, in the form of six lively beagles with twelve lively ears. One day, the President got playful and lifted up one of the dogs by the ears. The dog yapped—the yap heard round the world. Douglas Cornell of the AP wrote the ultimate "Man Bites Dog" story. The zealous AP also promptly solicited comments from humane societies. Weary postmen cursed as they struggled in with heavy sacks of protesting mail. I know because dog mail was, unfortunately, my department. We answered the correspondence with a tender photograph signed by the President and autographed with the paw prints of the beagles, Him and Her.

While the controversy raged, the President doggedly maintained that beagles enjoyed having their ears stroked and pulled. But the public wasn't convinced. About two weeks later, the President was playing with the dogs again in the garden, and reporters and photographers were present. To prove his point, he patted one of the beagles, gently took hold of his ears, pulled, and said to the dog, "Now don't you yap or one of those photographers will take your picture." The dog cooperated beautifully. When he was picked up by his ears, he didn't even open his mouth. He almost smiled with pleasure.

President Johnson had four press secretaries during his term of office and all of them sought to serve his best interests. Every time the President changed one there would be scattered rumors that I might get the job. And each time such a rumor appeared, it put the fear of God in both the President and me. I knew my limitations, and it would have been about twenty-four hours before I had an eyeball to eyeball confrontation with the President. And he has stronger eyeballs!

Pierre Salinger manned the barricades for a few months after President Kennedy's death. Then George Reedy took over until July 1965. Bill Moyers sat in that hot seat until February

1967. George Christian took the last stint until January 20, 1969. Each tried to serve the President in his own way. The roly-poly, cigar-smoking Salinger was an invaluable help in advising the President during the transition. LBJ relied on his advice because Pierre was well acquainted with the White House press.

One midnight, early in the Johnson Administration, Pierre Salinger called me to say, "The President wants some of us to telephone the columnists we know best and give them the following story." (I was in bed sleeping peacefully beside my husband—as any good woman should.)

I don't even remember what the story was, but it was something which was better announced indirectly than directly.

"He hopes you will call Drew Pearson and Dorothy McCardle of *The Washington Post* and any others you know particularly well and tell them about it."

"Okay, Pierre," I said, turning on the lamp by my bed. "I'll be glad to."

At this moment my eyes fell on Les—my Prince Charming and favorite columnist—snoring beside me. Flushing with a sense of power, I added, "Pierre, I'll bet I'm the only press officer in town who merely has to roll over to plant a story."

"Don't be so damned sure," he replied and hung up.

Salinger was adept with wisecracks and well liked by the reporters. He and the President parted friends. When Salinger offered his resignation so he could go to California and run for the United States Senate, Johnson reached in his pocket and pulled out money to pay the filing fee as his contribution. He campaigned for Salinger, and even tried to patch up—right on the campaign platform—a growing mid-campaign squabble between Pierre and his wife, Nancy. At a California Democratic rally, when Nancy conspicuously took a seat far away from her husband, Johnson the matchmaker literally yanked them together for the benefit of cameramen. It was probably the only time during the campaign they were photographed together. After Pierre was defeated, it was only a matter of time until Pierre, totally devoted to politics, and Nancy, totally devoted to art, separated. Fortunately, each lived happily ever after.

George Reedy, Press Secretary No. 2, was as lovable and lumbering as a St. Bernard. His unruly shock of gray hair and owlish glasses made him look like an oversized Quiz Kid. As press aide, he had worked for LBJ through his days as Senate Majority Leader with great success and helped the country get to know Lyndon Johnson the activist, the doer, the man who could bring men together. Against Reedy's own protestations, Johnson insisted that George become his White House press secretary. He was liked by reporters, but was more a philosopher than a generator of news.

Many times George found himself trying to double-talk his way between the President's penchant for secrecy and the reporters' desire to know.

One press briefing went like this:

> REEDY: As things now stand—I talked to the President about the Christmas situation—depending upon how far he gets on budget matters . . . it is possible that he may leave here Friday night after the Christmas tree lighting ceremony. This is still strictly off the record, not to be published and it is for planning purposes only because it is one of those things where the schedule is still fairly fluid, but I would recommend that whatever Christmas shopping you have to do in Washington be done between now and then.
>
> REPORTER: Would that mean then he would probably not come back until after the New Year or would it be a weekend trip?

REEDY: No. I think he would stay there over Christmas. However, I want to stress this is for planning purposes only and it is still entirely possible that he will not go at this point, but we are all pretty prudent.

REPORTER: While we are off the record, it is pretty clear, still off the record, that he is going to Texas?

REEDY: You are getting into percentages now. It is sufficiently sure that I am telling you all that I think you should be ready for it.

REPORTER: We do appreciate the time of warning. On the record we certainly appreciate the warning a few days ahead.

REEDY: Not on this record.

REPORTER: On the record we appreciate the off-the-record warning.

After seventeen months with the President on one side and the press on the other hammering away, faithful George limped out of the White House press office with, of all things, a severe case of hammer toes.

Bill Moyers, like an evangelical Lancelot from Texas, rode into the press office to face a disgruntled array of reporters. Quick in wit, the dark-eyed, bespectacled thirty-one-year-old Baptist preacher relished the spotlight. He thought the President needed a translator and he tried to be one. This pleased the columnists and annoyed the President, but for a few exciting months, it worked.

Moyers, articulate and canny, became the darling of the top name columnists. He concentrated his energies on prominent newsmen, lunching cozily at the better clubs and restaurants to spread the Johnson gospel. He established himself as a power in government, second in his eyes only to the President.

The poet Tennyson wrote that Lancelot's strength was "as the strength of ten, because his heart was pure." The new knight of the press office was strong, too, because he loved the corridors of power and walked them with a sure tread.

The Moyers press briefings were never a bore. When the daily papers carried stories that China's Mao Tse-tung had been swimming in the Yangtze River, the exchange went like this:

REPORTER: Bill, is there any chance the President might go for a swim in the Potomac?
MOYERS: No, but he will send Hubert Humphrey.
REPORTER: Will you give us advance notice if the President does go swimming?
MOYERS: He won't.
REPORTER: What will he do?
MOYERS: He plans to throw a silver dollar across.

Like his predecessors, Moyers was plagued by the President's desire to keep his travel plans a secret. This irritated the press constantly, and once prompted the following exchange:

REPORTER: I understand the President is going to Kansas City.
MOYERS: I can tell you forthrightly the President is *not* going to Kansas City.
REPORTER: Thank God.
MOYERS: I'll tell him.

When the trip actually was announced, the memorandum to the press corps outlining the plans often ended, "All of the above subject to change."

But complaints are a normal part of the White House press

picture. Reporters griped if there was too little news, or too much. Once in a briefing, Douglas Kiker of NBC sarcastically asked, "Why are we getting so much news?"

Moyers replied, "I intend to confound you with the truth."

Other Moyers exchanges are as follows:

REPORTER: Bill, can you tell us if the President prays?
MOYERS: He does.
REPORTER: When? Before meals?
MOYERS: That depends on what he's eating.

REPORTER: (At a Saturday morning briefing) We don't expect anything today?
MOYERS: I won't disappoint you.

REPORTER: Bill, has General De Gaulle's message arrived here yet?
MOYERS: No.
REPORTER: Why do you suppose it is taking so long?
MOYERS: Maybe the General is chiseling it himself.

REPORTER: Will you try to get some reporters on Air Force One for the next leg?
MOYERS: I'll take it up with the President.
REPORTER: But if we're on the press plane, how will we know?
MOYERS: When the President opens the door of Air Force One and tosses me out, you'll know.

REPORTER: Bill, was the President on the lake yesterday?
MOYERS: Yes.

REPORTER: Boating?
MOYERS: He just went for a walk.

REPORTER: Bill, did the President see red when he heard you released that bill he had not signed?
MOYERS: He did if he saw my face!

Moyers managed to cut most of these exchanges out of the public transcript, and thus they were never read by the President. But a few choice copies survive.

Bill also had a sense of humor about housing the press, when they needed to be on round-the-clock duty. When the President went to Bethesda Naval Hospital for his gall-bladder operation, Bill arranged to have thirty-six beds for the overnight press set aside in the hospital—in the psychiatric ward. The President asked Bill what became of the patients. Bill replied, "We gave them press cards."

News was fast-moving in the Moyers era, but it never moved fast enough for Johnson—literally. He would hold a press conference in his Oval Office and before the reporters were out the door, running for the phones, the President would be waiting impatiently over the AP and UPI news tickers. If the stories didn't click off fast enough, he would lift up the glass lid, reach down and pull the copy out—as though to speed it up. I was terrified he would get his arm caught in the machinery.

On one occasion, Al Spivak of UPI covered a Johnson announcement about a German Head of State who was coming to visit the ranch. Spivak dashed to the UPI telephone booth in the White House press room and was dictating his story to his office downtown.

"I reached about the fifth paragraph," Spivak recalls, "and suddenly I realized that Bill Moyers was pounding on the door of the phone booth. I stopped a minute, opened it a crack and Bill said, 'Al, the President is reading your story as it comes into his office. He feels you've given the wrong emphasis in the lead.'"

Spivak said he would have been indignant at such blatant news management, but he was too flattered by the instant high-level readership back in the President's office.

Another indication of the President's close attention to the news came one afternoon when he was watching TV as he rested in his bedroom. In a few minutes he was scheduled to greet his Ambassador to South Vietnam, Maxwell Taylor. Suddenly a newscaster was reporting in an excited voice that big black limousines were rolling up to the White House, and there was an extraordinary sense of urgency in the air. Johnson listened in disbelief, then said sarcastically to an aide, "Good Lord, we're at war and I've forgotten about it."

The Moyers era was not destined to last. The war in Vietnam was worsening. Johnson's popularity was declining. Tempers flared, and there was no turning back. The death of Bill's brother and increasing family responsibilities crowded in on him. Finally he left. It was a regrettable break, and one that caused suffering to both men. For Bill Moyers was the only press secretary who really attempted to interpret the President's acts and decisions and to influence them. The others saw their job simply as a mirror of the man. They followed the Boss's orders rather than endeavoring to question and argue. Johnson is a powerfully persuasive man. He respects those who argue against him, rare though they be.

Moyers was replaced by laconic George Christian, up from the Texas Political Establishment and Governor John Connally's rigorous training. He was exactly what President Johnson ordered—an efficient, understated spokesman, totally loyal, who preferred to say the minimum on any given subject. The times were turbulent, and perhaps a tight-lipped press policy was appropriate. George was scrupulously fair in his relations with the press. He never attempted to explain the President. He said what there was to say and no more. He was available to all reporters, not just the prima donnas of the world of journalism.

The Christian era was more inhibited and less inspired than the Moyers reign, but while there were fewer hits, there were also fewer errors.

It is too bad that, in the vernacular of the West, you couldn't cross-breed all four press secretaries. The perfect press secretary would have the camaraderie of Salinger, the knowledge of Reedy, the idealism and daring of Moyers and the cool of Christian.

Reporters who cover the White House domain hold a coveted assignment, and they seldom stray far from it. They are a profession of talented, sharp, witty, hilarious, congenital complainers. Most members of the White House press are good, really good, at their jobs. A few are lazy. And many, perhaps too many, are so impressionable that they get their news from each other. They like the security of agreeing with one another. As a result, there are many stories in Washington which are overcovered, and many which are never covered. To me, as press secretary, this was a constant source of frustration. There were some reporters, it seemed, who simply could not make the adjustment from the glitter of the Kennedy years to the hardworking—but no less exciting—pace of the Johnson era. There were some columnists who covered Lyndon Johnson by lunching with other columnists at downtown clubs. It disturbed me—as a Westerner by birth, and an Easterner by migration—to see the provincialism of Eastern journalists at work—to witness a real Eastern bias against the unfamiliar ways of a Western President.

What was the basic problem between the President and the press? Clearly they never understood each other. He made the mistake of assuming that reporters should be participants—more obliged to be citizens than critics. He never saw the press as a vast industry with hourly needs to produce a product in print or on the air, a need which requires some degree of planning. They never understood his desire to hold back news as it developed and wait until it was a fact. But a man is marked by what made him. Johnson had lost one election by 1311 votes; won another by 87. A man waits until all the votes are in.

While it can be said of the Johnson era that President Johnson was able to manage their news, it can also be said that they certainly never were able to manage him.

# *Forgive Them Their Press Passes*

## *PART II: HER PRESS*

No one ever offered me the job I had at the White House. I knew what I wanted. I asked for it. I got it.

It happened on a chilly afternoon in December 1963, when I sat before a crackling fire at the Elms, the Johnsons' Washington home before they moved into the White House. Mrs. Johnson and I were thinking out loud how the talent from LBJ's Vice Presidential staff could best be put to use in the White House. Finally I mustered up enough courage to say, "As for me, I would like to be your press secretary, if you'd let me."

"Of course, Liz, I'd love to have you as press secretary—and my staff director," Mrs. Johnson said.

I was delighted, for in my sixteen years as a reporter in Washington I had always been disappointed that no First Lady had ever named a professional newswoman as her press secretary. Instead, this duty had been left to just a secretary, who had little or no conception of the requirements of the news media—newspapers, magazines, book publishers, radio and TV—foreign and domestic.

I had the best of all worlds. I was in a position to serve the

President by serving Mrs. Johnson, perhaps to influence him from time to time, to lend a hand to his press relations in an indirect way, and yet not have the responsibility of that grueling daily job of briefing newsmen.

At one time, nearly all news was handled by the President's press secretary, out of his West Wing office. I always felt it lessened the dignity of the President's office to have a press briefing interspersed with questions about hamsters or the First Lady's clothes. The newswomen didn't like to ask them in the midst of discussion about Cuban missile crises and other world-shaking events. But before LBJ, they had no alternative.

Pierre Salinger had watched this happen during the Kennedy Administration and been rewarded for his labors with an autographed picture from Mrs. Kennedy which bore the inscription: *To Pierre, from the greatest cross you have to bear, Jacqueline Kennedy.*

I worked out a clear division of powers with Pierre. Under it, the President's press secretary would worry about all the news from the President, Kosygin, Vietnam and De Gaulle. I just had to worry about women, dogs, old brocades, Luci changing the spelling of her name, Luci becoming a Catholic, Luci having her ears pierced, Luci getting engaged, Luci getting married, Lynda and a broken engagement with Bernie Rosenbach, Lynda's engagement to Captain Charles Robb and Lynda's wedding; Peter Hurd and Eartha Kitt, a hot-tempered French chef and forty Lady Bird trips covering 200,000 miles.

My job as press secretary to the First Lady revolved around eighty-five women reporters who cover the family side of the White House. I may have had fewer reporters to worry about than the President's press secretary, but my newswomen work a seven-day week, and the big news always seemed to break on holidays. There is a good reason for this holiday disruption. This is the time when families—even First Families—get together and personal decisions are made. But that didn't make me any happier when, over July 4th weekend, Luci became a Catholic. On Christmas Eve, we announced her engagement to Pat Nugent. Over Labor Day, Lynda became engaged to Chuck Robb. I couldn't even put the phone down long enough to shoot off fireworks, open a Christmas present, or pay tribute to George Meany. But that's all part of being a press secretary.

When the Johnsons moved into the White House, I moved into the East Wing. During the next month, I gathered a staff of bright young women to serve the press in a manner to which they eagerly became accustomed. As one of their breed, I felt I knew what they wanted—insight into the Presidential family, entrance to the White House, and, most important, a First Lady who cared about her country. My own role was to be the link between the First Lady and the press.

My friends in the newspaper business were a tremendous help. Newspaper reporters are never shy about giving advice, and I sought it. At a series of meetings at my home, I asked each group: "How do you think the First Lady's press office should be run?" They didn't hesitate to answer:

"Never lie. Tell us you can't tell us, but never lie."

"Return our phone calls."

"Don't resent our intrusion. It's our job to know where the First Lady is and what she is doing. We resent being resented."

"Throw out the Renoirs and bring in the Remingtons," another advised. "If I have to write one more story about an antique clock, I am going to scream!"

Another recalled how one former First Lady spent all her time entertaining what she unflatteringly called, "the singing grandmothers." She entertained six hundred women a day and came out with the vaguest image of all.

One reporter told me of an unhappy experience with a former First Lady. "We would go to the airport to meet her when she was returning from New York. Even in the rain she never acknowledged us. Never even looked to the right or to the left. Never spoke to us, and it was our job to be there!"

With Mrs. Johnson, I knew this would be no problem. While she had never been a working newswoman, she understood a reporter's needs. From four years of journalism school at the University of Texas, she knew the language of the trade, the difference between an A.M. and P.M. deadline, that it is better to be accessible than evasive. She was never more than a telephone call away from me. She understood my problems and tried to ease them.

Most important, she wanted to be a working First Lady, not an ornamental one. Backed by the President's complete confidence in her ability—and his enthusiastic encouragement—she chose several projects which were ideally suited to her natural interest. In five years she busied herself underlining the War on Poverty with countless meetings in the White House. She created the First Lady's Committee for a More Beautiful Capital; she made national and local causes of rescuing the environment through White House meetings, trips and speeches; she encouraged her fellow citizens to Discover America through a series of delightful safaris.

"Call it corny if you will, but I want to boast about America," Mrs. Johnson said firmly.

She did these things, not only for her own pleasure and education, but also to serve a highly useful purpose: to share the story of America's beauty and potential with dozens of reporters—and, through them—millions of her countrymen.

"Perhaps I can just draw the curtain back a little bit wider so people may see and, I hope, act," the First Lady explained.

The President thought it was marvelous. He thought she was marvelous. He just hoped I wouldn't get her into too much trouble. He would kid me whenever these trips received good press coverage.

"Well, Liz, I see you got out your bullhorn and have Lady Bird all over page one," he said.

Or, if we hit a snag, as we often did, like meeting someone who would use Mrs. Johnson's visit to air criticism of the President, he wouldn't let me forget it.

One painful incident occurred on a dairy farm near Avoca, Wisconsin—the "Big Little Hill Farm" to be exact. It was owned by one Joseph Johnson and had been selected for the First Lady to visit by dozens of experts in the Department of Agriculture. But the experts missed one important point. The farmer was not only a successful dairy farmer, but also an outspoken critic of the government and, alas, LBJ.

The purpose of the trip, inspired by Secretary of Agriculture Orville Freeman, was to show how young farmers, under the Democratic Administration, had a golden opportunity in staying down on the farm. Hopefully, this would inspire other young couples to do the same. But while the experts did find the young farmer, they failed to ask him what the reporters asked: "Would you recommend farming as a life for young people?"

"Hell, no!" he said bluntly. "Not at today's prices."

The First Lady blushed. I was ready to kill our advance man.

Then, insult was added to injury. The farmer, we discovered, had been part of a big "dump milk strike" against Freeman the previous year. Reporters couldn't resist asking what political party the family supported. The farmer's wife replied tartly, "I'd just as soon not say."

Mission: Impossible.

After that, before we set out on any trip, the President

would chide me, "Are you going to see any more farmers on this trip, Liz?"

Despite this ribbing, I always knew the President was our enthusiastic backer. When we were out on a trip, I always awakened early and phoned the White House to find out how the New York and Washington papers carried the story of our activities. First, I would try to get hold of someone in the press office, and most likely I would find that the President's assistants were still home in bed at the ungodly hour of 6:30 A.M. So, in desperation, I would say to the switchboard operator, "Well, who *is* awake?"

"No one, Mrs. Carpenter, except the President. He's been on the phone the last half hour."

"Well, then, give me the President," I would reply.

The President would have read the papers already and understood completely why I was so eager to know how the story went in print. He could tell me succinctly. For instance, when we were in the Big Bend National Park on a Discover America trip with Secretary of Interior Stewart Udall, he summarized the coverage this way:

"You have a nice story on page one of *The New York Times*. There is a four-column picture above the fold. Lady Bird has on a Western hat and looks like the Lone Ranger. Udall is standing beside her looking like Tonto."

"There was a good story last night in the *News* by Wauhillau LaHay," and he would read her salty, down-to-earth story with expression. He told me about the interesting telecast on NBC by Nancy Dickerson.

Mrs. Johnson, on the other hand, seldom read her own press, which surprised and slightly annoyed me. But the President and I read every line. We are the kind of people who, after every performance, wait up for the reviews.

In addition to the President's support, I was blessed with

the knowledge that most newspaper reporters, male and female, admired and liked the First Lady. This wasn't hard to do. She was considerate. She was doing something. And she treated reporters with warmth and respect. The President was far less patient with his constant inquisitors—but then he had more to lose as their victim.

Idle typewriters are the devil's workshop. This long-held belief prodded me to find stories at the White House which would keep the press busy writing articles we could live with—rather than to leave them the time to write the ones we couldn't. I kept a "bank" of story ideas and pulled them out to divert a reporter who was, for instance, demanding a personal interview with Lynda or Luci when the girls were too busy with school to give them. It worked most of the time, for the White House is filled with unwritten feature stories. They may not be page one combat, like an Eartha Kitt visit, but with some digging there was plenty of copy to go around, and it was my feeling that I should never send a girl away emptyhanded.

So when some reporter would call up and ask, "Does Luci really dye her hair?" I would reply, "Oh come on, what kind of story is that? There is a really good story here about all the animals that have lived at the White House. Did you know Woodrow Wilson kept sheep here? Did you know William Howard Taft had a cow named Pauline Wayne? Did you know Teddy Roosevelt's children had a one-legged rooster?"

My diversionary tactics didn't always divert. The definitive history of animals in the White House, for instance, remains unwritten. But I tried, and the world still doesn't know whether Luci dyed her hair. For that matter, neither do I. Nor do I care.

The "generation gap" between a press secretary in her forties and two teen-age Presidential daughters was narrowed successfully by younger assistants on my staff throughout the five years in the White House.

First, Wendy Marcus, the savvy daughter of Mr. and Mrs. Stanley Marcus of Dallas merchandising fame and longtime friends of the Johnson family, promptly cancelled her trip to Europe on November 23, 1963, and arrived at the Elms volunteering for any task. A graduate of Harvard Law School, Wendy was also an expert organizer and she immediately took on the task of the voluminous correspondence which poured into the new First Family. In makeshift offices on the third floor of the Johnsons' Vice Presidential home, she kept a group of Congressional wives busy sorting and answering the mail so it would not be an added burden to the White House mail for the Kennedys. Incidentally, one of these volunteers was Abigail McCarthy, wife of Senator Eugene J. McCarthy of Minnesota who later became such a sharp critic.

Wendy stayed on with us for two years, traveling with the Johnson girls when they made public appearances. Other young women who helped from time to time with the mail and trips for the Johnson girls were Kristin Anderson and Helene Lindow. Marta Ross, a permanent member of the press office, was a lifelong friend of Lynda and Luci and could always be useful in that department when she wasn't involved in other office duties.

I held briefings whenever a trip was coming up, or there was a great deal of news to announce. For these sessions, I used the family library of the White House, a cozy room on the ground floor filled with books, antique furniture and a fireplace—which was always crackling in the winter. There was just enough space for everyone to sit, and we improved the atmosphere by having White House butlers serve tea and cookies from a handsome silver service.

There is no recorded text of these briefings. If there had

been, my tenure at the White House would have been much shorter. At first, Pierre Salinger wanted to send over the official White House stenographers to make a written transcript of each briefing. "Not on your life!" I told him. "I want to be in a position to deny everything."

Some questions at press briefings taxed my ingenuity to the limit. For example:

REPORTER: Why has Luci changed the spelling of her name from Lucy to Luci?
ME: How many of you have ever been sixteen?
REPORTER: How do *you* spell her name?
ME: *I* spell it *both* ways.

That stopped the questions.

My slaphappy answers are, of course, not really in the great tradition of press secretaries. If I had come into my job from one of these big advertising agencies on Madison Avenue or a public relations agency for Disneyland, I'd have known better and answered with a casual, "I'll check on it," or "That matter is receiving the highest priority, and I'll be back in touch with you." But I came into my job through the uninhibited path of the newspaper profession.

However, after a few of my flippant answers showed up in print, I knew I had to do something. So I lettered a big sign across from my desk which read: REMEMBER. YOU ARE A NEWS SOURCE. It helped.

Our press office in the East Wing was the scene of purposeful bedlam. Besides me, there were three young women assistants and two secretaries in our three-room suite. Evening gowns and cocktail dresses to provide quick changes for social events overflowed from a rack behind the door, and laughter and action spilled out from our office over to the spit-and-polish military office across the hall.

Early in my tenure I realized that a television expert was necessary for a Twentieth Century press office. I confiscated Simone Poulain from the Department of State where she had been giving TV advice to Secretary of State Dean Rusk. Being strictly a pad and pencil reporter myself, I needed someone who knew the language of the television networks. Simone spoke it with kindness and competence. Slender and blond, she was as correct as a French second arranging a duel, sometimes deploring the whole business. She was respected by the networks, and she was also the reason that Mrs. Johnson made two hour-long TV specials, which brought the role of the First Lady more vividly to her countrymen.

My other assistants were Marta Ross and Marcia Maddox. Both in their early twenties, they had graduated from Wellesley and Smith and exemplified the bright minds, ready charm and terrible spelling for which those schools are famous. They combined Junior League manners and Chamber of Commerce know-how. Marta was breezy, beautiful and possessed the happy air that made you feel that if you missed one ring on the Washington merry-go-round, you would catch it next time around. As far as I was concerned, Marcia met her test one day in the middle of the main street of Lincoln, Nebraska, when she singlehandedly moved an entire sheriff's posse of twenty men and beasts up the street to the head of the parade, while the whole town watched and waited.

The two secretaries, Oghda O'Gulian and Lenora Haag, were twins, too, at least in height and ability. Both were tiny and slender, tidy and capable. Lenora had been a career White House secretary, beating out letters when they were signed by FDR. She possessed that invaluable trait of a secretary: she was in the office by 7:30 A.M. every day. Oghda was a chipper, cheerful person and her long office hours upset her evening church work considerably, but she said, "The Lord will forgive me because it's for you and Mrs. Johnson." Nothing brightened her day as much as questions about the dogs. She adored all animals.

Bryson Rash, the NBC newscaster, came one day to interview me about the President's mongrel dog, Yuki.

"Do you know Yuki can sing?" Oghda bragged as she escorted Bryson into my office.

Instantly, Bryson insisted that we capture Yuki's voice on a tape for NBC radio. To get Yuki to sing, however, requires much human encouragement. This, Oghda gave unstintingly, getting down on hands and knees to howl so that Yuki would sing back into a microphone.

It was one of our finer hours.

My work was done primarily over the telephone. My office averaged 150 phone calls a day which impressed even a marathon telephone talker like LBJ. In fact, once when Marvin Watson, on one of his periodic fits of economy was trying to reduce the number of telephone lines in the offices, he had a check made on all calls to the White House. I came in third—with Watson and Bill Moyers topping me. (He didn't check on the President.) I kept my twelve lines, and the President gave me a salary raise.

The two most persistent callers, understandably, were the two women reporters who cover the White House for the wire services, Frances Lewine of the AP and Helen Thomas of the UPI. I averaged talking to them four or five times a day, either to tell them what was happening on "our side" of the house, or to convince them that nothing was. They never gave up. I would groan at their persistence. My husband would occasionally urge me to unplug the phone at our home. But as I told him more than once, "They wear me out, but I like them. I'd probably choose them to be my pallbearers."

His indignant reply was, "That's what they're going to be."

The phone calls from newspaper people often brought helpful tips on something I should know about. "Liz, this story has just come over the wire, and I suspect you're going to need an answer for it," was a frequent greeting on the phone. Or from my husband, Les, who would read the news ticker at his office in the National Press Building, a warning, "You all must be out of your minds over there." This brought me out of my ivory tower fast, and frequently from these conversations, I gleaned advice which I passed on to the President's staff.

The telephone brought a variety of unusual questions. Once I was startled when the AP called and asked tartly, "Does the White House grass have cancer?" I had learned to take nothing for granted in that house. It was wiser to check out even such an unlikely rumor as that. My call to our head gardener, Irvin Williams, affirmed that the grass did indeed have something like cancer.

"What are the chances of recovery?" I found myself asking anxiously.

"We are treating it around the clock," Mr. Williams replied. "We have isolated the diseased areas and hope to have it under control."

I sought some kind of solace. "Are there other cases of grass cancer along the East Coast?"

"Yes, it's the hot muggy nights that have done it. It is a widespread problem right now," Mr. Williams said.

I was greatly relieved and phoned to give a medical bulletin to the AP. The AP was so touchingly sympathetic that the reporter even said, "I'm sorry, Liz."

"That's all right," I replied. "Everything that's humanly possible is being done."

Newswomen tracked the two Johnson girls wherever they went, even when the girls hoped for privacy.

On occasion, both resorted to disguises. Luci wore an elaborate blond wig, prepared with much cloak and dagger intrigue by hairdresser Jean Louis, when she tried to escape publicity at a dance at Marquette University.

"Reporters were all over the place," Bob Kohler, Luci's Secret Service agent chuckled. "One of them could have reached out and touched her, but he never recognized her."

The President's older daughter, Lynda, was not so lucky. A budding writer, she undertook an assignment with *National Geographic* to take a canoe trip in the rugged Minnesota-Canada boundary lake country. Eleven canoes and twenty-eight people in the entourage, including one Presidential daughter and the Secretary of Agriculture and Mrs. Freeman, were not easy to hide for eight days, even when Lynda tried to disguise with a large, floppy Madras plaid hat and dark glasses.

The two reporter-photographer teams from Midwest newspapers, who picked up her trail and followed her, promptly dubbed her "The Greta Garbo of the North Woods."

*The Milwaukee Sentinel* had pitted a resourceful reporter, Marian (Toni) McBride, mother of seven children, against the resources of the White House staff, Secret Service, United States Forest Service, the *National Geographic* and the wilderness.

"President Johnson may be famed for his arduous press conferences," Toni McBride pointed out, "but no eighteen laps around the South Lawn of the White House in the Washington heat, or careening in a jeep over the back 48 at the LBJ Ranch quite compares with Lynda's canoe press conference in the mosquito-laden dusk on Nina Moose Lake."

For five days and nights, Toni and the press had stalked their prey by canoe and portage, camping each night a short way up the bay from her, and placing a crudely lettered charcoal sign on a tree, proclaiming "Press Room," just in case she wanted to make a statement.

"What we obviously needed was a chance to interview Lynda, and we were determined that after five days of rowing and slapping mosquitoes we couldn't go home empty-handed," Toni recalled.

Finally, Toni took steps. She scribbled a note on a rain-soaked tablet and placed it in an empty bourbon bottle.

It read: *"We four sunburned, mosquito-bitten, muscle-sore members of the press have tried to respect your desire for privacy on this trip. But as the sun sets on the last evening of the canoe voyage, we are beginning to worry more and more about our editors back home. Could you spare a few minutes to chat with us?"*

She dispatched her photographer down the bay in the press canoe to float the bottle into Lynda's camp. Through the woods, he could hear the Secret Service warning of his arrival on the walkie-talkies: "Canoe sighted. Pulling into camp. Threw something into water."

Back at the press camp, Toni recalls that she had put on her heavy red pajamas to fend off the cold and had borrowed a lighted cigar to discourage the mosquitoes. Squatting by her campfire and puffing away at the only effective measure against the bugs, she suddenly realized that a canoe had pulled into shore and "Greta" was sitting midsection with two Secret Service men paddling.

"Your message was so ingenious, I just couldn't resist coming over," Lynda said, adding, "Several members of the party rushed out to grab the floating bottle—thinking it was full. It gave us quite a laugh."

The conversation became known as the "Bourbon Bottle Press Conference." But it came so unexpectedly, the reporters didn't have time to find their notebooks, and it was too dark for photographs. The best story of all—as is often the case—was the hunt rather than the kill.

The best opportunity for newswomen to get to know Mrs. Johnson well was on trips. Then we were away from interruptions and phones, and she was out doing a public chore that was worth covering. She put her own reportorial education to work helping them get their story, asking the right questions of her hosts at the Head Start Center, or the Park Ranger on a raft ride, and being sure that newswomen were within hearing range to get the point being made.

Her trips were actually the best way I could find to get a success story covered. Editors would assign their top women reporters to cover the First Lady. By going to see the Teachers Corps in action, or a Head Start project that worked, Mrs. Johnson could focus the national spotlight on it. Unless, alas, some pickets were out in front. Then our chances of getting the basic story told were slim. The TV and newspaper reporters would more often let the pickets get the lead.

I look back on those unhappy incidents more in sorrow than in anger. I would search for the reason. Was it the competition of the instant media—TV—that drove some reporters beyond the realm of truth and taste? Did they realize the harm done by a capricious pen?

One October Sunday a few weeks before Lynda and her United States Marine captain were to be married, I awoke to find Maxine Cheshire's column in *The Washington Post* headed: *Vietnam on Waiting List for Captain Robb.*

This was hardly news. He had asked for combat duty, and he had known since August he would be departing Washington at the end of February 1968. It was a matter of record. It was his desire.

I read on in disbelief: "Lynda Bird Johnson's fiancé, Captain Charles Robb, may not be going to Vietnam until sometime next summer. Robb told British Princess Alexandra's businessman husband, Angus Ogilvy, here last week that his scheduled tour of combat duty will be moved from February to at least 'seven or eight months' hence.

" 'We are hoping to have some time together first,' said Robb.

"Ogilvy's reply was to tease the President's daughter that she ought to have some influence with the Commander-in-Chief."

I knew this couldn't possibly be true. If Chuck Robb had made anything clear to me since his engagement, it was simply this: he had a commitment to go to Vietnam and he was going.

I grabbed the phone and asked a White House operator to find him.

"He's out on the football field in front of the Marine Barracks," the operator reported, "playing touch football."

"Well, get some Marine to get out there and tell him to call me. It is an emergency."

In three or four minutes, Chuck was on the phone. He hadn't read the column. I read it to him. Even over the phone, I could tell that his temper was rising.

"It's just not true. No such conversation ever took place," he said. "Why would she say that when it's just not true?"

"I'll take care of it," I told him. "Go back to your football game and don't let it worry you."

I called the British Embassy and discovered that Lord Ogilvy had gone on to Canada, but the Ambassador, Sir Patrick Dean, located him and called me to say Ogilvy was at a loss to know how a reporter could write something which didn't happen.

I called the President, related what had happened and said, "I'm going right to the top. I'm going to call the publisher of the paper and register a formal protest."

He was as furious as I. "Go ahead," he said. "Don't they

know that Chuck Robb is no Johnny-come-lately? He's been a Marine for six years."

The phone calls went out—first to the publisher.

"Out of town for the weekend," the switchboard operator reported, "and the publisher left no phone number."

Then to the managing editor.

"He's down in the country, and there is no way to reach him by telephone," the operator said.

"Well, get me the associate editor or whoever is on the desk," I said.

When I reached him, I tried to keep the fury out of my voice, but I told him plainly, "I have checked with Robb. The conversation never took place. I have talked to the British Ambassador, and Lord Ogilvy is writing a denial. The Ambassador says no such incident occurred. I want an apology for that story."

To my tremendous disappointment and surprise, he said, simply, "Well, we just have your word against hers."

"You have the word of the White House. You have the word of Captain Robb. You have the word of the British Empire. Now, I think we are due an apology," I said.

"I'll look into it," he said warily, but I sensed his reluctance to take action.

We didn't get an apology. We did get an unobtrusive article giving Chuck's denial. "The conversation never took place. It was never considered, never said, and is strictly a figment of someone's imagination. Nothing concerning my orders has changed. Nothing will change. I want very much to go to Vietnam, and I am very disappointed something as totally inaccurate as this alleged statement should ever get into print. On something as important as this, I am also disappointed that no attempt was made prior to publication to check the facts."

The article included, however, this statement: "In submitting the column, Mrs. Cheshire told her editors it was based on a conversation between Captain Robb and Ogilvy which she heard while standing nearby at a party in honor of Princess Alexandra and Lord Ogilvy at the British Embassy."

Meanwhile, I let the AP and the UPI and everyone else know that nothing like that took place. Knowing Robb's sense of duty and character, they never carried the story.

Marrying into the limelight of the White House—as Chuck Robb and Pat Nugent did—posed problems for them. They handled them well. It also posed problems, the stickiest kind of problems, for my office. There was one particular period I recall when Chuck was in heavy fighting in Vietnam. We kept getting calls from newspapers. *The Milwaukee Journal* reported, "A mother in Wisconsin whose son is in the service with Chuck has written her that Captain Robb is in the hospital. He was wounded."

From the London *Daily Mail:* "We have it on a very reliable source that Chuck Robb was injured in the face during a heavy battle last Monday."

I carefully checked each story with the Pentagon, and each was totally incorrect. In the case of the second rumor, it turned out another soldier named Robb had been injured. I will always be grateful that the newspapers did bother to check. That made all the difference—particularly for Lynda, who was expecting their baby. I was constantly afraid a radio broadcast might reach her with a rumor story before she knew it wasn't true.

Chuck Robb, with all the organizational ability of a superior Marine officer, had taken care of some of the grimmest possibilities before he left for Vietnam. He knew I would be likely to get the calls, if he should be captured, and certainly this was in the realm of possibility—for the Viet Cong would have liked nothing better than to capture the son-in-law of the President of the United States.

Shortly before he left for Vietnam, he asked for a private conference with my assistant, Simone Poulain, and me. With the door closed, he told us that death wouldn't cause as many complications as capture. "If I am seriously wounded, killed or missing, I want you to know I have made a new will, my insurance is in order, and, from a legal point of view, there will be a minimum of personal problems." His manner was matter-of-fact.

I didn't feel matter-of-fact at all, but he continued in a brisk Marine cadence.

"Capture seems reasonably remote," he said. "I believe I can take care of myself in battle, and I don't think I will be captured, but you should know—and I have also given a statement to the Pentagon—that my political philosophy won't change. I believe in what we're doing in Vietnam. If the enemy should try to broadcast some phony statement or claim, you and the Pentagon know my views and can release them. My statement would disclaim any claims they might make."

He continued, "The press will undoubtedly be looking to see if I am coddled. I won't be. It is not my wish. I have asked for nothing. I will proceed under normal circumstances."

The conversation had all the air of an impersonal discussion between three business-like people. But when he walked out, Simone and I wept. And then we typed up the grim but necessary notes, sealed them and wrote on the envelope: "*Re Chuck Robb—To be opened only in the event of death or capture.*"

Thank God it never had to be opened.

# *Dog Days at the White House*

I don't mean to bitch about dogs, because I know they are man's best friend. But they are *not* a press secretary's best friend. The dogs we had at the White House were terrible publicity hounds. History will undoubtedly show they even appeared in more pictures than Jack Valenti.

They quickly learned how to upstage the First Family. Not only would the dogs yelp when their ears were pulled, but if a week passed by when they hadn't been making the papers as regularly as usual, they would try anything to get into print.

One morning Mrs. Johnson's hairdresser, Jean Louis, arrived at the White House with this news: "As I was driving into the grounds, I saw the cutest thing. One of the dogs was up in a tree."

Mrs. Johnson burst into laughter, but I headed for the door and Traphes Bryant, the dog-keeper. Mr. Bryant is to White House dogs what Steve Hannegan was to Miami Beach. He was always trying to get the dogs into pictures, and I suspected that he trained them to show their best profile on camera. His wife entered into the wretched plot with enthusiasm. She would take out her sewing machine and whip up doggy coats and sweaters for the occasion. The prize outfit was a doughboy hat which Yuki wore to the American Legion Auxiliary parade. The only inhabitant of the White House able to compete with the dogs—for press coverage—was little Lyn, who came later. Mr. Bryant suspected me of getting Luci's buoyant and photogenic baby from Central Casting.

When I found Mr. Bryant, I growled, "Have you been teaching the dogs to climb trees?"

"Well, I didn't have to teach them much," he replied proudly. "Yuki can go right up the Andrew Jackson magnolia."

"Climbing is not what dogs are supposed to do to trees," I replied.

"Why I just thought that with practice, Yuki's talents would make a wonderful cover for *Life* magazine," Mr. Bryant said doggedly.

"Listen, Mr. Bryant, I don't want to hear one more thing about Yuki climbing trees. We can't even keep up with the beautification mail, and you are starting something else," I said. "Those dogs have simply got to learn their place around here."

As far as Mr. Bryant was concerned, their place was in front of grinding cameras. He could hear a lens click clear across the South Lawn.

The dogs in residence varied from time to time, but during our stay these were the principal ones:

*Him and Her*—a pair of oversexed beagles belonging to Luci. After a short but active love life, both died at the White House. One swallowed a stone; the other chased a squirrel under the wheels of a car.

*Blanco*—a male white collie, highly pedigreed and more tempermental than Maria Callas. Blanco was given to the President as a watchdog by a well-meaning child in Illinois.

*Edgar*—a beagle, given to the President by J. Edgar Hoover.

*Freckles*—a beagle, one of Him's children.

*Dumpling*—a beagle and offspring of Freckles.

*Little Chap*—a beagle, an offspring of Edgar.

*Crasher*—a beagle, offspring of Freckles.

White House dogs are always news, and someone has to be available to answer all sorts of questions about them, their past, their future, their hopes and dreams. When I look back through my "dog files," I am amazed at the extent of public interest.

For instance, when "Her" died, we received hundreds of condolence letters from dog lovers. One man even wrote and confessed that he was responsible for the dog's death. The poor man was so confused, he even admitted to the accidental killing of the wrong dog. His letter is as follows:

> Dear President Johnson,
>
> I have gotten enough courage to finally admit the accidental death of your dog Him. I am not absolutely sure about this but I am almost sure I did it. I was visiting Washington during Thanksgiving vacation. We saw many interesting places including your White House. As we were going back to our hotel from the Washington Monument we passed your place. About between your place and no farther than Lafayette Park we saw the keeper of your dogs. He brought the dogs up to the gate and let us pet them, Her was on a leash and Him was running around the grounds. Before we left I had a peanut and I tossed it to Him. He sniffed it put it in his mouth and he ran away. Then I left the White House. It was bad news when sometime later I heard of Him's death. This all happened on the day of its death. So I sorrowfully confess the accidental death of your dog.

Children's letters were particularly enjoyable. After Her's demise, one six-year-old wrote to the President,

Dear President Johnson,

My beagle named Gypsy is old enough to get married now. I heard my Daddy tell about Him's wife eating a rock and going to Heaven. Him is lonely and Gypsy will make a good wife. They will have to get married this week so they can have babies in the spring. Gypsy is a very special beagle. There are pictures of her grandparents in the library book. They are all Field Champions and she will be too some day.

There is, for instance, a note from Marcia Maddox, my assistant marked *URGENT*: "Blanco is about to smother to death from too much hair. Mr. Bryant wants you to find someone who can clip the dog here at the White House. He even brought Blanco up here today to prove he needs a hair cut."

A rush job was done on a hair cut.

Then, there was the letter that arrived one August day from an enterprising publicity man, Sheldon Ritter, for a dog food company:

"As I told you the other day, we are giving a 'Gourmet Doggie Party' in the Sheraton-Carlton Hotel in conjunction with a reception for Miss Gypsy Rose Lee, who, because of her great interest in dogs, is being made a vice president of a pet food company that believes that dog food should be of the highest quality.

"We would like to invite the White House dogs, Yuki, Blanco and Edgar to be the honored guests among all of the dogs. We are having the dogs appear at a press conference at 4:30 P.M. and again during the reception at 6:00 P.M. The attendance of the White House dogs, with perhaps a member of the Johnson family, would certainly bring the house down."

For the menu at the gourmet party, I envisioned squirrels

under glass, rabbits on the half shell and an old slipper with béarnaise sauce. This was a tempting invitation, but the White House dogs always held their press conferences at the White House; so a regret was sent.

Yuki was the top dog with the press. Microphones or cameras didn't bother him. Having been picked up at a filling station by Luci, we had no clue as to his background, but his antics led us to believe he had been a circus dog at one time. He could turn flips, leap into the air and climb trees. He had stage presence, and no matter what happened, always felt that the show must go on.

One of the most unusual records in White House lore is a copy of the transcript of an interview with Mr. Bryant and Yuki, by a reporter in Greenville, South Carolina. Thanks to Tom Johnson, assistant press secretary to the President, the notes of this interview serve as a transcript.

Herewith the text:

MR. DUPREY: Mr. Bryant, Marty Duprey in Greenville. How are you today?

MR. BRYANT: Fine, thank you. How are you, sir?

MR. DUPREY: I understand you have a job in addition to being White House electrician there. You also take care of the canine population around the White House.

MR. BRYANT: Yes, I do, and it is a pleasure.

MR. DUPREY: I bet it is a lot of fun. A few months ago, I was in Washington and driving by the South Lawn and saw a little beagle running around there. Which one was that?

MR. BRYANT: Oh, that could have been either one of four. I have Freckles, Dumpling, Edgar and Little Chap. Those are all beagles. Then I have a white dog, Blanco—and we have the number one dog. His name is Yuki.

MR. DUPREY: The number one dog?

MR. BRYANT: That is the President's choice right now.

MR. DUPREY: Why do you call him the number one dog?

MR. BRYANT: This little dog takes to the President. He goes right to him. He leaves me and goes to the President. Luci found him in a filling station down in Texas. She brought him up here just for a visit with her beagles.

MR. DUPREY: He is not pedigreed. He is just "dog"; isn't he?

MR. BRYANT: He is just a plain old dog. That is one of the best kinds sometimes.

MR. DUPREY: You say President Johnson really likes him?

MR. BRYANT: He does. I have him here with me now.

MR. DUPREY: Is that a fact?

MR. BRYANT: Yes, sir.

MR. DUPREY: Will he ever bark or anything like that?

MR. BRYANT: Sometimes he will sing a little bit.

MR. DUPREY: See if you can get him to bark. This is the top dog now.

*(Yuki barks and sings.)*

MR. BRYANT: Sing Yuki.

*(Yuki sings again.)*

MR. DUPREY: Who taught him to sing like that?

MR. BRYANT: The President.

MR. DUPREY: The President taught him to sing? That is fabulous.

MR. BRYANT: He just picks him up and he starts to sing. I take him down to the shop and let him take a nap.

MR. DUPREY: Does he have the run of the House pretty much?

MR. BRYANT: Well, I keep him down here and let him take a little nap. When the President calls for him, we hop up out of here and go upstairs to the second floor.

MR. DUPREY: Does the President ever feed him from the table?

MR. BRYANT: Once in a while, he will feed him scraps from the table, yes.

MR. DUPREY: He eats pretty high on the hog.

MR. BRYANT: He eats mostly table scraps. I have my beagles and white collie; they eat regular dog food.

MR. DUPREY: You know, only in America could a regular dog like that live in the White House and receive top attention. There is something symbolic about this to me. I don't know exactly what, but there is a message in there somewhere.

MR. BRYANT: Well, he is a lot of comfort to the President. The President has all these world problems and operating the government and everything, and if he can get just a few minutes consolation out of petting a little dog, I know it is worth all the trouble to me.

MR. DUPREY: I know it is a lot of fun for you to take care of him then. You have got your hands full. Say, look, we want to thank you very much for filling us in on this. If we ever get up to the White House and are walking around, we hope we see that top dog, Yuki, there. By the way, how did he get that name?

MR. BRYANT: That means white or snow in Japanese. Luci named him. If you are ever up around Washington or any of your friends from down around that country, just come up to the policeman at the gate and ask for Bryant. I will bring the dogs out there and let you see them.

MR. DUPREY: All right. We will take you up on that. Thank you so much, Mr. Bryant.

MR. BRYANT: You are welcome, sir.

MR. DUPREY: Goodbye.

The dogs were forever getting into my own press briefings. Mary Packenham, a reporter for *The Chicago Tribune,* was diligent on inquiries about Blanco because he was, after all, a dog from her circulation area. One exchange went as follows:

MARY: How did the First Family acquire Blanco?
LIZ: He was a gift from a little girl in Illinois.
MARY: Is he an Illinois dog?
LIZ: That's right.
MARY: Is he a Chicago dog?
LIZ: No, he's a northeastern Illinois dog.
MARY: Where does he live?
LIZ: In the White House doghouse.
MARY: Is he happy?
LIZ: Yes.
MARY: How do you know?
LIZ: Because I'm in there most of the time.

Mary later asked me for a personal interview with Blanco, explaining that "*The Chicago Tribune* is crazy about dog stories."

I granted the interview. Democrats have such a hard time

getting a good press in the *Tribune* that I thought we might—through a yaller-dog Democrat.

The name "Him" kept creating confusion at the White House. Once a Hollywood producer came to see me about filming a TV show on "Him." I spent the first thirty minutes trying to send him over to Bill Moyers because I thought he was talking about the President. It turned out the "Him" he wanted was the dog.

My staff became accustomed to ridiculous questions about the dogs. For instance, when District of Columbia Dog Tag No. 1 was issued to "Him," and No. 2 to "Her," a woman reporter called up and said, "How do you reconcile this with the President's pledge to give women equal opportunity?"

The death of "Him" created a whole barrage of questions, including the most minute details of what we would do with the body. Luci, who was heartbroken, decided she wanted him buried back in the family cemetery at the ranch. This meant cremating the dog and preserving the ashes until the next trip to the ranch. With some mischief, I thought, a British reporter called and asked crisply, "Will 'Him's' ashes be buried or strewn?"

"Buried, of course," I replied solemnly.

(Actually, few people grieved more than Mr. Bryant about the death of the two beagles, for despite his flair for public relations, he was really devoted to the dogs, and he realized what a source of pleasure they were for the First Family.)

The White House was constantly a forum for Mrs. Johnson's favorite project—conservation. And one time the dogs got into the act when Lassie, the most famous bark on TV, came to the White House for a ceremony.

Secretary of Agriculture Orville Freeman felt that in Lassie, he had a newsworthy recruit for his campaign to keep the

National Forests clean, just as Smokey the Bear kept them from disappearing in flames. "Let me bring Lassie over one day to meet Mrs. Johnson," Secretary Freeman said. "It would really boost the new anti-litter poster 'Help Lassie Keep America Beautiful.'"

If Tom Mix could bring his favorite horse, Tony, to the White House during the Coolidge Administration, I saw no reason why Freeman couldn't bring Lassie. So, I assigned Cynthia Wilson to handle the dog show. With foresight, she arranged this animal summit meeting in the East Garden, where there are no hydrants. Mrs. Johnson would meet Lassie, the litter dog, and unveil the new poster.

To make this *the* social event of the Year of the Dog, there would be tea and cookies after the ceremony. The planning moved along smoothly, and the event was widely publicized in advance. Not since Princess Margaret came for dinner had so many people called demanding an invitation.

Another problem was our own white collie, Blanco, whose image was, of course, jealously guarded by Mr. Bryant. Blanco looked very much like Lassie.

Came the great day for Lassie's party, and Cynthia Wilson was determined that Blanco would not steal the show from Lassie. In the process of extensive briefings from Lassie's trainer, she had discovered evidence of a Hollywood credibility gap. "Lassie is really not a lassie at all. Lassie is a male dog," she said. "And the trainer warns us to keep all other male dogs away. Males do not mix with males."

She gleefully reported this message to Mr. Bryant, hoping he would keep Blanco, a temperamental dog at best, in the background. After all, what had Blanco ever done for litter?

I had been worried about getting press coverage of the Lassie presentation, because the President had a very newsworthy schedule that day. I needn't have worried. The whole West

Wing—some forty photographers and seventy reporters—abandoned the President and his affairs of state and invaded the East Garden with cameras to capture each wag of the tail and microphones to record every bark.

Seeing all this equipment from the communications media roll into the garden was too much for Mr. Bryant. He appeared with Blanco newly bathed and brushed. Cynthia glared at him, and I motioned for him to stay back behind the holly tree, out of sight.

Meanwhile, Lassie performed nobly. He trotted up to Mrs. Johnson with a nosegay of flowers, carrying it in his mouth. He picked up several pieces of paper that his trainer tossed on the ground, and showed he knew a trash can when he saw one.

The cameras ground. The reporters kept a running record on this historic event. Mrs. Johnson smiled approvingly. Secretary Freeman glowed. Hollywood press agents rubbed their hands in glee. And Mr. Bryant sulked behind the holly tree.

But right after the ceremony, Mr. Bryant got his revenge. He brought Blanco up importantly. I was surprised he hadn't arranged for the Marine Band to herald their entrance. Blanco descended on Lassie, and for three tense minutes, there was silence. They were eyeball to eyeball. Then, a low growl from Blanco. Cynthia envisioned a law suit if Blanco so much as touched one hair of the million-dollar TV dog. I envisioned headlines that said: DOG FIGHT LITTERS WHITE HOUSE LAWN.

"Get that dog out of here," I said to Mr. Bryant more sharply than I have ever spoken to anyone in my life.

Both Mr. Bryant and Blanco tucked their tails and left. Mr. Bryant sulked for two weeks. So did Bill Moyers, the President's press secretary, who opened the next day's papers to see that White House coverage had literally gone to the dogs.

# *The Last of the Big-Time Whistlestops*

I have sipped champagne by moonlight at the Acropolis. I have thrilled to the beauty of the Taj Mahal.

I have watched two White House brides come down the aisle on the arm of the President of the United States. I have danced under the crystal chandeliers in the East Room beside Princess Margaret, Lord Snowdon, Christina Ford, Hoss Cartwright (right out of *Bonanza*) and the Shah of Iran.

But for the ultimate in sheer joy and exhilaration, give me a Whistlestop train and head me down the track through Dixie. That's what happened to me in the campaign of 1964.

I am a political animal by nature, a Southerner by birth and a P. T. Barnum by instinct. So when that train whistle blows, I'm mentally already down the track with bands playing, bunting waving, buttons and bullhorns, balloons flying in the wind.

For me, there is nothing which can top it—the local high school band playing, "Hello, Lyndon," or "Happy Days Are Here Again" not quite in tune; a First Lady named Lady Bird on the back platform waving and saying, "I'm mighty glad to be here and see all you folks. You-all may not agree with what I say, but you sure can understand the way I say it."

Congressman Hale Boggs, professional Southerner and New Orleans aristocrat, warming up the crowd and shouting a question to them. "How many of you-all know what red-eye gravy is? Well, so do I. And so does Lyndon Johnson!" The people and the placards all along the track, kids held aloft on their fathers' shoulders; women in their best sunbonnets standing up in the back of the wagon so they could see better.

Into town they come from the back roads and the coves, and the forks of the creek, the sand hills and the river bottoms. There, from the back of the train, standing in the depot, is where the government and the people meet. It is politics, U.S.A., served up just the way I like it best with the flavor of fried chicken and mustard greens and cornbread.

Harry Truman knew what campaigning by Whistlestop meant, and he was the one who recommended it. "You may not believe this, Lyndon," he said, "but there are still a hell of a lot of people in this country who don't know where the airport is. But they damn sure know where the depot is. And if you let 'em know you're coming, they'll be down and listen to you."

We took his advice in the campaign of 1960. And Lyndon Johnson carried the South for Jack Kennedy, the Harvard graduate, the city-slicker who had voted against subsidies for the cotton and peanut farmers.

In 1964, it was a salvage operation in the wake of the Civil Rights Act of 1964. The bill had been engineered by LBJ and signed three months before the Lady Bird Whistlestop rolled through Dixie. Our star attraction was a Southern-bred First Lady. We were supposed to blow kisses and spread love through eight states and make them like it, forget about Barry Goldwater and vote for "that nigger-lover in the White House." Miraculously we held half the South for the Democrats.

Mrs. Johnson had always said placidly, "Lyndon is the kind of man who stretches you."

Well, she can say that again. We stretched ourselves over 1682 miles, 47 stops and four "slow downs" from October 6th to the 9th. Do you know you can get votes just by slowing down and waving?

"Don't give me the easy towns, Liz," she said. "Anyone can get into Atlanta—it's the new, modern South. Let me take the tough ones."

Thanks a lot, Mrs. Johnson!

That meant the places neither LBJ nor HHH could get in and out of with their hide on—or they couldn't take the time to visit because it was a lost cause. Ours was simply a holding operation.

"But we must go," Mrs. Johnson insisted. "We must let them know that we love the South. We respect them. We have not turned our backs on them. I don't think there's much chance of carrying it for Lyndon, judging by the letters I get from my Alabama cousins. But at least we won't lose by default."

Fortunately, I had been on the 1960 Whistlestop with LBJ and learned a little bit about it, but this was a whole new ball game. I was in charge of organizing the mammoth undertaking primarily with women.

Kenny O'Donnell, who had been Jack Kennedy's principal political adviser and had stayed on to help in the 1964 campaign, turned up his nose at the whole thing. He sat sphinx-like in meetings with me—half laughing at the whole idea and obviously feeling that neither the South nor women were important in the campaign. He suffered from the same attitude I had seen so often among the Irish Catholic politicians. Women are good for licking stamps and sealing the envelopes down at campaign headquarters, rounding up the votes on Election Day, casting their own ballots—and then, back to the kitchen and the bedroom, girls, for four more years.

Hell hath no fury like a woman scorned! But I would be less

than honest if I didn't credit the O'Donnell attitude with whetting my appetite to make that Whistlestop a spectacular political happening like he'd never seen in South Boston.

And on Operation Whistlestop, I had LBJ all the way with me, backing up every plan, as excited about it as I was, sorry he wasn't along for the whole thing!

Not since the inimitable Dolley Madison dropped her Quaker primness and her neckline and held bi-partisan Congressional salons to help her husband with Congress, have the walls of the White House seen a First Lady involved in such political intrigue and planning of a major campaign effort.

Maps and schedules were scattered all over the West Hall of the family quarters. President and Mrs. Johnson pored over them together. I told them the latest suggestions we were getting by phone and telegram.

"A little town—only 4583 people, Ahoskie, North Carolina, wired in today, DEAR MRS. JOHNSON, PLEASE STOP IN AHOSKIE. NO IMPORTANT PERSON HAS VISITED HERE SINCE BUFFALO BILL, AND NO PASSENGER TRAIN HAS STOPPED IN 12 YEARS."

"Stop there!" the President ordered. "If they want you that bad, you'll get everyone out from three counties."

Ahoskie went on the schedule. Lynda chimed in, "Well, we *will* have a kind of Wild West show."

"You've got to have plenty of advance men," LBJ advised, "and I don't mean just men. They're all right, but use some of the women around here who are can-do women."

The South may have its shortages—in nutrition and education—but I will match the political talents of Southern women against any others, anytime and any place. They have the uncanny ability to look fragile and lovely as a magnolia blossom, and still possess the managerial ability of an AFL-CIO organizer.

Lindy Boggs of Louisiana, Betty Talmadge of Georgia, Vir-

1. *Over my shoulder!* (Photograph by Ray Lustig © 1969, *The Washington Star*)

*2. I asked LBJ for pictures of me, and he sent this. That's me in front of the old grey mares, if you look closely.*

*3. Some of Mrs. Johnson's Congressional friends helped us to sort the mail at The Elms during the transition period. Mrs. Eugene McCarthy is sitting at the end of the table.*

*4. Mrs. Johnson shows the camel driver, Bashir Ahmed, and his translator Saeed Khan around the Capitol during his trip to visit with Vice President Johnson.*

*5. A pre-trip briefing in the White House Library gives the travelers an idea that we are going to Marlboro Country.*

*6. Whistlestopping through Dixie on the Lady Bird Special was my favorite form of action. We took 4 days, 47 speeches, and 1682 miles down the track from Washington to New Orleans as a holding operation.*

*7. Lady Bird Johnson loved meeting the people on the great Whistlestop Campaign and they loved her.*

*8. The LBJ Ranch house with the President in residence. His standard flies from the flagpole.*

*9. The 1964 election, with the two winnahs, prompted an instant celebration barbecue at the LBJ Ranch. President Johnson and Vice President Humphrey receive a few directions from me.*

*10. Blanco and Him and Her are "all ears" for the President.*

*11. One of our finer hours comes when my secretary, Oghda O'Gulian, tries to get one of the Presidential beagles to howl into a microphone.*

*12. My favorite fringe benefit—the handy government Mercury—delivers me, and evening dress over my shoulder to the East Wing of the White House.*

ginia Russell of South Carolina, Carrie Davis of Tennessee —all of these women, wives of Southern officials—combined the characteristics and fortitude of the women in *Gone With the Wind.* They had the manner of Melanie Wilkes and the mind of Scarlett O'Hara.

Virginia Russell—Mrs. Donald Russell, the wife of the then-governor of South Carolina—moved into a guest room on the third floor of the White House for three weeks to work on the Whistlestop with Mrs. Hale Boggs, wife of the Congressman from New Orleans and Democratic whip. Whistlestop headquarters were opened at the Democratic National Committee to organize the politicking that would go on in the VIP lounge cars as we rolled from town-to-town, picking up local politicians for part of the ride.

I made a quick run through four Southern states with Joe Moran, a Washington lawyer who was to coordinate the train schedule; Bill Brawley, Southern regional coordinator for the campaign; Jack Hight, an advance man; and the Secret Service.

Small Southern towns are made to order for Whistlestops. The depot is still downtown, right in the middle of the main street. J. C. Penney is on one side and International Harvester, with its shiny red tractors, on the other. A cotton gin is down the street. With strength and will, we could see that it was possible to make thirteen stops in North Carolina alone.

These were sleepy little towns when our advance group went through, but it didn't take long for word to spread that strangers were in town from Washington. The routine was the same. Joe Moran would get the depot master and figure out the exact spot for the train to stop. Bill Brawley would call the local politicians. Jack Hight would touch base with the civic leaders. The Secret Service would scout the KKK situation. I would go into the depot and telephone the newspaper editor to get his advice. "We're thinking about coming," I said, making it very tentative. "Could we get a good crowd here in Turnip Green?"

I knew many of the Southern editors from my years as a reporter in Washington. Their advice was invaluable. They had their fingers on the pulse of their town. They could measure how much goodwill the Democrats had in the town. I made copious notes and got their promises for future help if we decided to come through that particular town.

Necessity is the mother of crime. I filched phone books from depots all over the South simply because I knew how vital those names and addresses could be when I got back to Washington, and there was no time to write Southern Bell Telephone Company for them. This required real talent. Most phone books were tied to the booths with dirty string. But a fingernail file served nobly. I hope the Lord will forgive me. It was for a good cause.

On this preliminary run from Washington through Georgia, I met my first taste of red-necked bigotry and hate. Governor Donald Russell had invited our advance party to spend the night at the governor's mansion in Columbia, South Carolina. When we landed at the airport in the early afternoon, I noticed a carload of six men in shirtsleeves there. No other planes were scheduled to arrive. We had come in a small charter. And no other car, except the governor's, was on hand. They sat, silent, sullen and stared at us. "What are six men doing in a car just sitting at the airport in midafternoon?" I asked my fellow travelers. The governor didn't answer. I had an eerie feeling I was seeing the face of hate.

We met that night at the governor's mansion with a group of Democrats and planned the stops in South Carolina. The day after we left, the governor woke up to find a burning cross on his front lawn—a warning. Three weeks later, we were to meet our first organized red-neck protesters in Columbia.

Back in Washington, I reported all the findings to the President and Mrs. Johnson, plus a proposed itinerary that Joe Moran and the railroad men had figured out. And we began a series of meetings.

"How many advance men have you got?" the President demanded.

"Fifty-five," I replied.

"That's not enough," he said. "Get those women. Have them hold meetings in each town, send out postcards, put ads in the newspapers inviting people to the depot."

This was pure Johnson—cajoling, beating the maximum effort out of you. It always worked. I redoubled my effort.

I called a meeting of advance men and women at the White House Mess—a large room in the West Wing we could use at the end of the day. There, we would rally their enthusiasm, assign towns to them and get them out on the road.

"Where's the meeting, Liz?" Mrs. Johnson asked me to my surprise. "I want to drop in."

She charmed them all, thanking them for giving their time to help her husband get re-elected, and then she said somewhat wistfully, "You know I always wish I could advance my own trips. I wish I could go there once to learn and then go back again for the event. I feel at home in the small towns, and I want my speeches to make the people feel I am at home, too. It always helps if you know something about the town. I know how proud I am when people come to Austin, Texas, and know that it is the City of the Violet Crown, that it was the home of O. Henry. I hope you will be telephoning these things in to Liz so we can use them."

She continued, laying out the line: "I know the Civil Rights Act was right, and I don't mind saying so. But I'm tired of people making the South the whipping boy of the Democratic Party. There are plenty of people who make snide jokes about the cornpone and red-neck. I'm no hard-sell person. But what I want to say to those people is that I love the South, I'm proud of the South. I know there have been great achievements there. And I want them to know that as far as *this* President and his wife are concerned, the South belongs to the United States. For me, it is going to be a journey of the heart."

Advance men are, by nature, a cynical, rollicking group, but there was a long silence, and then—standing applause. There wasn't a man there who wouldn't have gladly gone all the way to Appomattox for her.

She left us to start planning the stops and various gimmicks and color that are so much a part of the American political scene. The meeting continued, and I tried to convey LBJ's feeling of the importance of a successful Whistlestop.

We knew Barry Goldwater was strong in the South, and growing stronger every day. He had voted against the Civil Rights Act. The Republicans were well organized and pouring money into the region they knew was vulnerable for the Democrats.

"Don't waste a minute," I warned the advance men. "Those sweet-talking Southerners will honey-chile you to death. And they're always trying to get you to sit down for a Coke. Don't do it. Coca-Cola is the opiate of the South!"

One advance man spoke up. "Mint juleps, maybe?"

But they got the idea. The next day they were off by plane to their destinations. One advance woman had the ideal name: Mrs. Robert E. Lee. I yearned for a dozen more of her, and even contemplated giving this name to all advance women because it read so well in Southern newspapers.

By now the schedule was final. There were to be forty-seven stops in eight states and we were ready to announce them for Sunday newspapers.

"I don't think it's courteous for a Senator or governor to pick up the paper and read I'm coming to his state without hearing it first from me," Mrs. Johnson said on Friday. "I want to call them all personally."

My mental arithmetic told me this was twenty-four calls to twenty-four busy men. But she was right. They should hear it from her. What's more, she wanted to invite them to ride the Whistlestop with her.

"I don't think I'll have many takers. Most of them were against the Civil Rights Act, but it's only polite to ask," she said. "And it would help."

During the next eight hours, sitting there in the West Hall of the White House by the phone, the First Lady telephoned the governors and the Senators of the South. The White House switchboard operators are the greatest of all sleuths. As Ernie Cuneo put it, "They could find a Senator in a whorehouse—and have!"

But that was no problem on this occasion. The problem was persuading them to come along.

Mrs. Johnson was at her best, in her most beguiling appealing manner. There is not a phony bone in her body, but when she is talking to Southerners, her childhood wells up in her with such memories of honeysuckle and watermelon cuttings and graveyard cleanings that her voice grows increasingly Southern.

"Guv-nuh, this is Lady Bird Johnson," she would say. There would be a pause in which I could overhear him saying, "Howdy, Miss Lady Bird. How's the President?" Or, more often, "How's Lyndon?"

"Fine, just fine, Guv-nuh. I'm thinking about coming down to your state."

Thinking about it! That was the understatement of the year. We already had seventy people down there working on it!

"I called to ask your advice."

Pause for five minutes while he told her how tough things

were for the Democrats. They would have been fine if Lyndon hadn't been so gol-darned hardheaded about the Civil Rights Act. But these comments were softened with affection for her.

"Well, I know there is a long education process that is necessary," she would add, "but I was thinking about coming through on a Whistlestop train. You see, I don't want the South to be overlooked in this campaign. And we have lots of good friends and kinfolks there. Matter of fact, some of Lyndon's ancestors came from your state in the early days."

Pause for more comparing kinfolks.

"Well, Governor, I was hoping that you and your wife would join us and ride the Whistlestop through your state." (She would always take a deep breath before that one.)

At this point, there were two possibilities.

"Oh, that's too bad. I'm sorry. Well, do give my best to your nice family."

Or, "That's wonderful. I'd appreciate your advice, and it will just add so much to the trip if you are aboard. I'll be sending you a schedule, and it will tell you where you can board. The President asked to be remembered to you."

I would tabulate the results, and then get the operators to make the next call.

The results were surprisingly good—five governors and four Senators—a number that was to grow as we rolled southward and the crowds swelled.

But some of the excuses were memorable.

"That's too bad," Mrs. Johnson said, smiling and chuckling when she hung up the phone with Senator Willis Robertson of Virginia. "The Senator is going to be away antelope hunting."

Another politician begged off because he was still in mourning for his wife. She'd died two years before.

Our advance men, who were phoning in each day, were having a varied time. Enthusiasm was high for the Democrats in many places, and for Lady Bird in others. But in South Carolina, and especially Charleston, it was a different story.

We had two of our very best advance people in Charleston —Jack Hight, a tall, courtly, gallant young businessman, and Mrs. Cecil Burney, a talented veteran of campaign organizing in Texas.

"How are things going down there?" I asked in a checkup call to Charleston. "Are we going to have a successful stop in Charleston?"

"Frankly, Liz, it's a little lonely," Jack said. "We had a meeting of local Democrats last night. It wasn't exactly a sell-out."

"How many?" I demanded.

"Well, as a matter of fact, two. Me and—you aren't gonna believe this name, Liz—Cummingball Gibbs the Third. Yes, that's his name. In fact, it was so small and lonely that we moved the meeting to Cummingball's yacht in Charleston harbor."

"Good grief, Jack, do something! I can't believe those people feel closer to Barry Goldwater than they do to Lady Bird Johnson."

"Down here, Liz, they feel closer to George the Third than they do to anyone," he replied. "You see, there are two Charlestons—old Charleston along the Battery, and suburban Charleston out by the shipyards where the population is. To get a crowd, we'll have to have the stop in a suburban shopping center."

"But Mrs. Johnson can't come to Charleston and ignore the beautiful, historic part of the city. Fix her up a horse and buggy ride through old Charleston, and we'll do both," I said.

"I'll see what I can do," he said, not very hopefully.

The President was following every move. He loved Whistlestops, and I could see that our plans were to him like a siren to an old firehorse.

"I can't make the whole trip, but you tell me where it will help the most for me to join you and I'll be there," he said. "The girls want to go along. Lynda can take the first part and Luci the second. This way they won't miss too much school."

My concern was keeping the story sustained for four days, and I knew the presence of the President would be vital at three points: the first stop in nearby Alexandria, Virginia; halfway down the tracks at Raleigh, North Carolina; and in New Orleans, the last stop.

I chose Raleigh for the midway Presidential appearance because the nominee for governor, Dan Moore, had brought into power a new array of very conservative Democrats who were flirting with the Republican organization. Moore's aides kept telling me that if we came down, they would arrange an event "befitting a lady"—perhaps a large tea with petits fours. I seethed as I listened to this kind of outmoded thinking. The situation was so bad that when our advance team visited Raleigh, we had to confer with the lame-duck Democratic governor, Terry Sanford, separately from the Dan Moore team.

"How many press do you think you'll have?" the President asked me.

"I would guess about fifty for the entire trip, but lots of local reporters along the way," I replied.

Even with my enthusiasm for the trip, I greatly underestimated the power of a woman and a Whistlestop. The press list reached 225—the capacity of the train—and I put "a lid" on it. Many veteran male political reporters signed up because they knew it would be a colorful political story. Others came along because they are—let's face it—frightened fliers, like me. The train offered them a chance to travel in the style they liked, as well as cover a political story. A surprising number of foreign journalists—some thirty—wanted to come along because there is no comparable campaign technique abroad.

Bess Abell, the Social Secretary and one of the savviest political women I know, had not been idle. Her crew of painters and upholsterers was down at the Union Station train-yard transforming the *Queen Mary,* a tremendous Pennsylvania Railroad lounge car which had the necessary back platform for speeches, from drab green to red, white and blue. This car would serve as the hospitality car for Mrs. Johnson and high-ranking guests. A speaker system was installed, and Bess arranged to have excellent recordings made of "Happy Days Are Here Again" and the political version of "Hello, Dolly!" These would be heard over the speaker systems as we pulled into each town. It took all the legal genius and characteristic canniness of David Merrick, a stalwart Democrat, to obtain the rights for us to use the very popular "Hello, Dolly!" number. Jerry Herman, the composer of the original song, had come up with the new lyrics: "Hello, Lyndon! Hello, Lyndon! It's so nice to have you there where you belong!"

Our hostesses for the train were a group of Southern-born beauties in their twenties and thirties. Their "denmother" was Mrs. Dale Miller—better known as "Scooter"—who is, as she put it, "more than thirty." Bright blue shirtwaist dresses, white gloves, and white roll-brim hats were the hostesses' uniform. Against the backdrop of Bess's red-and-white striped tin canopy over the back platform of the train, the effect was colorful cheesecake.

On the morning of October 6, at 7:45, the Lady Bird Special was boarded by three hundred people, including the President of the United States and the Whistlestop star, Lady Bird Johnson. The whistle blew and our nineteen-car train was off for its first stop across the Potomac River in Alexandria, Virginia.

An early-morning, cheering crowd of Virginians and government commuters welcomed us to the town. Proud and beaming, the President escorted Mrs. Johnson to the back platform. Our blue-uniformed hostesses, waving their Lady Bird pennants and carrying balloons and baskets of "All the Way With LBJ" buttons, were off the train and circulating among the crowd. Photographers, TV cameramen and reporters scrambled for positions.

The President raised his hand to shush the band. Mrs. Johnson began her first Whistlestop speech:

"Because this is the beginning of a four-day trip, that will take me down the railroad track 1682 miles to New Orleans, I want to tell you some of the reasons I am going," she began.

The voice was soft, but the words were strong and the crowd listened and cheered as she clicked off her reasons.

"I wanted to make this trip because I am proud of the South, and I am proud that I am part of the South. I'm fond of the old customs—of keeping up with your kinfolks, of long Sunday dinners after church, of a special brand of gentility and courtesy," she continued.

"I'm even more proud of the new South, the spirit of growth, advances in economy and progress in education," she said, "and I share the irritation when unthinking people make snide jokes about us. None of this is right. None of this is good for the future of our country. We must search for the ties that bind us together, not settle for the tensions that tend to divide us."

She recalled that Robert E. Lee, no less, had advised his fellow-Southerners: "Abandon all these local animosities and raise your sons to be Americans!"

She ticked off the proud record of Southern statesmen: twelve Presidents, twelve signers of the Constitution, fifteen Secretaries of State, from Thomas Jefferson to Dean Rusk.

And then to the sticky point: "We are a nation of laws, not men, and our greatness is our ability to adjust to the national consensus. The law to assure equal rights passed by

Congress last July with three-fourths of the Republicans joining two-thirds of the Democrats, has been received by the South for the most part in a way that is a great credit to local leadership—to mayors and ministers, to white merchants and Negro leaders, to all the Mr. and Mrs. John Citizens who live in our communities. This convinces me of something I have always believed—that there is, in this Southland, more love than hate."

She told them that the "hard duty of assuring equal and Constitutional rights to all Americans falls, not only on the President but upon all who love this land. And I am sure we will rise to that duty."

The President let it be her show. He said a few words, introduced Lynda, gave them both goodbye kisses as he left the train, and we were on our own—rolling down the tracks.

An extra engine was fifteen minutes ahead of us—a Secret Service precaution in the event the tracks might be bombed.

Then came our tremendous engine, two communication cars, and six Pullman sleepers, followed by two dining cars which remained continuously open around-the-clock and offered campaign specialties like the *"LBJ Steak Platter—Please specify: raring to go, middle of the road, or all-the-way."*

The cars were numbered starting with the last car. Cars number 6, 7 and 8 housed the staff, the hostesses, and campaign material, including two helium tanks to inflate balloons. Cars 4, 5 and 5A were working press rooms with a Western Union filing desk, and Air Express for shipping film. There were mimeograph machines and tape recorder outlets—and bars for the daily "Happy Hour."

Car number 3 had the office bedrooms of me, Bess Abell, and other top staff, plus a large lounge space which was the receiving area for groups of invited VIPs who came aboard the train one stop before reaching their home area.

Car number 2 was occupied by Mrs. Johnson and her personal

secretary, Mary Rather. It included a dining room and the only bathtub on the train. A chef and assistant prepared dinner for the First Lady, special guests and top staff during the trip.

Then Car number 1—the *Queen Mary*—complete with its own mailbox, and an array of colorful postcards of the Lady Bird Special which our visiting VIPs used to write home between stops.

Each section had its own busy schedule and assignment. The hard political talk emanated from Car 3 where John Ben Shepperd, veteran Texas politico, Congressman Hale Boggs, and Tennessee's Governor Buford Ellington, and Bill Brawley, Southern regional director for the campaign, visited with local politicians. Mrs. Bill Brawley dispensed warmth and hospitality. I think she and Shepperd, the master of ceremonies, stood in the center of that car all the way from Virginia to Louisiana. It was a trip that swelled shoe sizes more than heads.

My assistant, Simone Poulain, and I divided our time between Mrs. Johnson's needs and the working press cars, trying to keep 225 reporters happy and well-supplied with stories. We made the most of a large press bulletin board. I concocted a Dixie Dictionary "for folks from the Nawth covering the South." This rapid course in conversational English read as follows:

Yawl—not a boat, but more than one Democrat.
Tall cotton—what the Southerners walk in, due to Johnson prosperity.
Grits—only staple available during Hoover depression.
Kissin' kin—anyone who will come to the depot.
Beri-beri—(pronounced Barry-Barry)—a disease wiped out in the South.
Yankee—object of good neighbor policy.
High on the hawg—the gross national product under the Democrats.

Everyone got a laugh out of it except the sober-minded Associated Press. When that press association's Frances Lewine wrote a story, the AP later messaged its clients: PLEASE ELIMINATE THE DIXIE DICTIONARY—OBJECTIONABLE MATERIAL.

Translated, I suspected that meant some Goldwater publisher had filed a complaint.

Some hint of the hectic time ahead was also given in my memo of warning:

> A whistle will blow two minutes before the train starts moving. We hope we won't be scattering you over the countryside but the train does not wait. In case you get left, look for the advance man. He can easily be identified as the happiest man at the depot because all of his problems have just left. See if he can work out your transportation to a nearby town. If he can't, just take out residence, register and VOTE!

Our mad, merry Whistlestop rolled on down the tracks spreading Southern accents and Dixieland music along the way—through the crossroad villages of Virginia, on into the tobacco farmlands of North Carolina. Bands played. Pennants waved. The people turned out in thrilling numbers: 20,000 in Norfolk, 7500 in Ahoskie, 12,500 in Durham, 8000 at Rock Hill, South Carolina. The crowds and momentum snowballed; the news coverage blanketed every town in the South. Smiling faces and happy signs, one bearing the picture of two beagles saying, "You can pull our ears anytime, Mr. President." Receiving gifts of home products, our train filled up at every stop—bags of peanuts at Suffolk, hams and beaten biscuits at Richmond, boxes of hosiery in the milltowns, a jar of May haw jelly in Valdosta, Georgia, and roses, roses, roses. Mrs. Johnson was smiling, waving, saying her howdy-dos and thank-yous, bragging about each town and its heroes and Democratic candidates, and between stops, turning over to her secretary, Mary Rather, the handful of notes and telegrams pressed into her hands from well-wishers. One woman on the back of a wagon called out, "I got up at three o'clock this morning and milked twenty cows so I could come to see you, Lady Bird."

Mrs. Johnson blew her a kiss. She loved seeing the Southland this way. They were homefolks. In the privacy of her car, she was aglow. I praised the tremendous job she was doing and she confessed, "I love it. I'm like Br'er Rabbit in the briar patch."

All along the tracks were clusters of people waving and cheering the red, white and blue train. The pretty hostesses took turns standing on the back platform and waving back to the people in the fields or the schoolchildren along the way. Secretary of Commerce and Mrs. Luther Hodges—those grand old Southerners who had helped turn North Carolina into a progressive state while he was governor—were with us to greet old friends along the way.

At Raleigh, the President joined us. We left the train for a tremendous downtown rally, which netted us the support of Mrs. Dan Moore, wife of the taciturn Democratic nominee for governor. Mrs. Moore had been riding on the train during the day. She got so carried away with the crowds that when she met the President that night in the jam-packed hall she flung her arms around him and declared her full support for the Johnson-Humphrey ticket. Her husband stood silently by.

In Raleigh, we had a head-on collision between the President's and the First Lady's press. There just wasn't enough room for all the pool photographers in the convertible automobiles that carried them from the train station to the rally. The collision was literally head-on. Stan Weyman of *Life* magazine and a CBS photographer got into a fistfight. *Life*'s tooth was broken, and I spent the entire rally searching for Dr. Janet Travell, our Whistlestop physician. Behind the bleachers, she administered Novocain, and we called ahead to make a date with the dentist at the next overnight stop. The tooth was repaired. Stan brought the dentist and his family down to the station and lined them up for a picture with Mrs. Johnson—a method, I strongly suspected, that Stan used to aid the expense of his dental bill.

For the press, the whole trip was a brutal physical endurance test. I accused Dr. Travell of dispensing more drugs than I did press releases. There seemed to be an epidemic of laryngitis and sprained ankles. But the reporters seemed to thrive on the pace. As the train would stop, they would jump off the cars, race down the side of the track to the back platform, record the happenings, the color and the speech—and, if they were on a deadline, grab one of the phones we hooked up at each stop and dictate a story.

Two toots of the whistle, and they boarded again. We were off for the next stop. Sometimes there were thirteen stops in a day. Their tennis shoes (I had warned them to wear tennis shoes for the cinder-covered tracks) were being mutilated. But their stories were making page one, and the messages from the editors—"More on Lady Bird train"—were tonic to them.

The staccato of typewriters of all shapes and sizes never stopped. It was a noisy backdrop for the TV commentators also working in the rolling press rooms.

The railroads hospitably furnished a daily Happy Hour with a free bar from 4 to 5 P.M. Bess Abell and her helpers would serve the Southern dish of the day—beaten biscuits and ham in Virginia, hush-puppies in the Carolinas, shrimp and avocado dip in Florida.

At Charlotte, North Carolina, we had another medical crisis. Veteran newswoman Doris Fleeson suffered a mild stroke. My husband, bless him, volunteered to accompany her back to Washington by plane. As we said goodbye at the train platform, where Doris was lying on a stretcher waiting for the ambulance to the airport, I tried to think of something cheerful to say. "You're the only woman in the world, Doris, whom I could trust flat on her back with my husband," I said.

She lifted up her head from the stretcher, glared at me and shouted defiantly, "Dammit! I'll never be that sick!"

Our first trouble in the South came in Columbia, South Carolina, and it was so surprisingly ugly, it left all of us aghast.

There was a tremendous crowd waiting at the station as Governor Donald Russell introduced, in gallant and glowing terms, the First Lady. And then, before she could even begin talking, there was a rumble, a drum beat and a chant from a group of boys bunched together, heckling, "We want Barry! We want Barry!"

Shocked, the crowd looked to see how the First Lady would handle this startling discourtesy. She did not disappoint them. One hand raised gently, she said, "My friends, in this country we are entitled to many viewpoints. You are entitled to yours. But right now, I'm entitled to mine."

It worked. That time it worked, and every network that evening carried the filmed story of the First Lady's courage. Newspapers all over the country remade their editorial pages. And at Republican headquarters in Washington, Barry Goldwater's top aides denounced the attack on the First Lady and tried to deter heckling, for they knew it did them no good.

Something else happened in South Carolina. At Orangeburg, heart of the black belt, 5000 Negroes—cheering, arms reaching out in adoration—screamed their praise of LBJ. Ironically, we had been advised not to stop in Orangeburg because of recent racial incidents, but we stopped anyway.

It was a black rally. Keeping at a distance, a few white men eyed us suspiciously. Emotion-packed, the crowd of cheering Negroes had arms uplifted, reaching to grasp a hand, and to cry forth praise and adoration of the President. To his wife, they were expressing their thanks for the man who had given them the first real hope since the Civil War—a Civil Rights Law.

Here in Orangeburg, the First Lady and her press entourage were seeing the front lines of the civil rights battles. As she had promised, she had come to the "land where the pavement runs out and city people don't often go." And it was here "that people want a personal part in this election—for they all have an equal share in their government."

On into Charleston the Whistlestop rolled. Our advance man, Jack Hight, had been hard at work. By now, he had located a valuable friend—a Democratic lawyer of good standing, Getney Howe, who helped persuade the mayor to show up for the First Lady. Howe literally forced a shopping center, one of his clients, to allow us to have a rally there on the outskirts of Charleston. Representative Mendel Rivers, the long-maned Congressman and powerful chairman of the House Armed Services Committee, was on hand to let the people of South Carolina know the economic dangers of electing a Republican President. The hecklers came again, some of the same group who had been in Columbia, and they had their drum and ugly chants: "Johnson is a Communist. Johnson is a nigger-lover." Despite efforts of many Southerners to quell the hecklers, they continued, but the bread and butter message got through despite their noise. When Isabelle Shelton of *The Washington Star* asked one man whom he would vote for, he replied, "Johnson, because I'd rather stand beside a Negro in a factory than stand behind a white man in the soup line."

The flurry of open animosities by this crowd of suburban

shipyard workers and their families was not as chilling as the ride through historic old Charleston the next morning.

The First Lady was somewhat reluctantly accompanied by the mayor on a horsedrawn carriage ride through the picturesque old Battery to see Charleston's historic homes. Through empty streets, she rode past stately mansions graced with delicate grillwork—monuments to a lost day. On each door the blatant indignity of a sign that said, THIS HOUSE IS SOLD ON GOLDWATER. They didn't say, GO HOME LADY BIRD. But they might as well have.

Occasionally, there would be a Catholic school. How I came to appreciate those Catholic schools with their schoolyards of cheering children and sweet-faced nuns.

The hour-long drive ended. The mayor bowed a courteous farewell. And we were back on the train.

"What did you think of it?" I asked Mrs. Johnson when we were alone.

She laughed and said philosophically, "It was a rather frosty morning. I kept feeling that I was looking at a beautiful corpse."

Where was the hospitality of aristocratic old Charleston that morning? In retreat, nursing its bitterness, quarrelsome with one of its own. Like the moth to the flame, I have always yearned to go back there in search of some—even a few—who might remember that day and are a little bit sorry.

Betty Talmadge, the wife of the Georgia Senator, joined us and carried a ham aboard. We left Charleston and we munched on that ham through the red clay timberlands of Georgia. We met Savannah, first cousin of Charleston, and just as petulant and cold. But Luci took on the hecklers. In Johnson Square, named for a long-ago governor, under the shade of giant oaks, she told the crowd, "It seems to me that it is easy to holler a lot and make a lot of noise when you're not the one having to handle the problems."

She was only seventeen years old at the time, but the crowd of young Goldwater campaigners quieted down.

"We're the generation that is going to have to handle the problems later on. All the emotion in the world isn't going to help us when the time comes for us to lift up our banners and take the reins of government," she continued. She was interrupted only once, and when she finished, the hecklers remained quiet.

Congressman Hale Boggs and some of the men traveling aboard had been so indignant at the discourtesy to the First Lady as we rolled deeper into the South, that Mrs. Johnson had to stop them from rising to the defense of Southern womanhood.

"Look, I appreciate your kind words," she told them in a hastily called caucus in her Pullman car, "but the effect is simply this. We are doing more talking about the hecklers than about the candidates. So, really, I can handle any ugly moment, and I do think it would be best if we each ignored the hecklers as much as possible in speeches."

Congressman Boggs decided the best way to fight for civil rights in the South was chitlin-for-chitlin. He dispensed with the facts and figures in his speeches and began serving up verbal Southern cooking at each stop. It was a show-stopper.

His face smiling with a hush-puppy grin, Boggs would begin by saying, "You know what we had on this train this morning? Hominy grits. About noontime we're gonna' start servin' turnip greens and black-eyed peas. Later on, farther South, we're gonna' have some crawfish bisque, some red beans and rice, and some creole gumbo."

Then he continued, "Now about this race. You're not gonna' turn your back on the first Southern-born President in a hundred years?"

By this time, the black-eyed-pea-eating crowd was wild with

laughter. They loved the rhetorical questions and they screamed, "All the way with LBJ."

One of the growing problems of travel with three hundred bodies and no bathtubs on that train for four days was sanitation. The press cars looked like slums, with newspapers scattered everywhere, among the leftover snacks from the daily Happy Hour. Only one reporter—Mary Packenham of *The Chicago Tribune*—had been farsighted enough to bring along her own makeshift bathtub. It was a large plastic sack which she filled with water, slipped into and swished about, emerging better than before. Our stop in Tallahassee, where the train would sit on the tracks overnight, looked like the best prospect for improving the atmosphere.

The advance man, Bill Bates, a delightful Georgian who cut his political teeth in the campaigns of that master of Dixie politicos, Senator Richard Russell, was a little startled with the message we wired ahead: PRESS STINKS. PLEASE RESERVE THREE ROOMS AND 150 TOWELS FOR BATHING PERIOD AT NEARBY HOTEL. But he produced. The press took turns, and we cleansed ourselves of our dirt—if not our sins—in Tallahassee.

On the press bulletin board, I posted this message: "On the theory that the press that bathes together stays together, we have reserved three rooms, baths, showers and 150 towels at the DuVal Hotel in Tallahassee tonight." The gratitude of the train's grimy passengers was touching. The entire atmosphere was literally sweeter.

Next day, at tiny Flomaton, Alabama—the first stop as we rolled into Alabama—half a dozen of Lady Bird's cousins boarded to ride with us. Also waiting for us at Flomaton, much to our surprise, was a large bouquet of red roses sent by Governor George Wallace who was certainly no supporter of LBJ.

But Alabama had many ties with Mrs. Johnson. She had spent her summers there as a child. So Governor Wallace sent the wife of the lieutenant governor, Mrs. James Allen, to present a beautiful bouquet of red roses. Although she boarded the train in Flomaton, she wanted to make a public presentation of the roses two hours later when we arrived in Mobile for a major stop.

In any campaign, there is always the danger of overorganizing—becoming a victim of your own efficiency. That's what put Governor Wallace's roses in peril that day. Because the train couldn't carry all the gifts heaped upon Mrs. Johnson at each stop, we set up a little-known operation. When Mrs. Johnson received flowers, her secretary, Mary Rather, would then take them and walk nineteen cars through the train to a window by the engine. By previous arrangement, a police car would be waiting. She would toss the bouquets to the police car, including nicely written notes from the First Lady. The policeman would dispatch the flowers to hospitals in the town. This obviously accomplished two things: (1) It furnished an opportunity for Mrs. Johnson to share the flowers with many people, and (2) It disposed of the mounting mound of flowers which gave the train's hospitality car a distinctly funereal appearance.

All over the South, Mary would gather up the roses, attach the notes, wait a decent number of towns, and then go running back through the train and pass the bouquets to the waiting policeman.

"I feel like a bride every day," she said gaily.

Just as we pulled into Mobile, and our Alabama dignitary, Mrs. Allen, prepared for her big moment—presenting the roses to the First Lady—she turned around to look for the bouquet.

"Where are Governor Wallace's roses?" she asked me.

I glanced furtively around. "They were right here," I said. "They must be here somewhere."

"I just laid them down here. I've got to have them," Mrs. Allen said.

I rushed to find Mary, suspecting what had happened.

"Where are Governor Wallace's roses?" I demanded.

She turned ashen. She started out in a dead heat through the train to overtake an emissary she had just sent to the front of the train. In what seemed like hours, while we slowed to a stop in Mobile, she was back breathless—with roses. She had rescued them just as they were being handed out the window. This was one time when it was *not* better to give than to receive.

Governor Wallace's roses were finally presented. Mrs. Johnson's trek through Mobile, through masses of wildly cheering crowds, was perhaps the most sentimental stop of all. This response was the reason why George Wallace had bothered to send flowers. He didn't want to ignore a popular daughter of the South.

She met friends and cousins from Atmore, Mobile, Billingsley, Prattville—the towns, she recalled, "that are filled with memories of watermelon cuttin's and pallets on the floor."

By the time we arrived in Mississippi, we found another group of dissident dignitaries waiting to welcome her: Senators James O. Eastland and John Stennis were on hand. They said their polite hellos quickly and didn't linger.

Last stop—New Orleans, the Crescent City—the end of the ride. The President joined us there. The station was jammed and the streets were lined to the Jung Hotel where he would make a major speech.

Our trainload of bedraggled reporters and staff, and an exhausted First Lady, packed our tumbled suitcases, took one last deep breath, and mustered enough strength for the final appearance.

We stood there on the back platform waiting for the President to join us. I could see the President pushing through the crowd, taller than anyone, stopping to shake a hand or give a hug to the newswomen whose by-lines he had been reading so avidly and proudly during our trip. He was pulling two Louisiana Senators along with him—Allen J. Ellender and Russell B. Long. When he reached the train, he kissed Luci, and enveloped Mrs. Johnson in his arms. She happily yielded the microphone and speechmaking to him. He was buoyant, glowing in praise of all the dignitaries who were there, trying to get the message over to Governor John J. McKeithen who timidly stood back in a corner.

It was an unusual sight. Here in New Orleans' Union Passenger Terminary, thousands of Negroes chanting "We want Lyndon." In front of the platform the races mixed together, all cheering together.

"I'm going to repeat here in Louisiana what I have said in every state of the Union. As long as I am your President, I'm going to be President of all of the people. And your President is going to protect the Constitutional rights of every American."

The crowd went wild, black and white alike. And LBJ's enthusiasm was contagious. Senator Ellender, certainly no supporter of civil rights, was swept up in the mood. But, in his excitement, he got his tongue twisted and yelled: "All the way with LJB!" (sic). The crowd roared.

An hour later, at his formal speech in the Jung Hotel, LBJ threw his prepared text away, took off his coat, rolled up his sleeves, and made a civil rights speech like the South has never heard before—or since.

He told the story of a Southern Senator who, sick and weary at the end of his career, had said: "I wish I felt a little better. I would like to go back home and make 'em one more Democratic speech. I feel like I have just one more in me. The poor old state! They haven't heard a Democratic speech in thirty years. All they ever hear at election time is nigger, nigger, nigger!"

The President's arms were outstretched, slicing the air for emphasis. The audience gasped, and it was the Negroes who started the applause.

"There is only one real problem that faces you," he said defiantly, pointing his hand toward the audience. "It isn't an economic problem. It isn't a Negro problem. It's whether you're going to live or die!"

We left New Orleans that afternoon, flying back to the ranch feeling, as Mrs. Johnson said, "like cooked spaghetti." The President was bursting with pride. For a week the stories had blanketed the nation. He had watched his wife take on an assignment that no other woman had done in history, and perform it with skill and with heart—and with courage in the ugly hours.

Everytime he looked across at me, he would shake his head and laugh and say, "Now, Liz, that's the way to run a railroad!"

Throughout that afternoon and into the evening, the Lady Bird Special sat on the tracks in the New Orleans Station. Porters swept out the accumulation of trash, copy paper, carbons. In the working press cars, a reporter, her bags packed and waiting beside her, finished her story.

"New Orleans, Oct. 9—Together, the President and the First Lady made an assault on the heart and the mind of the South that must be the most remarkable joint campaign effort in American political history.

"Perhaps they had changed some votes; perhaps they had altered none. But they had given it everything they had."

This was, I felt, the appropriate epitaph to the Lady Bird Special.

## *Home on the Range*

The city limits sign of Johnson City reads: POPULATION, 854. Eighteen miles down Highway 290—past Ranch Road 1—the sign of Stonewall reads: POPULATION, 175.

Pardner, out there it's Marlboro Country. The ranches and pastures between Johnson City and Stonewall have 515 dry creek beds, 1071 cattleguards, 1001 gates—not to mention innumerable deer, tarantulas, horned toads, stinging scorpions and jackrabbits.

I know. And when you've seen one dry creek bed, you've seen 'em all.

Henry Ford II once rode over this rugged terrain as guest of You-Know-Who, and after four hours of dusty roads, and opening gates, and climbing in and out of the back end of one of the President's station wagons, he rubbed his behind all the way into the ranch house. I suspected he privately made plans to recall all his Lincoln station wagons to install more foam rubber padding.

The President was very generous with his ranch, and he liked nothing better than to fill all the guest rooms with friends or staff members, especially if he felt they needed a rest. Did

I say *rest?* Relaxing with LBJ is like getting a massage on a roller coaster. His idea of a good time is to put eight people in a car which holds six comfortably and go see the deer and the antelope play. Not just one deer and one antelope, either! But herds and herds of them through pasture after pasture.

The problem about taking a drive with the President was that he was Mr. Hospitality Incorporated, and he just couldn't bear to leave anyone behind or to pass anyone by. So the car became more and more crowded as you drove along picking up neighbors, hitchhikers, cousins and grandchildren until finally even LBJ realized it was too crowded. Then he was likely to say to a staffer, "You just hop out and let Judge Moursund ride with us a while, and we'll be back in about ten minutes and pick you up here in Johnson City."

This happened to Ervin Duggan, whom the President had hoped would take a job as a researcher at the LBJ Library. Unfortunately, LBJ forgot all about Ervin standing patiently in Johnson City. Ervin did everything he could think of to kill time. But after he had visited the LBJ Boyhood Home, walked around the courthouse, and whittled a while at Truman Fawcett's Drug Store, he was getting more and more conspicuous as the stranger in Johnson City. In fact, Ervin became so conspicuous by his lengthy presence that the Tax Assessor almost served notice on him. Finally he flagged down a car, headed for the airport in Austin and flew back East—to stay. It took months for him to laugh about this oversight.

After my first trip to the ranch for one of those hilarious weekends, I learned to carry along a survival kit which included: a good book (something about the length of *The Decline and Fall of the Roman Empire*), an extra pair of slacks for tromping over hill and dale, lipstick (you never could tell when he was apt to take a look at you through the wind and dust and say, "You need lipstick"), and snake bite prevention kits. As an added precaution, I always notified my next-of-kin before I left.

Some Presidents relax on the golf course. Some like to sail or fish. Some go to the Kentucky Derby. Some chop down cherry trees. Others have collected stamps. This President loved to roam the countryside, stopping off here and there at neighboring ranches to visit Cousin Oriole, or Mr. Hodges, or Lela Martin.

Once his father had described this country as the part of the world where "people know when you're sick, miss you when you die and love you while you live." LBJ kept up with the family news on all of his neighbors—births, deaths and ailments—and fulfilled his father's description exactly.

When he became President, the ranch changed from a pastoral setting of trees and cattle and the lonely sound of the hoot owl to the "Week-End White House" with Secret Service, Signal Corps, the United States Air Force and, occasionally, members of the National Security Council in residence. To behold Walt Rostow in a red checkered shirt and blue jeans is to get a new insight into the whole international situation.

The kitchen of the ranch house was the visiting place for many of the entourage, especially the dozens of Secret Service, who liked to sip coffee and talk to Mary Davis, the cook. The President had a hard time getting used to seeing so many able-bodied men around the ranch seemingly idle. One morning, he came through the kitchen, caught one glimpse of this relaxed scene, and couldn't believe his eyes. All that manpower going to waste! All those idle hands! Conversation stopped. He glanced furtively around looking for something to tell them to do. Then he bolted through the door shouting back defiantly to the Secret Service: "Swat flies!"

Rufus Youngblood, in charge of the ranch SS detail, finally broke the stunned silence: "Well, I guess flies could be a security problem." He picked up a swatter.

When it comes to empire building, Napoleon could have taken a few tips from the Secret Service. Every agent comes in multiples of four, several for every eight-hour shift, and an extra in case of illness. By the end of the Johnson Administration, flies were no longer a problem at the LBJ Ranch.

LBJ knew every inch of his pastures. He wanted them to look their best and produce their fullest. Talking ranch language about weather and crops—rainfall, yield per acre and what kind of grasses grew best—was a diversion that restored his spirits; so everyone encouraged the President to "play ranch" when he was home.

If something didn't work or a fence was broken down, he'd get on the car radio to talk to the ranch foreman by intercom, with an order: "Dale, this fence over here at the Haywood place is out, and we're going to lose every cow we've got if you don't get it fixed."

Or, as we walked through the various empty ranch houses, the assignment went to Mrs. Johnson. "Bird," he'd say, "we've certainly got better paintings than that stuff. Let's get them over here." Or, "These curtains need replacing."

It was no secret that Dale Malechek liked it a lot better when the President was in Washington involved in other business. But at the ranch, Dale would just nod, do what he was told, and tuck his chaw of tobacco deeper into his jaw.

Dale had only one escape from listening to orders. Once a year, when the grapes were in purple, he would make wine. This process was accomplished in the basement of the house of a nearby German farmer. It took longer and longer every year. Dale would stomp grapes, uninterrupted by the sound of human voices. In a week, he would emerge with a few bottles of wine of recent vintage that he gave the Secret Service agents at Christmas.

Mrs. Johnson didn't have this outlet. She just responded, "Yes, dear," and ultimately got the assigned chores done. I did hear her sigh once, "I wish, I just wish that one time we would come home and find that everything at the ranch worked!"

But she was too realistic, too experienced at rural life to believe this would ever happen. There is not a farm or ranch in the United States where everything works all at one time. Show it to me, and based on my experience with the LBJ Ranch, I can instantly find a windmill that doesn't turn, or a cattleguard that is down. Cattleguards! The word still makes me shudder. We lost dozens of tenderfoot reporters from some of the nation's best publications into cattleguards in those five years.

In fact, when Bonnie Angelo of *Time* magazine was warned to look out for the cattleguards, she asked, "Why? Are they handsome?"

A cattleguard is a series of six or eight parallel pipes several inches apart which are suspended over a ditch to separate one pasture from another. This contraption keeps the cattle, who have sense enough not to cross it, in their proper place.

But newsmen didn't have sense enough. They didn't know that to cross a cattleguard you have to step gingerly from pipe to pipe, or jump the entire thing. So they would go forging ahead—forward together, if you will—and first thing we knew, the New York *Daily News* would have one leg wedged into the ditch below and the other hanging above the pipe and would be bellowing as if the world were ending.

Dipping vats were even more hazardous for the press. A dipping vat is a deep hole filled with liquid insecticide. Two wooden slides on either side force a calf or sheep to slide down into a smelly substance below and come out on the other side free from ticks, fleas and other insects. The most interesting dipping vat I know was located at Betty and Tom Weinheimer's ranch, nearby the Johnson ranch. This vat was a favorite, photographically speaking, for the newsreels and magazines who occasionally published color stories about the President's Hill Country and its inhabitants.

I think the best laugh the President got in his entire five years in the White House was when Betty Weinheimer called from Stonewall and reported with dismay, "*Life* magazine fell into the dipping vat this morning." The President slapped his sides and laughed until he cried. His only regret was there hadn't been room for the entire White House Correspondents' Association.

The President loved the ranch, and he liked to share the things he loved with everyone in the vicinity. Sometimes his hospitality got him in trouble. In fact, most of the time LBJ got burned by the press was when he was trying to do a favor for some correspondents. The famous "beer can incident," for instance, never happened in the wild manner in which it was incorrectly reported. The story began when Marquis Childs, a columnist, sent word to the President, via George Reedy, that he would like to drive out from Austin and see the ranch with the President. Johnson—being Johnson—invited Mark and, in the process, filled his car with other reporters who had come out to the ranch for a press conference. None of the reporters in the car wrote the ugly story, but their tales of a Johnson safari around the ranchlands—an event so strange to their Eastern breeding—were enlarged with every retelling. The weekly news magazines reported all the rumors. Pressure began for the AP and UPI reporters in Texas to write about the beer cans. Al Spivak of UPI checked out the damaging part: had the President tossed beer cans out of the car while driving at a reckless speed? He found no confirmation. But by this time, the wire services were picking up the *Time* and *Newsweek* stories. How much of them were fact and how much were fiction, therefore, remained a mystery to the public. There is no question that the beer can story hurt LBJ.

Aside from this incident, many Eastern newsmen did not share the President's love of the land. They were only at home in a concrete society of town houses and art collections—of the quips and quotes from Georgetown. They found no joy in blue skies and enough rainfall, or the beauty of a shiny, fat white-faced Hereford. The only way they would respond would be to get out a pencil and pad and make lists of the number of ranches, ranch houses, and head of cattle this big, strapping Texan owned. They relished the Super Texan image because it was so different from anything back East. The President's ranches—small by Texas standards—were larger than life to them. They couldn't understand why a man would prefer pastures to Picassos. I always wondered if when they dined at a Kennedy residence or with the Harrimans or Rockefellers, they got out a pad and pencil to list all the paintings, all the avant garde sculptures, all the priceless antiques, boxes and bibelots which these men enjoyed possessing.

But there were others who really enjoyed the friendly atmosphere of the Hill Country. Take the time the powers of *Life* magazine decided to give a park to Johnson City. Well, I wouldn't say they exactly decided all by themselves. But Mrs. Johnson had written an article for them, and she couldn't accept a fee. So, in lieu of a fee and in honor of her, *Life* transformed an old broken-down lot on Highway 80 in Johnson City into a lovely park with grass, live oaks, picnic tables, a water fountain for the thirsty and a beautiful stone wall. There was only one drawback. Johnson City had never had a park before, and the residents didn't know quite what to do with it. So the hometown folks would just walk by and look at it, but never use it.

"We must let people know how pleased we would be if they would make use of that park," Mrs. Johnson said to me one day. "For instance, there is a group of elderly domino players who have been in the same game for about eight or ten years. They sit around the corner from the park, playing on an absolutely disreputable-looking table every day, all day long. I think it would be nice if they moved to the park. I would buy them a new domino table. Anyway, Liz, figure out something so the people in Johnson City know that the park is theirs—it is open for their pleasure."

I called my longtime college friend, Jimmy Pitt, who handles public relations for the *Time-Life* empire. Unlike the rest of the *Time-Life* hierarchy, Jimmy is a real country boy from Quanah, Texas—slow-talking, but sharp as a newly whittled stick—as they say in Quanah. He had helped me work on the park.

"Mrs. Johnson wants us to get some domino players for the Johnson City Park," I told him.

"Well, I think that would be fun," he said and arranged to meet me in a few days in Johnson City.

We invaded the domino table next to Casparis Cafe and pulled up two nail kegs to sit on, and watched and waited until the time came to speak. I wouldn't say that we exactly blended into the shirtsleeve, tobacco-chewing atmosphere—after all, we'd both been away from Texas a long time. Strangers driving by *would* have picked us out as city-slickers. But we tried to be patient.

After an hour or so, Jimmy said, "Nice game you've got going."

Not a sound from the domino players.

"Must get hot over here with no shade trees," I offered.

Still no sound, and the game continued.

"Ever notice the live oaks over in the park on the highway?" Jimmy suggested.

"Yep," one of them yepped.

"Well," I said, "Mrs. Johnson thought you might like to

*13. Our children, Scott, and Christy: I did all the work and Les got the by-line. They have his brown eyes and long, lean look!*

*14. Liz and her best beau, Les.*

15. *"Do you read me?"—With walkie-talkie, you can bring almost anybody in.*

*16. Working on the State of the Union message with LBJ and Presidential Assistants Marvin Watson (left) and Joe Califano (right).*

*17. Air Force One calling.*

*18. "How many raisins in the wedding cake," asked a reporter at a press briefing before Lynda Johnson Robb's wedding. The reporter was assigned to count the raisins.*

*19. Wedding Daze and 500 romantic-minded newspaper reporters interested in one bride and one groom prompted this scene in my office with assistant, Marcia Maddox.*

*20. The day before Luci's wedding, I held an impromptu briefing on the steps of the National Shrine of the Immaculate Conception.*

*21. Here Comes the Groom, and Best Man: Captain Charles Robb and Douglas Davidson arrive on December 9, 1967, just before the wedding.*

22. *In the White House dog house, I get the straight stuff from Him.*

23. *Christmastime Reunion for Mom and the children, Christy (left), Scott, and my new daughter-in-law, Joyce.*

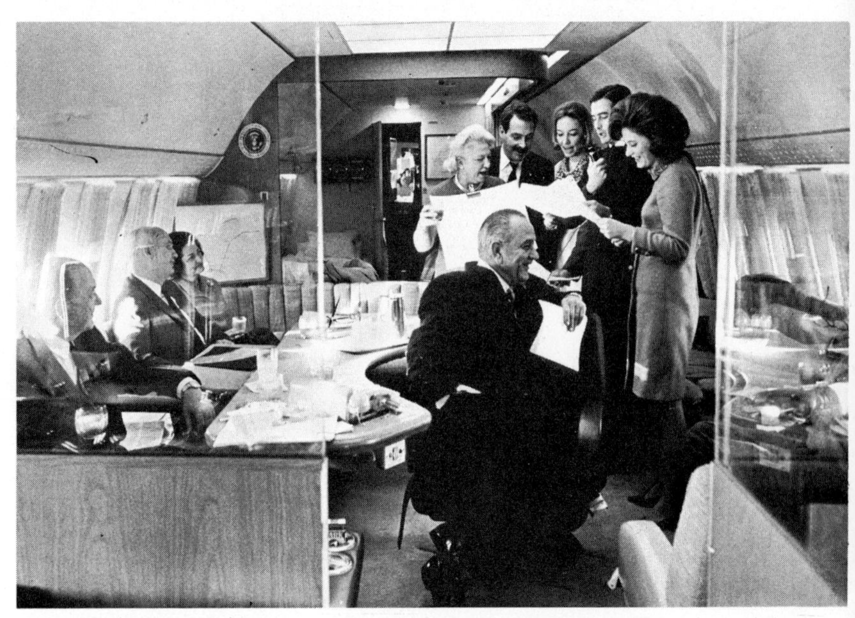

24. *Aboard Air Force One, the President listens as we tell the trials and tribulations of traveling around the world with LBJ, to our own musical presented at 35,000 feet.*

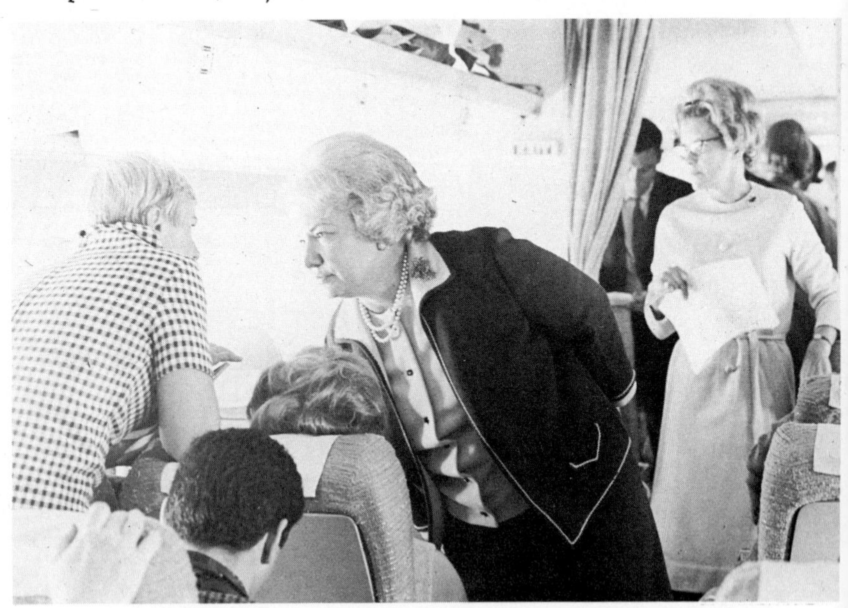

25. *High-flying Liz answering a press question with fear from Nan Robertson of* The New York Times. *Simone Poulian, my assistant, is in the background.* (Photograph by Fred J. Maroon)

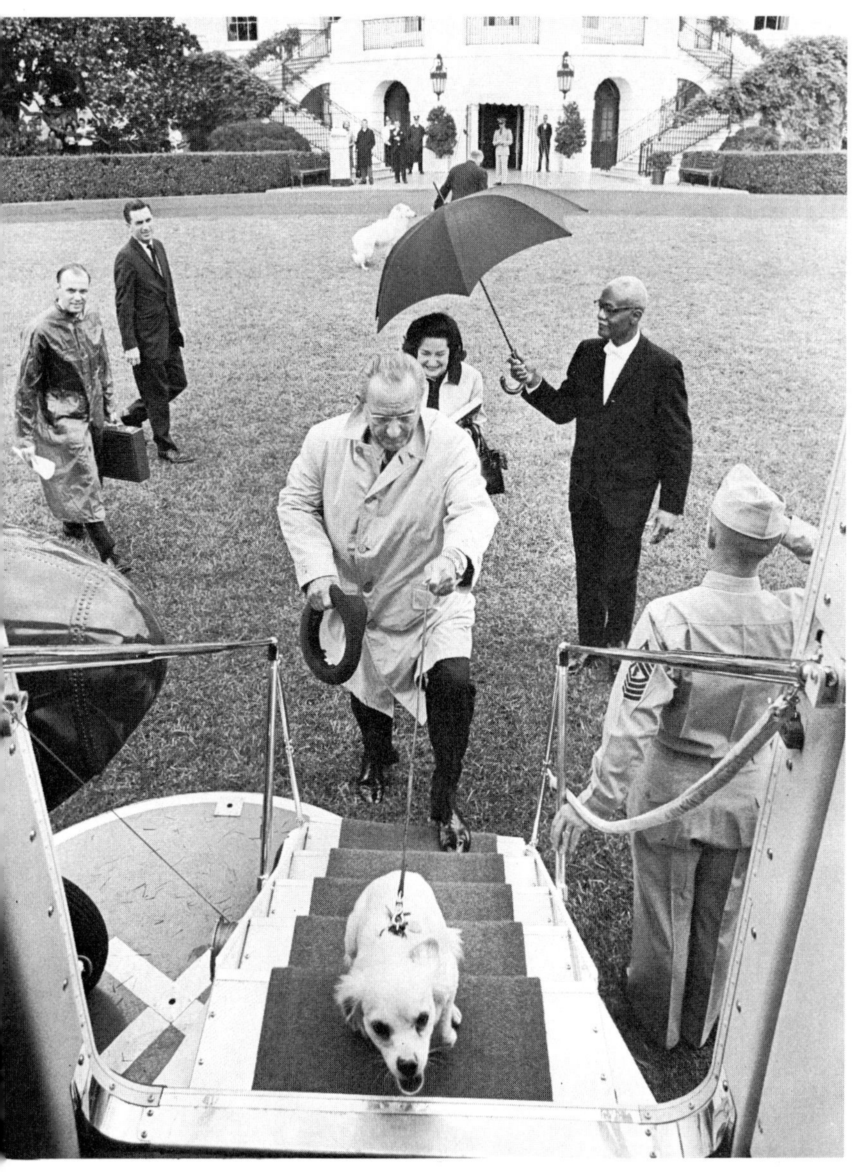

*26. Yuki's enthusiasm for departing the scene of pomp and splendor was always marked when the President and Mrs. Johnson boarded the helicopter.*

*27. The Lone Ranger (Mrs. LBJ) and Tonto (Secretary of Interior Stewart Udall) show their countrymen how to discover America in the Grand Tetons on a raft ride down the Snake River.*

28. *During the last week, Mrs. Johnson met with all of us in the press office. Left to right, Lenore Haag, Marta Ross, Mrs. J., Marcia Maddox, me, and Oghda O'Gulian. Simone Poulain had already departed.*

29. *Moving Day, January 1969. I pack the accumulation of five years of work and memories to exit smiling.* (Photograph by Ray Lustig © *The Washington Star*)

30. *On a trip, the photographers often came between the First Lady and the scenery. But here I am in my natural habitat.* (Photograph by Fred J. Maroon)

bring your game into the shade. As a matter of fact, she would find a suitable table for you."

"Like this table. Besides, we can move into the cafe if it rains," the domino player added.

"Well, the park is just around the corner. It couldn't be more than a hundred steps away. Besides, how often does it rain here?" I said.

"Too fur," said the domino player.

"Well, think about it overnight," Jimmy said and motioned to me to leave.

Three hours had been totally wasted, I felt, and so we went across the street to our only oasis in Johnson City—the coffee pot of Judge A. W. Moursund, longtime friend of the President.

The former judge—still addressed as judge—is a tremendous man, in height and in character. He is the kind of man you'd want around in an emergency, because he could fix a flat or carry your casket.

Lots of people felt the same way, which is the reason he does the most business of any lawyer in five counties. Your troubles seem to disappear in his presence. We related our tale of woe to the Judge, and he threw back his head and must have laughed for five minutes.

"You don't stand a chance," he declared, once he was able to talk again. "Those old coots wouldn't change their location for all the tea in China. They want to be where they can see who comes in and out of my door, so they can tell everyone in town. Nope, Liz, you better find something else to make people come to the park."

Jimmy and I took our worries up the road about eight miles to the Ranch House, a restaurant with the best barbecue in the world. It is run by Mr. Cecil Presnall, who used to be a carpenter, but decided one day that he would build a barbecue pit and take advantage of the growing number of tourists visiting Blanco County during the President's term of office. Business got so good that he finally replaced the privies with indoor facilities. Somehow that detracted from the original charm.

During a bountiful meal of barbecue, pinto beans, thick slices of onions and dill pickle, we came up with an idea worthy of our finest talents: a bake sale.

It was three weeks before Christmas. If all the ovens of Blanco County started baking their delectable goodies, they could have a sale in the park, churches and other local groups could make money for their organizations, and people would see that the park could be utilized for worthy purposes.

We enlisted the aid of Jessie Hunter, a redheaded middle-aged woman who knows all the women in the town and is the curator of the LBJ Boyhood Home. She'd invited Jimmy and me to the Women's Club that evening to enlist their aid.

When I told Mrs. Johnson of our determination, she said, "I declare, Liz, I just can't get over how you and Jimmy have taken to Johnson City." She suggested that we see the Home Demonstration agent.

It took three days, a subscription to the Johnson City *Record Courier,* two paid memberships in the Blanco County Historical Association, and a call to the Texas governor's wife and the state commissioner of agriculture. But Johnson City had the biggest bake sale in its history. One important reason is that it was the *only* bake sale in its history. There were thirteen tables of cakes, pies, cookies, German sausage. Each table was sponsored by a different church or organization—like the United Daughters of the Confederacy.

The day of the sale, Jimmy and I were there, waiting at 6 A.M. to greet every soul who passed that way. Having persuaded the good women of Johnson City to do their best, we were determined they should have customers. And just to be sure, Jimmy had negotiated a large loan from *Life* magazine in case he had to buy them out himself.

"I wouldn't want them to be disappointed, and I can always take my children out of college and pay the loan off slowly," he said.

It wasn't necessary. The customers came from Austin and Fredericksburg and San Antonio, and we stood there just as pleased as if we had been slaving over the oven all week. Mrs. Johnson brought preserves and homemade bread from the LBJ Ranch. By the end of the day, the ladies had made $2400 which was divided among their clubs. That was big money in Johnson City.

Since then, the park has been used for an art show, picnics, afternoon marble games. The *Life* magazine hierarchy came down, and Andrew Heiskell, Jerome Hardy, Hedley Donovan and Jim Linen, who had never quite seen anything like Johnson City, were so pleased with the park they contributed lights and a cement stage for dancing and roller skating.

But the domino players can still be found at Casparis Cafe.

There is no doubt that the 36th President of the United States put Johnson City on the map, just as Harry S Truman made Independence known, and Dwight D. Eisenhower, Gettysburg.

With the booming new tourist trade, came the accompanying cheap souvenir stands, stocked with rattlesnake ash trays, bottles of water which were said to be from the Pedernales River, a jar of LBJ Ranch dirt, and plates and cups with pictures of the President and Mrs. Johnson that make portrait artist Peter Hurd seem like Gilbert Stuart.

But there was absolutely nothing the First Lady could do about it, except to encourage these stands to stock tasteful crafts.

Jimmy Pitt and I explored the possibility of finding someone who would start a shop of tasteful crafts and souvenirs, thereby setting the example.

"One of the handsomest buildings in town is the jail," Jimmy observed. "Maybe it could be used as a showcase of crafts."

We called on the sheriff.

"Nope, no one has been in jail for nearly five years now. We'd have closed it up if it weren't so handy for folks who get stranded here in Johnson City," the sheriff said. "Lemmesee, I guess the last ones we had was a widder woman who came through here with a whole carload of kids heading for California. The car broke down and she ran out of money. So I found some blankets and cots and let her spend the night in the jail. Some of the ladies bought them groceries and packed 'em a lunch, and they went on the next day."

This seemed like such a worthwhile purpose that Jimmy and I didn't want to disrupt the Johnson City Sheraton. But one day maybe we'll try to buy it, and put some worthy souvenirs on the market.

The LBJ Ranch also served as a meeting place for many Heads of State. This was constantly being encouraged by foreign policy adviser McGeorge Bundy and discouraged by Mrs. Johnson. After all, the only thing "Mac" Bundy had to do was to pack up his papers in a fashionably shabby brief case and arrive. But not the working class like Bess Abell, the First Lady and me. We well knew the pitfalls of running a State visit eighty miles from the nearest fresh head of lettuce.

We also were aware we had a temperamental water system and a precarious source of electricity. In fact, once when CBS came down to film a show, the technicians plugged their cameras into a wall of the main ranch house and blew out the entire electric system all the way up and down the Pedernales River. After that, we asked all networks to bring their own batteries.

One thing in Texas is more unpredictable than LBJ. That is the weather. So, when you start planning a barbecue on the picturesque banks of the Pedernales River, you have to be prepared to move it seven miles down the road to Stonewall High School's gymnasium.

To help us cope with the uncertainty of the skies, Bess Abell had her own secret crystal ball reader—Dr. Irvine Krick, a meteorologist, who chooses to live in Palm Spring, California, because that's where the weather is best, with or without a prediction.

Thus, when Chancellor Ludwig Erhard of Germany decided to come call on the President in December of 1963, and when McGeorge Bundy decided the meeting should be held at the ranch, Dr. Krick got out his ouija board, his willow branch, or whatever he uses, and told us to plan the barbecue inside.

The Stonewall gym isn't exactly the State Dining Room of 1600 Pennsylvania Avenue. Bess and I decided to cover the holes in it by tossing some bales of hay here and there in an artistic rustic fashion. We hauled in some old saddles. With red checkered tablecloths—and with Walter Jetton's succulent barbecue—it was a scene and a feast fit for a Chancellor.

The Chancellor is a frustrated concert pianist. Well, I couldn't actually swear that he's frustrated, but his biography indicated he would rather play the piano than chancel.

Texas' own pianist, Van Cliburn, agreed to come and perform. The day before the barbecue, Bess called Van Cliburn to check his arrival time. Yes, he would be there on time. Yes, the piano tuner from San Antonio was satisfactory. Our suggestion about his clothes?

"A red checkered shirt and blue jeans! Certainly not!" Van Cliburn said. "I'll wear white tie and tails, just as I always do for a concert."

"But, Van, they haven't ever seen a tuxedo in Stonewall," we pleaded.

"But this is a concert for the Chancellor of Germany," Van insisted.

"But you haven't seen Stonewall," we shouted.

Finally, a compromise was reached. He consented to wear a business suit.

He came. He played. And the Chancellor, whose early ambition was to be a concert pianist, was charmed. The occasion was so informal that Pierre Salinger, also a frustrated pianist, took to the keys. That was before he took to the horse. He did much better with the piano.

(This was not the only time I was to become involved with Van Cliburn on the subject of white tie. Once he arrived in Washington for a concert in Constitution Hall, and the airline lost the clothes bag with his white tie and tails. The tuxedo rental places were closed, for it was Sunday. He phoned me to see if he could borrow my husband's white tie, since Les and Van are both tall and lean.

(While Les had several black tie outfits in the closet, the truth of the matter is he doesn't own a set of tails. They are rarely worn in Washington, and the few times an invitation says, "White tie," Les rents tails.

("I know someone who is just your height and does own a white tie," I volunteered. "Let me call him and see if he won't lend a set of tails to you."

(A quick call to LBJ. "Sure, he's welcome to them. Tell him to come on over, and I'll get Paul Glynn down here to help him get dressed," the President said. Van rushed to the White House. It took a major pin-in—because the President is many pounds heavier. But soon the Texas-born artist was off to Constitution Hall to play his concert in an outfit borrowed from his friend—the Texas-born President of the United States.)

The German visitors, including about thirty-five German writers, had let us know they would love to go home with

Texas hats. In one corner of the gym we had the forty beautiful Stetson hats, all boxed and ready to present, but the President decided he wanted each man to try his hat on. The problem about new Stetsons is creasing them. Someone who knows how, has to whack them in just the right place in the crown so they shape up nicely.

I tried two or three times and obviously was an amateur. "A.W., get on over there with Liz," the President called to Judge Moursund over the microphone, "and show her how to crease a hat."

The Judge creased most of the hats. Sitting there rejected, I again realized how wonderful it was to hold a high policy position in Washington.

After this early experiment in instant barbecues, we became quite adept at it. It's fortunate, too. Because on Election Day in 1964, we had another challenge. The President and First Lady were riding into Johnson City to cast their vote, and they invited Bess and me to go with them. Down past the barbecue grounds in front of the ranch house, we passed some remnants of Walter Jetton's left-over-from-last-week campaign barbecue. There was a chuck wagon with a sign reading LBJ OR BUST, a few scattered tables and chairs.

"What's all that junk?" the President asked.

"It's left over from the barbecue last week," I replied.

There was a silence. Then, the long, slow curve: "We just might have a barbecue tomorrow for all those reporters who've been traveling with us. Might ask the Humphreys down, too."

Bess pulled out her pocket telephone book and began looking up the phone number of Walter Jetton. I was watching the President as he slowly drove through the streets of Johnson City, waving and stopping at each corner to give an LBJ fountain pen or pencil to the children of Johnson City who followed him along in Pied Piper fashion.

We parked in front of the voting place—the Pedernales River Electric Cooperative—and more than a hundred reporters and photographers were swarming all over waiting for the President and First Lady. At the curb were neighbors and friends, proud of their local boy.

The President began unfolding his six feet, three inches from the car. I saw him put his hand into his pocket for another souvenir fountain pen just as I also spied a sign that said: "AGAINST THE LAW TO CAMPAIGN WITHIN TWO HUNDRED YARDS OF THE POLLS." I leaned over to him just in time: "Don't campaign at the polls, Mr. President; please don't campaign at the polls!" The hand withdrew, and he went on inside, smiling, to cast his vote.

The pen-pusher had reason to smile when the votes were counted.

The LBJ Ranch is a small working ranch, not a showplace, and the ranch house (the oldest rock portion of it was built a hundred years ago by a man known only as Polecat Meier), has been added onto and stretched to accommodate a growing family and visiting dignitaries. Even the two servants rooms have been converted into small guest rooms. The couple who handle the Main House—Mr. and Mrs. James Davis—moved up the road to a place of their own. Their hands were multiplied by the efforts of a dozen Philippine stewards from the White House detail when the President entertained visiting Heads of State.

In all, the Main House has six bedrooms on the second floor and a wide upstairs porch which looks across the gray-green live oaks to the winding Pedernales down below. The first floor has two living rooms, a dining room with a large picture window framing the fields of deep coastal Bermuda grass in the back pasture. There is also the President's large office, and a tremendous kitchen with a table for breakfast and coffee at any hour of the day or night. And there are two bedroom suites occupied by President and Mrs. Johnson.

At the door of the house is the welcome mat given by the Women's National Press Club. It reads: ALL THE WORLD IS WELCOME HERE, and its letters have to be repainted frequently. A large mounted deer head, its horns affording a resting place for the President's hats and caps, is on the wall by the door. The visitor enters to a cool, restful atmosphere, a sense of grays, greens, beiges and burnt orange—the colors of the surrounding land which Mrs. Johnson has brought into the house in curtains, pillows, wall-paper choices.

In winter, the fireplaces crackle with cedar logs. Mrs. Johnson's collection of copper vases and kettles are set near the fireplace, catching the flame's light. There are always spicy smells from the kitchen—homemade bread baking or pies and cakes and lace-cookies spread out to cool along the counters.

The rooms are all "floppable"; that is, you feel the urge to flop down and get into a long conversation or devour a good book. Each wall and corner holds a treasured keepsake, usually with a story—patchwork quilts from the needle of a cousin or aunt, Mexican provincial paintings, a corner cabinet from Finland. And the flowers and fruit on the low tables come from the land—a big wooden bowl of ripened peaches from Stonewall when they are in season, a profusion of bluebonnets or daisies and thistles.

At night, the ritual after dinner is to walk down the road to Cousin Oriole's, who lives just the right distance for a pleasant stroll. You can almost reach up and touch the stars. But it is still and velvety and comforting, with only a hoot owl or the crickets, or a dog's bark across the river, to break the silence.

There is a saying in the West that the best fertilizer is the heel of the owner's boot. This land knows the owner's boot.

# *Guess Who Came to Dinner?*

The State Dining Room of the White House is where Buckingham Palace and Broadway meet.

I don't mean that we had the Queen of England confronting Gypsy Rose Lee. But we did have the Queen's sister, Princess Margaret, and the Great White Way's enchantress, Carol Channing.

During those five years, 200,000 people received the beautiful engraved invitations, hand-addressed in banknote script, which read: "The President and Mrs. Johnson request the pleasure of the company of . . ." The Johnsons invited a cross-section of America—not just the rich and powerful, the glamour names in the newspapers, although there were many of those—but also the people who make up the heart of this country. For instance, when Queen Frederika of Greece came for a luncheon, a Greek restaurant owner from Texas, who is a longtime friend of the President's, was invited, too. And when the Prime Minister of Italy came, Steve Martini—the President's barber—was invited, because the President knew how much this would mean to him.

We had parties in sweltering heat, hailstorms, blizzards and on starry nights. We had a carnival on the South Lawn, dinners in the Rose Garden, a steak fry on the roof. Guests included the great, the near-great, the halt, the lame, the pregnant, Eartha Kitt and a tribe of Indians.

Like hospitable old Andy Jackson, Lyndon Johnson invited "all creation" to the White House. He was naturally gregarious. But he also wanted to share the glamour of that great House with thousands of people who helped him in big and little ways throughout thirty-four years of public life. The Johnsons were the first Presidential couple who regularly invited members of their staff—secretaries, letter-writers and calligraphers, as well as special Presidential assistants—to White House parties. This opportunity was deeply appreciated by the staff, for no matter how long you have worked at the White House, being a guest is always a treat.

The Johnsons had come to Washington as an unknown couple, and they knew the thrill of a White House invitation. In an old diary which Mrs. Johnson kept as the young bride, she tells (in her own handwriting) of the excitement of attending a dinner at the White House during the Roosevelt Administration. The date was February 13, 1941.

> Tonight, I went to my first (will it be the last and only!?!) Dinner at the White House! Everything managed with watchmaker's precision! Rep. Joe Casey was my dinner partner and very handsome and attractive. On the other side sat Sen. Sherman Minton. Was as far from the President as possible. The dinner was in honor of the Duchess of Luxembourg and her family—the President's houseguests. After dinner the ladies and Mrs. R. (Roosevelt) went to one drawing room and the men somewhere else. We had coffee and visited and Mrs. R. moved from group to group. Then we went upstairs and saw "Philadelphia Story" —big day!!

At the time of that diary, her husband was a young Congressman from Texas.

Twenty-eight years later, it was Mrs. Johnson who managed the state dinners with "watchmaker's precision," and who opened the doors of the White House with warmth and imagination. She wanted the experience of coming to the White House to be more than a perfunctory handshake for each visitor, and she was willing to work long hours to this end. She studied her guest lists for hours, knew some bit of news about each guest and would make the receiving line a personal experience for every visitor. Thus, receiving lines in the Johnson Administration moved slowly. The Johnsons wanted to chat with each guest, many of whom had come from across the country for that moment. Author Paul Horgan was delighted when the First Lady remembered his latest book, *Everything to Live For*. A winner of a beautification award—a secretary at a lumber company—was dumbfounded when Mrs. Johnson asked her about her forthcoming trip to the Virgin Islands. A staff member had mentioned it in passing, and Mrs. Johnson remembered. A friend of Luci's couldn't get over it when the First Lady wanted to talk about the days at Camp Mystic which Luci and she had shared.

Mrs. Johnson did her homework diligently for State visits. She would study maps and the exhausting briefing papers and talking points prepared by the Department of State for her husband. She wanted to learn, and she wanted to be a more interesting dinner partner for the Prime Minister, King or Shah who would be on her right for three hours or more at a dinner. She learned what country bordered each side of the visitor's country, what was the annual rainfall, what prominent Americans, Senators or artists had been there, what subjects were taboo.

A White House State dinner is a production. There is just no other word for the effort that goes into serving a superb cuisine of lobster or beef to violin music under the brooding portrait of Abraham Lincoln in the State Dining Room, and then escorting the guests down the red carpet of the Great Hall to the chandeliered East Room to hear Isaac Stern play the violin, or watch Hugh O'Brian and a costumed cast dance and sing several numbers from *Guys and Dolls*.

Bess Abell, the Social Secretary, was our Cecil B. De Mille. Tall, blond, poised, Bess has an easy Lauren Bacall air about her. She is one of those women who wears clothes well and can tie a scarf artfully—which I always envied! Bess had grown up in Kentucky politics—as unpredictable and uncertain as the racetrack—where her father had been governor and Senator. She combined shrewd political insight with creativity. Someone once aptly described her as an "iron butterfly." The President really put Bess's tranquil nature to the test.

I remember one evening about six o'clock when he decided to have a luncheon the next day, for two Prime Ministers and three Foreign Ministers, who happened to be in the country.

The comments made by the chef and the head butler when they learned the news are unprintable. A stag guest list of 180 was drawn up, and Bess and her assistants worked until midnight telephoning the guests. Invariably when the girls had finished their spiel: "The President hopes that you will be able to attend a luncheon at the White House tomorrow at 1:00 P.M. . . ." the invitees would say, "Did you say tomorrow?" Most of the guests were so startled that they forgot to ask who was being honored. This was fortunate, because Bess was not certain until the next morning which of the guests of honor would definitely be able to attend. But the luncheon went as smoothly as if it had been planned for weeks, and the next day LBJ wrote personal thank you's to the chef and head butler.

Usually we had at least three weeks to prepare for a State dinner. At planning meetings in the Situation Room, Bess would ply Walt Rostow, the National Security Council adviser, with questions about the background and interests of the visitor. This helped shape guest lists as well as determine entertainment, gifts and menus, for she literally tried to offer an evening fit for a King.

On the day of a State dinner, the White House was something to behold. In the morning, while heraldic trumpets announced the foreign visitor's arrival on the South Lawn, down in the kitchen, Chef Henry Haller would be whacking away at a barrel of live lobsters. The pastry chef would be gingerly placing finger-size rolls on a bread sheet. In the flower room, pollen-covered florists—true artists of the flora—would be arranging anemones, rubrum lilies and roses into the vermeil bowls which would be the centerpieces of each table.

In the Social Entertainments Office, the calligraphers, with a flourish of fine-lined pens, would be finishing up the place cards under magnifying glasses. Detail-expert and artist Sandy Fox and Bess would be studying a mock-up of the seating arrangements, and making last-minute changes.

On a rainy or foggy day, we were always prepared to lose a few guests in La Guardia Airport or circling over Washington National Airport. An invitation to the White House was of such importance to most guests that nothing would keep them from coming: raging fever, the last stages of pregnancy, or a heavy snowstorm. One woman arrived at a large reception with her nursing baby in her arms. When feeding time came, in front of the horrified but poker-faced Marine Band, she provided the child with her own ample supply of what nature had given her. At one dinner, Mrs. Silvio Conte, wife of the Congressman from Massachusetts, hobbled in on a swollen bandaged foot and explained, "I was rushing to fix the children's supper before I got dressed tonight, and I dropped a fork on my foot. But I wouldn't let that keep me away!" On another occasion, there was a paralyzing snowstorm a few hours before the dinner. Planes were canceled. Even trains were canceled, but—like excelsior—one man arrived in a taxi from New York. His bill to the White House was $280.

Rehearsals for the entertainment for a State dinner were held in the afternoon in the East Room under the exacting stopwatch of Barbara Keehn. You might see Carol Channing wearing an outrageous white fox hat and white jumpsuit rehearsing her *Hello, Dolly!* entrance or Helen Hayes reciting the lines of a play appropriately named *The White House* or Gregory Peck looking gorgeous. When Gregory Peck came, the rehearsals always attracted twice as many women reporters as usual.

In the press office, we prepared the background releases about the dinner—the menu, guest lists, gifts, performers and any advance copies of the exchange of toasts.

The pressure of perfection—as well as the grinding pressure of other activities being simultaneously planned—created frenzy in the hours just before a State dinner. Phones would still be ringing while Bess and I and our assistants were trying to change into evening gowns in our offices. The desire for a perfect evening made us all worry about every tiny detail, but somehow—despite many last-minute snafus, everything would always turn out all right. Sometimes the President would throw Bess's carefully arranged seating plan into chaos by deciding he wanted it rearranged. And occasionally, he would call her at the last minute and casually say that he had invited two more people to dinner—when every seat was already filled! But Bess was accustomed to the unexpected and never lost her cool. In a way she enjoyed testing her ingenuity to solve the problem.

As the dinner hour drew near, the social aides, bachelor military officers who were always immaculate in their gold-braid-trimmed dress uniforms, would be getting their briefing from Bess, who was often having her hair arranged while giving them instructions. Special care was given to guests who were handicapped in limb, language or the capacity to hold three kinds of wine.

Up in the Yellow Oval Room in the family quarters, Carol Carlyle—one of Bess's assistants—would be arranging the gifts which the President and Mrs. Johnson would give to the visitor during the twenty minute private reception they held for the visitor's immediate entourage. Bess was under instructions from the President to "spend more imagination than money" in selecting the gifts, and she did. Often she would consult on Presidential or White House history with those two experts, J. B. West, head usher, and James Ketchum, curator, and come up with original gifts. For instance, a walnut pipe rack for one foreign visitor was designed by calligrapher Sandy Fox and built by the cabinetmaker, Bonner Arrington, all in the White House. Gifts might be a handsome map case, a framed color picture of the visitor's country photographed from space by the American astronauts, a replica of an historic American antique. Two favorite antiques were a copy of the octagon-shaped file table designed by Thomas Jefferson and a replica of the brass candelabra by which George Washington wrote his farewell address. Sometimes the gifts would relate to the visitor's hobby: a set of golf clubs, skin-diving equipment, gardening books or a camera. Sometimes the gifts from the foreign visitors to the Johnsons would not arrive until the last moment, and Carol Carlyle would be frantically unpacking them while the visitors were driving up to the North Portico.

By 7:45 P.M., when the first guests started to arrive, everything was in readiness. In the Great Hall the Marine Band would strike up a medley of show tunes. A social aide would gallantly offer each lady his arm and escort her into the East Room, where there would be cocktails, conversation and a brief wait for the arrival of the President and his guest of honor.

Small emergencies often occurred. Forgotten cuff links were quickly replaced by Bess's office, and a rip in a suit or dress was promptly mended.

Synchronizing the arrival of a visiting dignitary and the President for dinner at eight o'clock gave ulcers to the Chief of Protocol and Bess. The visitor, housed across the street at Blair House (the Presidential guest house for Heads of State), would usually be punctual. But if some world development held the President in his office overtime, it was up to the Chief of Protocol to smile and try to keep the visitor happy in Blair House as the minutes ticked away. The President became expert at striding from his office to his bedroom and into the tuxedo which his valet, Paul Glynn, had waiting in hand, and getting downstairs in twelve minutes, if necessary.

But on one occasion, it was the President who had to wait. The President of Malagasy, one of the smaller countries in the world, for some unexplained reason was forty-five minutes late in arriving. Meanwhile the guests in the East Room were having cocktail after cocktail after cocktail. We never served hors d'oeuvres in the predinner reception because there are no tables in the East Room and no place to put the toothpicks and napkins that go with the tidbits.

As time lagged, with the President waiting upstairs, and the 140 guests impatiently imbibing below, there was still no sign of the President of Malagasy. Bess went to the pantry and prevailed upon John Ficklin, the head butler, "You've just got to find some nuts or something for these people to eat, or all of them are going to be drunk by the time we serve dinner." Fortunately, John located some nibbles, and promptly to the rescue went the butlers. Thus ended another flirtation with disaster.

The most electric moment at State dinners came when the President and his guest of honor walked down the Grand Staircase. At the foot of the steps, they paused while photographers from around the world snapped pictures. Then the official party would go into the East Room to greet the other guests as the Marine Band rolls the drums to begin *Ruffles and Flourishes* and *Hail to the Chief*. All eyes are upon the entrance.

After the receiving line ended, and the guests had all gone into the State Dining Room, the President and First Lady would escort the guest of honor down the Great Hall, led by the Chief of Protocol. When James Symington was Chief of Protocol, he added a wry wit to the usual formality by mumbling to those of us standing on the sidelines watching, "Make way for one President and one King. Make way for one President and one King." Fortunately, the President and his guest could not hear him.

Religious dietary requirements occasionally affected our menus. Muslims, for instance, do not drink wine; so their champagne goblets are filled with orange juice when it is time for the toasts.

King Faisal of Saudi Arabia had a very sensitive stomach. Perhaps he had been reading all those exaggerated stories about a President who loved chili and barbecue and panicked. The King sent word that he would be glad to have his royal chef prepare the entire dinner (in his honor) at the White House. Our chef was royally indignant! To keep the King happy and healthy, we worked out arrangements for his chef to prepare the King's dinner. Bess Abell suggested he prepare it in four courses to coincide with the White House menu. So he prepared the meal in Blair House and shortly before eight o'clock, the white-turbaned royal chef and royal taster arrived with four brief cases, each containing a neatly packaged course. They set up their service on a table in the corner of the State Dining Room. When the President was served a course, John Ficklin, the head butler, would nod to the royal chef, who would open another brief case and hand the plate to the royal taster who would serve his King.

Bess initiated a system of making the beautifully engraved menus more personalized and more of a collectors item for the guests by naming the dishes for the guest of honor, his capital or his country. For instance, the dessert at the dinner for the King of Nepal was Coconut Sagarmatha (the Nepalese name for Mount Everest). But I thought she got carried away when she named a dish in honor of Vice President Humphrey's wife "Breast of Pheasant Muriel." However, this did not have the diplomatic implications that Bess encountered when the President of a new African nation came to call. Bess had named the roast sirloin of beef for the African President. As she read the menu, she suddenly said, "Ye Gods! We can't do this. It just dawned on me that it hasn't been too long since his ancestors were eating each other!" By a frantic telephone call and a cooperative printer, she got the menus changed before dinnertime.

Every detail of a dinner was scrutinized by the society writers. The President and Mrs. Johnson invited more newspaper people as guests than any President ever had. These guests usually simply enjoyed the dinner and didn't cover it—that was left to the society writers who appeared at the East Gate in their evening gowns at 9:30 P.M. to cover the toasts and the after-dinner entertainment. Usually this group consisted of about fifteen ladies, looking far more glamorous by candlelight than by daylight. Doyenne of the social writers is Betty Beale, a patrician and exacting syndicated columnist, so competent at her job that her copy is read by all of the Washington press corps. The *Washingtonian Magazine* once described her as "the Super Society Reporter," who stands alone, "flicking social acceptance, like Holy Water, on the faithful below." She covers a social event as though it were a summit meeting, knowing that in this company town (U. S. Government, Inc.) it frequently is. Miss Beale, who attends an average of 1200 parties a year, is not above letting her host know what she feels should be done to improve the party. She kept a watchful eye on our social aides and occasionally criticized them in print for "holding up the walls" when they should have been dancing with the ladies present—including her.

Such a seemingly simple matter as providing entertainment is fraught with peril when a State visit focuses the spotlight on world problems. There was the day when Prime Minister Harold Wilson of Great Britain came to call, and the hypersensitive foreign policy advisers tried to find meaning in the musical program we planned. Robert Merrill, the great Metropolitan Opera baritone, gave me his list of selections for the evening, and I put out a press release. No sooner did the news come over the AP and UPI wires than Bess Abell came running into my office. "Walt Rostow just called me and says we've got to change the songs," Bess exclaimed. "He says we must be out of our minds!"

Rostow, a sometime songwriter himself, didn't see how Merrill could sing "On the Road to Mandalay" when Great Britain had just pulled out all their troops east of Suez. And he didn't think "I Got Plenty of Nuttin'" was appropriate when Great Britain had just devalued the pound!

There was a brief flap among reporters and staff members, and Robert Merrill began pondering what to do about changing his program. In the meantime, I ran into the President and Prime Minister in the corridor. To my surprise, the President looked at me and winked and said, "Liz, do you know what the

Prime Minister and I have been talking about the last two hours? We've been talking about songs!"

The Prime Minister spoke up before I could utter a word. "Look," he said, "don't change those songs. I like them."

So Robert Merrill sang them with fervor that evening, and then added another number: "It Ain't Necessarily So"—as a musical disclaimer. The Prime Minister led the laughter of the guests.

Another time that our entertainment caused a flap was during the visit of the Prime Minister of Thailand. In his country, fireworks are very popular. So we arranged a great American fireworks display on the South Lawn. The Prime Minister loved it, but the White House switchboard operators didn't. Washingtonians, still nervous after riots in the city, heard the noise and saw the flashes of light and thought the White House was being attacked. Naturally, hundreds telephoned to find out what was happening.

Entertainers are very unpredictable, and although they may behave perfectly during the dress rehearsal, sometimes they pull a surprise during their performance in the stately East Room. Tony Bennett was invited to sing for the Prime Minister of Japan, since American popular music is so well-liked in that country. Bess carefully explained to him, "Don't take off your coat and tie and unbutton your shirt when you're singing. I know you usually do that in your night club act, but this is the White House." The rehearsal was dignified enough, but, to our horror, by the end of the performance before the guests, Bennett was in his shirtsleeves. The next day the press gleefully reported his "strip-tease" act.

At some social functions, there was after-dinner dancing rather than entertainment. The annual Diplomatic Reception is always one of the most colorful and prestigious events, and the President made an extra effort to see that all of the guests from all 114 countries enjoyed themselves. The President, a good dancer, was happy to dance for diplomacy's sake. When the music started, he whispered to Mrs. Angier Biddle Duke, the beautiful and efficient blond whose husband was then Chief of Protocol, "Go bring me a lady from each continent."

She went off in a mad dash for an African, an Asian, a Latin American, etc. But he went even further than each continent. By the end of the evening, he had danced a few steps with nearly all the 114 ambassadors' wives.

Dancing had its hazards, of course. One evening while the guests were dancing in the Great Hall, Mrs. Johnson spied a woman's petticoat on the floor. She chuckled, picked it up and put it on the huge Steinway piano nearby. About thirty minutes later, she looked again, and it was gone. We never did learn to whom it belonged.

At some State dinners, dancing would follow the entertainment. The President liked to dance, but like most people, he didn't want to be alone on the dance floor. So he would tap the nearest social aide or staff member on the shoulder and urge them to "get out there and dance." So dance they did.

Having worked behind the scenes on so many parties, I thoroughly enjoyed being a guest at the dinner honoring Princess Margaret and her husband, Lord Snowdon, for it was one of the most glamorous parties ever given in terms of guests and excitement.

The star-studded dinner list included such dazzlers as Happy Rockefeller, Christina Ford, the second wife of Henry Ford the Second, and such personalities as George Hamilton, dress designer Mollie Parnis, Ambassador John Kenneth Galbraith. We dined on Atlantic pompano amadine, roast squab White House, artichokes with vegetable purée, hearts of palm salad, Brie cheese and praline glace.

The salad came complete, as always at White House dinners,

with twenty strolling violinists from the U. S. Army, who I always feared would spear a lettuce leaf in their sweeping medley of show tunes.

My dinner partner was Henry Brandon, popular bachelor-about-town and correspondent for the London *Sunday Times.* He came complete with British accent and his own Sterling silver swizzle stick which he always carries in his inside dinner jacket pocket in case he runs into a glass of champagne.

The dinner coincided with the Johnsons' thirty-second wedding anniversary and the President used love and marriage as his text for the toast:

> "You are somewhat younger than I, Lord Snowdon," the President told the 140 guests, "and you have been married a few years less than I. I hope you will not be offended if I take this occasion to offer a little bit of advice. I have learned there are only two things necessary to keep one's wife happy. First, let her think she is having her way. And second, let her have it."

He praised the Princess for the goodwill she and her husband had created during their visit of the United States, and raised his glass to "Her Majesty, the Queen."

Princess Margaret returned the toast, and it must have been an old Xerox copy in the Buckingham Palace files catalogued under "Toasts Appropriate for Any Country at Any Time."

"We are having a most wonderful time," she said, "and we will take away the most superlatively happy memories of all we have seen and done. We only wish we could have stayed longer."

After dinner, Peter Duchin and his orchestra played and the

Brothers Four sang a song they had composed especially for "Meg" and her "Tony Jones."

The dancing lasted until 2 A.M. with the President and the Princess, as one pair, and Lord Snowdon and Mrs. Johnson, as another, starting it off.

The Princess "sat out" the frug numbers, but no one could have vied with Christina Ford anyway. The more spirited her dancing became, the more the strapless white crepe dress twisted and slipped. During the frantic beat of "Tiger Rag," the Italian-born Christina had to pause momentarily to secure nature's endowments in her gown. One woman guest delicately warned Christina of the dangers, but Christina gave her a withering glance that seemed to indicate, "When you got it—flaunt it."

Next day, the whole town buzzed with Christina conversation and every woman wished that she, too, could crook a little finger bewitchingly at her husband, as Christina had done, and say in throaty tones: "Bambino, come dance weez me."

Performers at the White House receive no fee for their talent. They perform as a public service, with the knowledge they are playing in a prestige location. In our five years, Bess booked such varied top entertainment that included Herb Alpert's Tijuana Brass for the President of Mexico, Isaac Stern who performed for Prime Minister Indira Gandhi of India, and Rudolf Serkin to play for the President of Israel. (He brought his own piano.) Maria Tallchief and Jacques D'Amboise danced to the music of the National Symphony Orchestra on the South Lawn for Chancellor Erhard of Germany.

Jazz is very popular with Kings. For the King of Thailand we served up Duke Ellington and Stan Getz, who played with an upcoming generation of musicians from the North Texas State Lab Band. The entertainment made such a hit with the saxophone-playing King that he lingered on after the usual departing time and talked for two hours with Getz and Ellington. The Dave Brubeck Quartet entertained the King of Jordan. When the combo was introduced to the King, the uninhibited drummer's greeting was simply, "Hi, King." When the King of Nepal visited the White House, guitarist Charlie Byrd performed.

There were many factors determining what entertainment would be offered: (1) the preference of the Head of State, (2) the language barrier (if the guest did not speak English, we often had music or ballet), (3) the availability of a performer, and (4) whether the artist had recently insulted the United States or the President. Bess soon found out which performers were most likely to be "safe."

Ballet dancers don't usually walk in picket lines, she discovered.

But we did have some problem children. One dinner guest, Joan Crawford, grandly arrived in Washington with her own hairdresser and came coiffed to the White House dinner ready for a big evening. She found herself outlionized by Carol Channing, Alfred Lunt and Lynn Fontanne, and, alas, by Douglas Fairbanks, Jr., her ex-husband.

This was an error on our part. We tried not to include divorced couples at the same party, but this is a real challenge with Hollywood people and four-times-married Supreme Court Justice Bill Douglas. We simply didn't luck out all the time.

At dinner, Joe Califano, then a new assistant to the President, was seated between Joan Crawford and Justice Douglas's newest wife, Cathleen, a twenty-three-year-old wide-eyed blonde, who had just arrived on the Washington scene to find Douglas's three ex-wives and other female tongues wagging against her. Fortunately, Joe's previous Washington training had been in the Department of Defense, for his evening proved to be a combat assignment.

According to other guests at the table, who dined out for weeks on the story, Miss Crawford spent the dinner discussing Justice Douglas's new wife in a voice easily overheard by the bride. In between her comments, she sent a note across the room via a butler to an old friend, John Daly, at another table, which said: "Come kiss me, John."

When the dessert plates were brought to the tables, guests reported later, Miss Crawford decided that Mrs. Douglas was not sufficiently prompt in removing her doily and fingerbowl. Joan reached across a startled Joe Califano to do the deed herself. Fingerbowl and doily were removed by Joan with a reprimand, reported duly by society writers as, "This is the way you do it, darling!"

The story was trumpeted in New York and Washington, and I began getting calls to confirm or deny. Miss Crawford told me, in a somewhat tearful call from the West Coast, that it couldn't possibly have occurred. Other reporters checked with the guests. I went holier-than-thou, and told the press: "The White House certainly will not discuss the dinner table conversation of its guests."

Of course, the Eartha Kitt episode made Joan Crawford look like Emily Post reincarnated.

The First Lady was holding one of her Women Doers luncheons, and the subject was "Crime and What the Average Citizen Can Do to Stop It." Miss Kitt must have thought we meant "start it." Fifty women were to be invited—experts in one way or another on the subject. In drawing up the guest list, we wondered if any famous personality from Hollywood (a guest who always stirs interest) had ever done anything in the field.

"Yes," said Congressman Roman Pucinski, chairman of the House Committee on Juvenile Delinquency. "Eartha Kitt has testified in favor of the President's anti-crime bill. She was articulate. And she's done a good job in Watts, teaching ballet classes."

Articulate is hardly the word for Miss Kitt's performance at the luncheon. Hardly had the three panelists finished telling how to combat crime than Miss Kitt executed hers. With ringing drama that would have done Katharine Cornell proud, she rose to tell her audience—and the press—that Vietnam was causing all the troubles in the ghetto. Her clarion tones rising, her audience sitting there in growing embarrassment, she even got motherhood into the act: "I know the feeling of having a baby come out of my guts," she snarled.

It was this treatise on motherhood that got Betty Hughes, the wife of the governor of New Jersey, to her feet. Betty has ten children, and no one can outmother her. Betty pointed out, quite sensibly, that no one was in Vietnam because he wanted to be, but rather because his country was there.

But no one needed to rescue the First Lady. She too had something to say: "Because there is a war on . . . that still does not give us a free ticket *not* to work on bettering the things in this country we can better."

Miss Kitt left without the usual thank-you, and no one delayed her departure. Perhaps the most surprised man in Washington was Colonel Rowland Beasley, head of USO performers. Driving home from the Pentagon that night, he heard on his car radio about Miss Kitt's performance at the White House. The colonel was startled because he had been waiting all afternoon for an appointment with Miss Kitt, who never showed up. That morning—a few hours before the luncheon—she had asked him to make arrangements for her to go to Vietnam to entertain the troops.

Mrs. Johnson was determined that we convert what appeared as a disaster into constructive action. She answered all of the 35,000 letters that poured in with specific suggestions for what could be done to combat crime in the community. Many women's organizations, such as the General Federation of Women's Clubs and the National Association of Negro Women, passed resolutions promising action on crime.

Perhaps Miss Kitt's behavior was a blessing in disguise. The Women Doers luncheon got more attention than luncheons usually do and more action followed it. But it was certainly the hard way to get results.

Another well-motivated event that prompted widespread controversy was the White House Festival of the Arts. The Kennedys had championed the arts, but it was President Johnson who delivered the legislation creating the National Council on the Arts. He went even further. He was willing to let the White House be a showcase for painting, sculpture, motion pictures, music, literature, the dance and drama, in a day-long festival to which hundreds of artists would be invited.

Robert Lowell, who writes poetry, produced for this occasion some blistering prose. He sent a telegram rejecting the President's invitation because of the war in Vietnam. He released the telegram to the press, and suddenly the Festival of the Arts became the Battle of the Artists. Caught in the middle was Eric Goldman, professor from Princeton on leave to the White House. He had arrived at the White House in the wake of Arthur Schlesinger, and reporters promptly transferred the title of "intellectual in residence" from Schlesinger to Goldman. Goldman's office was located near mine, and I came to know him well. I like Eric Goldman. But then I liked Margaret Truman's voice and Mamie Eisenhower's bangs. I always found him helpful, and I admired him as a writer. You could almost waltz to his words.

The social staff was not as admiring. When Dr. Goldman suggested that Duke Ellington play background music during dinner, they were violent in their objections. "A great composer and international figure does *not* play background music at the White House," Barbara Keehn said pointedly. Anyway, the social office had the last word, Duke Ellington brought down his whole band and they played the smashing finale of the Arts Festival on the South Lawn.

The Festival performances (inside the White House) were magnificent, and Mrs. Johnson attended every one, warmly applauding the artists. We didn't miss Robert Lowell at all, but the press, with their insatiable appetite for controversy, spent most of their talents on who wasn't there, rather than who was.

In contrast to Robert Lowell's performance was that of Sarah Vaughan, the great blues singer. She came to dinner and performed for the President of the United States and the Prime Minister of Japan, and for thirty minutes held the distinguished audience in her hand. Afterwards, the guests danced. Later that evening, when the party was over, Bess Abell found Miss Vaughan sobbing in her dressing room.

"What's the matter?" Bess asked her, distressed.

"Nothing is the matter," she said. "It's just that twenty years ago when I came to Washington, I couldn't even get a hotel room, and tonight I sang for the President of the United States in the White House—and then, he asked me to dance with him. It is more than I can stand."

# *Flying With Fear*

"In my heart, I know the Wright brothers were wrong," I once remarked.

*Reader's Digest* picked up the quote and paid me $25 for it. But that hardly took care of the stamps I needed to answer all the irate airline pilots who wrote in objecting. One of them said he'd like to get me in his plane alone and "loop-the-loop four or five minutes—that would cure you." I shuddered, tore the letter into tiny pieces and threw it out of my second floor window—which was one story too high for me.

A hypnotist wanted me to fall under his spell, and promised he would blot away all fear—permanently. And my friend, Betty Beale, a society writer who is an ardent Christian Scientist, sent me a booklet entitled *Fighting Foolish Fears*. I read it, and while Mary Baker Eddy put forth an appealing line, it didn't do the trick with an old psalm-singing Methodist like me. I remained terrified.

If LBJ and the Democratic Party ever question the extent of my sacrifice, they have only to look at the number of flying hours I put in. Real combat hours, too! Me versus the jitters. Most of the time I lost, even fortified with tranquilizers, alcohol and the hand of a traveling companion, which I squeezed into a bloody pulp during turbulence.

I confess that I am an illogical nut about flying, but I honestly believe that if the Lord had wanted us to fly, he would have given us wings. Just how illogical was illustrated on one bumpy flight from San Antonio when my seat companion, a young newly married secretary, was taking her morning birth control pill. She had just opened the pill box and was daintily reaching for one when we hit an air pocket. I reached across her, grabbed one and had flung it into my mouth before she said, "But those are *not* tranquilizers, Liz."

My one regret was that in all my hours of agony aloft, I never ran into Shelley Berman, the comedian. He once described himself as a "white knuckle flyer," and I knew we were soulmates. We could have been white knuckle flyers together.

Mrs. Johnson was a frightened flyer, too, but she was much more controlled and lady-like about it than I was. That is, she wouldn't grab a martini off every passing stewardess's tray and swallow it in one gulp.

But if the passengers were just the two of us, plus the pilot, and a Secret Service man, and the weather got rough in Texas, she didn't mind a bit if I demanded that we land, rent a limousine and drive two hours to the ranch instead of feeling our way down through the clouds. That's one reason why I will never be pin-up girl of the Secret Service.

And she didn't protest at all one rainy morning when we were scheduled to fly to Philadelphia to dedicate an Eighteenth Century garden at Independence National Historical Park, and I insisted we go by train instead. I called our advance team, Nash Castro and Marcia Maddox, and ruined their breakfast with the news. They scurried around and notified the entire City of Brotherly Love of the change in schedule, and we had a pleasant trip up on the train. Nash still says, "The weather wasn't that bad. Liz was just chicken."

But 90 percent of the time, we had to suffer through the flight. We were either on a commercial airline, where I couldn't pull rank, or we were on a press charter with a scheduled trip, and people waiting. Not just ordinary people, either. But busy people like governors and mayors, who represented votes.

The absolute worst flight we ever had (and I even hold onto my typewriter as I write about it) was a stormy day when we were going to Cleveland to open an old people's home. By the time I reached there, I had aged so much I could have qualified for admission. There were ten women reporters, Mrs. Johnson, gray-haired Dr. Janet Travell, the comforting White House physician, and me, plus the necessary Secret Service. It was one of our cut-rate trips because newspapers just don't get all worked up about the opening of senior citizens housing in Ohio. Instead of our own charter, we all had tourist tickets on United Airlines. And, we became more and more "united" as we bounced in and out of black stormy clouds flying the unfriendly skies of United.

I kept ringing for the stewardess, and she finally came, smiling the smile they taught her at stewardess school. Nothing offends me so much as some idiot stewardess who smiles when she ought to be sending out distress signals to the nearest airport.

"When are we going to get out of this?" I demanded.

"Out of what?" she asked stupidly.

Mrs. Johnson, who had sunk her head into a pillow and pretended to be asleep, roused and said shakily, "She means when will this plane stop jiggling?"

"I'll check," the hostess said and started forward to the pilot.

At this moment, there were two flashes of lightning, the plane shook like a leaf, and there was the loudest cracking sound I had ever heard. Mrs. Johnson came out of the pillow and sat bolt upright. With one thrust, I leaped across the aisle into the arms of the surprised Dr. Travell. A Secret Service agent moved into the seat next to Mrs. Johnson. Dr. Travell had been calmly sitting there doing a needlepoint pillow cover for her newest grandchild, but I didn't even feel the needle she had in her lap.

"There is nothing to worry about, Liz," she said, and she took both my hands and held them hard. I could see why Barry Goldwater and Jack Kennedy went to her for their back problems. However, my problem was a *body* problem—and whether it was going to be splattered all over Ohio in the next few minutes.

We bounced around about twenty more minutes while I said the 23rd Psalm. When I got to that line, "I shall not want," I really didn't mean it because I fervently "wanted" to get my feet on the ground and never get them off.

The Lord answered my prayers. The hostess' voice (she never stopped smiling) told us we were landing at the Cleveland airport. At last, we were down!

Until this moment, I hadn't had time to even glance at my charges—the newswomen—but now I did, and even the most veteran, hardboiled of the lot were pale and ashen. Frances Lewine of the AP and Helen Thomas of UPI moved into action immediately. They summoned the pilot and demanded to know what had happened. Yes, lightning had struck the plane but done no damage. They went out and inspected the motor which was blackened more than usual, and then headed into the airport to call in their bulletin, FIRST LADY'S PLANE STRUCK BY LIGHTNING. I gathered the rest of the group together to make the most important decision of all; to wit, how were we going to get back to Washington, because I knew I didn't want to fly. Mrs. Johnson nodded agreement. By some quick checking I discovered the weather would remain bad all day. I also discovered it would take eleven hours to drive to Washington via the Ohio and Pennsylvania Turnpikes.

"Let's all vote," Mrs. Johnson democratically said, and vote we did. I didn't let the Secret Service vote because I didn't want the cowards to be outvoted by the courageous. By rigging it, the vote was overwhelmingly to drive back to Washington. With disgust, the Secret Service agreed to rent some cars, find some blankets, and—I added, "Whiskey, too!"

Meanwhile, the newswomen were still shaking. I spied Dr. Travell who had stopped stitching and said, "Have you got something in your medical kit we can give to these women?"

"Do you want to slow 'em down or pep 'em up?" she asked matter-of-factly.

"Slow 'em down," I said quivering. "They need calming."

So out came a bottle of pills and she dispensed them around. I took two.

We headed for the senior citizens home. Somehow Mrs. Johnson managed to shake every hand, blow out one elderly man's seventy candles on his birthday cake and make a speech.

The Secret Service rounded up six cars equipped with pillows, blankets and, yes, a drink which we so richly deserved. We started down the turnpike about 4 P.M. knowing we would reach the White House eleven hours later. I began to consult with the Secret Service man in the front seat about arrangements for dinner. We discovered through his handy walkie-talkie that there are thirty-two Howard Johnson drive-in restaurants between Cleveland and Washington. We called ahead to one right outside Pittsburgh and made arrangements for dinner for some twelve assorted travelers who would be arriving at a certain hour. "Please reserve a large table for Mrs. Johnson and party," was the order. We dined on "Big Joes," cheeseburgers and some of the 28 flavors and paid our bill.

As we left the restaurant to continue our journey, one hard-working newswoman lingered a moment for a word with our waitress.

"How did you feel serving Mrs. Johnson?" she asked.

"Well, I was pretty nervous," the waitress said.

"Have you ever met a First Lady before?"

The waitress looked stunned. "First Lady?" she asked. "First Lady!"

"Yes," the reporter said, "that was Mrs. Lyndon B. Johnson, the First Lady of the Land."

"Oh, my God," she said. "Thank goodness I didn't know it. I would have fainted dead away. I thought it was Mrs. Howard Johnson—that was bad enough!"

We drove into the National Capital about 3 A.M. It was still pitch black, as we pulled through the White House gates. I felt a little sheepish, tiptoeing in, and wondered if the President would be disgusted with us for letting our fears get the best of us.

"You know what I'm going to do when I get in that house?" Mrs. Johnson said with determination.

"No," I answered, wondering what one could do at that hour and envisioning what I thought anyone would do—drink the biggest martini in history!

To my amazement, she said firmly, "I'm going to look under the bed and find that peanut brittle I hid from Lyndon, and then I'm going to eat it."

Poor lady. She certainly deserved all the peanut brittle she could eat.

As press interest in Mrs. J. grew, we were able to charter a press plane and ride in comparative comfort. One of those charters was something to behold—particularly if we were returning from a trip to a remote park where blue jeans and boots were the mode of dress. Newswomen are notorious pack-rats. They not only carry the essentials—typewriter, hangup bag and suitcase—but they gather all the "freebees" offered along the way. On our trips this was frequently various forms of flora—an unusual species of potted wildflower, a miniature redwood tree—or pieces of driftwood and seashells found while walking along the beach. At the end of the trip the plane took on the appearance of a refugee camp.

There are a number of press flying habits which are traditional. For instance, all photographers consider it mandatory to fly with a drink in their hand from the time of takeoff to landing. Seat belt and no smoking signs are more often ignored than heeded. Many of these press passengers have flown under wartime conditions in combat through all parts of the world, but no matter what the occasion of the flight, the ritual is always the same upon landing—everyone applauds loudly—much to the chagrin of the pilot.

Our trips were zany, with toasts, songs and much rollicking in the aisles. My staff—always bleary-eyed but relieved at the end of the trip—joined in the merriment. Our convivial group and their antics once gave quite a shock to two commercial passengers who ended up on our plane by mistake. They thought they had boarded a Mardi Gras charter for New Orleans, but they hadn't.

Flying on Air Force One spoils the frightened flyer. You expect all planes to run that way—with a tremendous crew, immediate clearance to land, no circling in the air, and the underlying confidence that nothing is going to happen to that plane. LBJ is such an overwhelmingly strong personality himself that when he is aboard I am almost without fear. Lightning wouldn't dare strike him!

Then there is another factor. You are busy. You are drafting speeches or reading briefing papers, or doing some chore that is necessary for the next stop; so you forget to be afraid. Air Force One is literally a flying White House. It is equipped with electric typewriters, speech typewriters, and a mimeograph machine, so that speeches can be written, typed and a press release run off between stops. And there are conference tables and telephone service reaching any spot in the world.

Watching the President's secretaries on a flight is like watching a bunch of acrobats. Often, they would be typing the final draft of a speech when the airplane began descending. Somehow they could keep their balance as we bumped down through the clouds to Mother Earth, never making a mistake and having the speech cards ready to hand to the President as we rolled down the runway toward the speaker's stand.

What does it take to run Air Force One? A crew of fifteen, and $766 an hour to operate.

The government owns four Boeing 707s, and Air Force One is the designated title for whichever one the President is using.

It is an impressive sight in a foreign country to see that great bird soaring in—the handsomest aircraft of any nation. Baby blue, it bears the seal of the President of the United States on its door and nose, and the American flag on its tail. After it lands, out steps the President, waving a greeting to the people of Korea, France, Greece, wherever you are.

Inside are all the comforts of home. The President has his own kitchen, and the food is prepared by an Air Force steward. His bedroom, his desk, newspapers and a TV set. And seventy-five aides can travel with him to assist. Always, of course, the physician. Usually, also one or more White House dogs.

LBJ was probably more conscious than any President of the high cost of travel to members of Congress. He had been there once himself and knew there is never enough travel expense money to take you back and forth to your district as frequently as you must go. So he thoughtfully alerted every Congressman who might be going his way and let them hitch hike back and forth to Texas or whatever his destination. Senator John Tower, the Republican Senator from Texas who had once campaigned on the platform, "Double your pleasure, scratch LBJ twice," was treated with the same courtesy as Democrats.

Johnson also gave out a memento of each flight—a special paper certificate which stated that you had flown on Air Force One at such and such a time. It papers the walls of many a Congressman and friend.

While he was generous with the space of a plane that had to fly anyway, he was economical about the food. Everyone—staff, Congressmen, VIPs—was billed for food and beverages aboard Air Force One. The taxpayer was not left holding this tab.

Air Force One was an instrument of strength and friendship around the globe. In 1966, the President decided she should make a real swing through Asia. In the broadest terms, Asia stretches from New Zealand to India. In ratio of world population, it is Asians seventeen to one. Many of the countries have never been visited by an American President, so we set out to win friends and influence the people who were helping our troops in Vietnam.

Eight countries and fifteen million handshakes later, we turned Air Force One home absolutely exhausted—but slap-happy and giddy. With no stops between Korea and Washington and many hours before us, we decided to give ourselves a party. The social staff, Bess Abell and Barbara Keehn, had laid in a supply of champagne and party hats aboard. Chief of Protocol James Symington wrote funny songs and a script. Now in Congress, Jim comes by his talent naturally. His mother was the socialite songstress of the Persian Room in the Plaza Hotel during the depression. When young Jim went to college, he helped pay the bills by playing the guitar and often singing his own lyrics in the Carnaval Room of the Hotel Sherry-Netherland.

I coordinated for our Air Force One skit.

The result was a musical spoof of Presidential trips, the briefings, the countries and the arrival statements. Flying at 35,000 feet over the Pacific, we presented a musical comedy in the aisles of the plane for the President and First Lady.

The show opened with a song, "On the Road With LBJ," squeakily but zestfully sung:

"In an old Moulmein pagoda
Lookin' eastward to the sea
There's some Asian king or other,
And I know he thinks of me.
Yes, a stir is in the palace
And the ministers they pray:
Won't you leave the Pedernales
And sidle out our way
And sidle out our way?

"On the road with LBJ
Even Bundy gets a lei
They don't dock it from our pocket cause
Bill Crockett has to pay.
On the road to LBJ
From the ranch to Mandalay
And where nothing is, but Bess and Liz
help make it all the way.

"Ship me somewhere west of Austin
Where a man can raise a thirst
And the pills of Dr. Burkley
Will help prevent the worst;
While the wind is in the speeches
And the temple bells they say
Come you back you Texas Ranger
Come you back you LBJ
Come you back you LBJ.

"Come you back you LBJ
Bring Clark Clifford, that's okay
Bring Bill Moyers, bring your lawyers
Bring your own communiqué
Cause we're with you all the way
And we've gathered here to say
If the dawn comes up like thunder,
it's no wonder, LBJ."

After the song, Jim Symington gave a mock briefing like the ones he gave to the President before reaching each country:

"We're landing Mr. President.

"No sir, we did Bumtoy yesterday. This is our last stop—Birdoo—capital of Sen Sen. What sir?

"Friendly, sir. Mr. Rusk says a quasi-constitutional monarchy. Contenders for the crown draw straws—the loser is King—the others are flogged and sent out as ambassadors.

"You will be met at the foot of the ramp by His Majesty, King Kumquat, and the Crown Prince, His Royal Highness, Spitin Imaj.

"No sir, you're not to deplane by the rear exit. No sir, not the forward exit either. By the emergency exit, sir.

"Didn't Watson tell you?

"On the inaugural flight of their national airline—Sampan Airlines—the aircraft, carrying the King, became lodged between two rubber trees, and the King was obliged to leave by the emergency exit. Since that time in deference to His Majesty's experience, all Heads of State are requested to deplane in the same manner.

"Mr. President—the moment you set foot on Sen Sen soil, five thousand pigeons will be released overhead. A parasol bearer is assigned to you.

"Also, a herd of goats will be driven toward you. You are

not to touch the goats as this is against their religion. Okie would like to get your picture running from them.

"In addition, five high-spirited water buffaloes will be drawn up and each member of your official party is requested to ride one by the reviewing stand. Actually, we'll have to double up —Rusk and Bundy, Watson and Jacobsen, McPherson and Rostow—Dr. Burkley gets his own with saddlebags. During this traditional procession they will be pelted with native fruits in a gesture of good will.

"The King will greet you in his native tongue—this requires the assistance of two interpreters, one to translate the King's native tongue into the national language, and another to render these remarks into English—also the Royal Physician will stand by. The King tends to swallow his tongue when he gets excited, and the Royal Physician is the only person permitted to remove it.

"Yes sir, we impressed strongly on their Chief of Protocol that it would be acceptable if the King were to limit his remarks at the arrival. Yes, we believe the Chief of Protocol delivered the message. Because we haven't seen him since. In the past two weeks, they changed Protocol officials six times.

"The King then takes you to the platform for the national anthems which will be played simultaneously on native instruments. They regret there will be no 21 guns. They were overloaded during the last State visit and blew up, collapsing the pavilion. McNamara is reviewing their request for replacements.

"Following the rendering of anthems, there will be a moment's silence during which the Grand Chamberlain takes three slow steps forward and breaks an egg on your head. That's good luck, and you are to smile.

"The King will then take you along the line of dignitaries. Here they do not shake hands. Their form of greeting is to step up smartly and dig their elbow into your ribs. Your response is to simply smile and say, 'Proy,' which means 'ouch.'

"You will know when you reach the diplomatic corps. They will be in shackles.

"After doing proy with the receiving line you will be carried to your car with the King. Please don't refer to the car as your 'bubbletop' because this happens to be the King's pet name for the queen.

"Mrs. Johnson, you deplane with the President, and are greeted by Queen Woesmee. Together you follow the President and the King throughout except the Proy greeting. Instead of proy, each lady hands you a bouquet. There are approximately fifty ladies so when you deplane you will be immediately fitted with a traditional native wicker basket which is strapped on your back by six schoolgirls singing their national song.

"Don't wear blue, Mrs. Johnson. It is the mourning color for women. No, ma'am, white is the mourning color for men. Greens, reds and yellows are permitted only on Holy Days. How about a nice mud color—it's permissible everywhere but in the Palace, and you can change in the car.

"Mr. President, Bill Moyers has laid on the flat bed truck. He's laid on it for the past week. We're trying to get him up. The truck will be well-positioned—directly in front of you—separated only by twelve security and staff cars and a Greyhound busload of the King's personal bodyguards.

"Jim Webb has arranged a flyover of Gemini 10 and they expect to get some good shots of the parade.

"When you arrive at the Royal Guest House—Put Upon—you are greeted by the Minister of Information, Wham That Gong, and the King will take his leave. He will take your watch, too, if the strap is loose. Bundy has gone over the lunch speech—he'd like to change Rostow's passage about these being the greatest people money can buy."

Next on the show came the President's arrival statement, a takeoff on the necessary formal speech at every stop:

"Your Majesty, Your Worships, your excellencies, your every day ordinaries and folks. Mrs. Johnson and I are delighted to be here. The United States prides itself on the cordial relations which have existed between us since the founding of your great nation—last month. And we know that this significant and friendly relationship is destined to last—for another month. Your Majesty, I have met your Foreign Minister, your Special Adviser on Domestic Affairs, your Ministers of Defense, Commerce, Labor, Agriculture and Health, and am deeply impressed to find them one and the same person, your son. Your Majesty, twenty years ago, with the help of American boys foreign imperialism was eliminated from this fair land, and you are now at the threshold of eliminating imperialism at home. Certainly, under your vigorous leadership many old institutions have been toppled. Some of them will have to be rebuilt. We have noted with admiration that under the prodding of your general staff your national currency, the poontang, has been pegged at 100,000 to the dollar, and that unbelievably rampant inflation has been reduced to mere rampant inflation. You have begun a great new page of history. Some say it is still blank. Your Majesty, some thoughtless persons have called yours a have-not nation. Well, if so, then ours is too, for we have not the courage and dogged perseverance to cope with Twentieth Century problems without an alphabet.

"Your Majesty, we know you are in the week of the Wallaby. And it's a heartening thing to see the whole nation hopping up and down for seven days. During this period you should know that America's hops go with you toward a better world for both our peoples, and both of yours.

"Thank you."

If only every flight could have been a continual musical comedy, I wouldn't have been afraid at all.

# *We Woke Up Sleeping Beauty*

To anyone working at the White House, the citizens of the United States quickly take shape into blocs or cults; i.e., the business group, labor, the clergy, educators, women, Irish and non-Irish.

I came to know intimately the Beauty Cult, which includes every species of conservationist, and I will pit them against any other group for variety, determination and a full share of both statesmen and kooks.

Just how far the conservationists go to protect nature was apparent one morning when a unique letter arrived on Mrs. Johnson's desk—right at one of those moments when all the world seemed to be falling apart. The President was immersed in a National Security Council meeting. The ghettos were restless. Water-thirsty Southwesterners wanted to dam up the Grand Canyon. And Congress was thundering forth daily on every subject.

"Dear Mrs. Johnson," the letter pleaded, "We earnestly solicit your help in preserving the blind salamander." No kidding, there are these poor blind salamanders swimming in the underwater caverns of San Marcos, Texas, and a group of well-meaning citizens felt they needed aid. Mrs. Johnson was sympathetic, but she decided she would stick with more down-to-earth measures: getting billboard legislation passed before some of the more ardent conservationists were jailed for their midnight attacks on billboards with hatchet, knife and saw; encouraging air pollution ordinances before mass suffocation depopulated the country; and urging better planning of highways before the whole country was paved with concrete.

Beautification affected my social life considerably. When the Beauty Cult couldn't snare Mrs. Johnson for dinner, I would be invited. I found myself dining among people whose worthy causes ranged from dirty air to dead birds. Their organized efforts included: saving the redwoods, salvaging Skunk Cabbage Creek, preserving the Great Swamp of New Jersey and defending the wild mustang.

"Where in the hell do these people come from?" my husband asked one night on our way home from a small Georgetown dinner party. "I try to talk to them, but it's impossible. Tonight, I made about three runs at conversation about what was happening on Capitol Hill, what was happening at the White House and even what is happening to sex in America. I struck out every time."

The discussion at his end of the table, he said, was a raging debate over which are the oldest trees in America. He swears that the most interesting comment during the entire evening was made by a woman who said in resounding, positive tones, "The sequoia sempervirens of California are *not* the oldest trees in America! They are only two thousand years old."

"Mere babies," he quoted his dinner partner, "when you consider the bristle-cone pines of Nevada were up and bristling four thousand years ago."

But I could top him. I had drawn as my dinner partner, Mr. Harold Coolidge, a cousin of Cal's and a descendant of Thomas Jefferson. He was devoting his energies and money to the preservation of the one-horned rhinoceros. He had encountered a number of obstacles in the pursuit of this goal. The main handicap is geography. Most of the remaining one-horned rhinoceros are in a remote part of India and there are only six hundred left there. "When you're down to your 600th one-horned rhinoceros, it's serious," sighed Mr. Coolidge with feeling.

What Mr. Coolidge also has working against him are some sex-mad natives of India who believe that the horn of the rhino, when consumed, has great value as a stimulant for fertility among males. So, according to him, frustrated natives are at this moment running wild all over India brandishing guns and sabers in pursuit of the rhino. Mr. Coolidge sold me completely on his Save-the-One-Horned Rhino Crusade. I was fully convinced that the one-horned rhino deserved all his hormones for himself.

During dinner, I tried to broaden Mr. Coolidge's interest in conservation to include ideas on what we could do on Capitol Hill to get his Republican friends to vote against billboards. This issue seemed closer at hand. He nodded agreement, but I am sure it was just a matter of lip service. Nothing will ever really hold his heart like that one-horned rhinoceros.

Soon after becoming First Lady when Mrs. Johnson selected the projects she wanted to undertake, she tried to choose what came naturally. And Mother Nature certainly did! For Mrs. Johnson becomes lyrical about every blade of grass, every redwood, every wheatfield, every mountain peak and every trackless plain from the Atlantic to the Pacific. She genuinely loves this planet and feels, like conservationist Paul Sears, that "it deserves kinder treatment" than it gets from the litterers, the bulldozers, the proprietors of junkyards and the purveyors of billboards.

Primarily, two people—Secretary of Interior Stewart L. Udall and Mrs. Johnson's good friend, Mrs. Albert D. Lasker of New York—convinced Mrs. Johnson that her voice in behalf of improving the natural environment could be effective. The President gave his enthusiastic nod.

"Let's make it a nationwide effort," Mary Lasker urged, but discovered that Mrs. Johnson didn't want anything that grandiose.

"I think I can be more effective if I just try to improve my own hometown, which right now is Washington, D.C. Maybe people will follow our example in other communities," Mrs. Johnson said. So she formed the First Lady's Committee for a More Beautiful Capital and tapped for its membership prominent architects, conservationists, government officials and philanthropists from throughout the nation.

One of the Committee's greatest assets was its meeting place—the White House. Another was that it had no by-laws, no rules, no executive order. Limited only by the physical endurance of its members, the group forged ahead with the First Lady as its prime mover, scattering rose petals all over Washington, so to speak.

"Plant masses of flowers where masses pass," admonished Mary Lasker, pulling out a checkbook. A practitioner of what she preached, she wrote out a check for $30,000 to line Pennsylvania Avenue with azaleas—only the beginning of many such gifts to the city of Washington. Mary doesn't believe in doing things halfway. And she was a little impatient when she discovered that her own large purchase had exhausted the azalea market as far south as Houston. Within a few weeks, Mary had planted 10,305 azaleas from the U. S. Capitol down Pennsylvania Avenue to the Department of Commerce. Some of the critics of flower-planting delighted in the fact that 362 of the bushes died. Actually, that is a small attrition rate for azaleas, and Mary's attitude was stalwart. When a reporter said, "But what if the plants die or get stolen?" Mary replied, "Think nothing of it. We'll just plant some more."

Since her purchases had already wiped out the current azalea market, the "more" were hard to find. Mary had a solution. "Let's go see Dr. Skinner out at the National Arboretum," she said. "He's got lots of azaleas he could share."

Dr. Henry T. Skinner, a scientist, likes to grow azaleas; he does not feel compelled to share them. In fact, he is something of a Scrooge about azaleas. His job is to nurture them, propagate them and write scientific papers about them. But he wasn't eager to get into dispensing them, here and there, up and down Pennsylvania Avenue.

"You have such beautiful azaleas here," Mary began, waving her hand toward vast hilltops covered with giant azaleas.

"Yes, you virtually have the Fort Knox of azaleas out here, Dr. Skinner," I chimed in. "First thing you know people are going to accuse you of being an azalea hoarder."

"We enjoy them," he said flatly.

"Wouldn't it be marvelous," Mary continued, "to propagate several thousand for use around the city of Washington?"

"I don't have the hothouses," Dr. Skinner replied frostily.

"Well, you *should* have the hothouses," Mary continued, "and we'll just see that you get them."

Dr. Skinner got his hothouses and became an important supply line for azaleas in the city.

"You know, Liz," Mary said, as we drove back to the White House from the Arboretum. "It's absolutely ridiculous that people just assume flowers cost a lot of money. Why, I planted a few tulips on Beekman Place in New York. I doubt if I spent more than $200 on tulip bulbs, and my neighbor, John D.

Rockefeller, came up to me and raved and raved about my great generosity. You would have thought I'd given him the Empire State Building. So I just said, 'John, that is nothing, absolutely nothing. Think of how many tulips *you* could buy. You could probably cover the entire state of New York with a tulip planting.' And you know what, Liz, he turned pale and fled—really fled. He probably thought I would ask him to do just that."

For one silent moment, I was very sympathetic with John D. Rockefeller. "How could he possibly think that?" I asked Mary.

Mrs. Johnson's beautification committee met each month, and the wand of beauty was rapidly waved over the Nation's Capital. There were many donations large and small. Columnist Drew Pearson even gave $100 worth of manure from his Maryland farm. A busload of schoolchildren from Nevada sent in $1.21 for the program. But the three musketeers of the beautification effort, moneywise, were all well-known New York philanthropists—Mary Lasker, Laurance Rockefeller and Mrs. Vincent Astor—who felt that Washington was part theirs, too, because it is the Nation's Capital. Interestingly, both Mr. Rockefeller and Mrs. Astor are prominent Republicans but devoted to the Johnsons and determined to help make beautification a bipartisan program. Another prominent New Yorker who dipped deep into her pocket to beautify the White House tastefully with paintings and other luxury items was Mrs. Charles Engelhard.

The First Lady plunged wholeheartedly into beautification, and we traveled the country planting trees, dedicating parks, saluting the green thumbs of others who did these things, too. Her plantings were as varied as a few pansies in front of the Smithsonian Institution, a horse chestnut tree at Monticello, Thomas Jefferson's home, a little-leaf linden (no relation to the President) at New York State University in Buffalo, an ancient piñon tree in Big Bend National Park, cherry trees too numerous to count on Hains Point in Washington, and Dutch tulip bulbs at Charles Young School in Washington, to name a few.

That old tree lover, Joyce Kilmer, couldn't hold a spade to Mrs. Johnson. We lost count of how many trees Mrs. Johnson had planted after the fifty-fourth, a dogwood. One day I wailed to her, "Not another tree planting ceremony! My limbs have begun to ache. My roots have begun to disintegrate. I'll bet I'm the first human being in history to get the Dutch elm disease."

She laughed and said, "You'll be all right, Liz. Just let Dr. Burkley prune you and spray you. You'll be blooming in no time."

We had countless ceremonies. The planting continued in spring, fall and even dead of winter, by sunrise and the full of the moon, on desert and even at Camelback Mountain in 110° heat with Barry Goldwater, who not only is a big conservative but also a big conservationist. We planted daffodil bulbs—two million of them. "The biggest daffodil planting in the history of the world," Nash Castro, regional director for the National Park Service, said proudly as the garden club ladies put the last bulb into the ground along the Potomac River.

Planting wasn't all. There was fixing up and cleaning up, too. One of the first gifts to Mrs. Johnson's committee was $25,000 from Laurance Rockefeller for experimental work on cleaning the green oxides from Washington's eighty-five sculptured memorials. The gift helped start us off, and then almost stopped us in our tracks, because the Department of the Interior had no judgment about which statues to clean first. They wanted to use the money to clean General Sherman, whose statue sits proudly on horseback in downtown Washington attracting more starlings than tourists. Interior's press release was scheduled to go out to newspapers just as Southern tempers were running high on school desegregation. I told Mrs. Johnson about the forthcoming release and the good news for General Sherman.

"Does it *have* to be General Sherman?" she asked plaintively. "He's my least favorite general."

"Apparently he is also the dirtiest and most in need of a cleaning," I replied.

"Well, let's go ahead and clean him up," she said. "But let's just don't announce it."

The voice of the White House on conservation grew stronger every day. In February 1965 the President sent a Message on Natural Beauty to Congress, serving notice that he put improvement of the environment high on the national agenda. In May the White House Conference on Natural Beauty was held, and a thousand experts came to Washington to discuss not only conservation of scenic wilderness areas, but also better design of buildings, increased park space for urban areas, better planned highways and pollution control. The First Lady opened the conference. The President made the final speech. Citizens all over the country rallied to the cause. The response came in waves. First, enthusiastic wires and letters from the "believers"—the garden clubs, the Audubon Societies, all the unsung heroes who had been working for these goals for many years without any help from Washington. Then came the "hardware" group, such as businessmen—General Electric, for example, which put large sums of money into research, the salvage companies seeking ways to crush junked cars more efficiently and economically, the neon sign companies wanting to look better if someone would just tell them how.

I realized beautification had really arrived when the public officials, Senators, Congressmen, governors and mayors began clamoring for recognition from Mrs. Johnson: a personal letter, a personal appearance, a dedication ceremony of some new project. Even Senator Everett Dirksen, Republican leader, wanted Mrs. Johnson to come see newly refurbished downtown Peoria! And it took the President all of one minute to tell us to go.

Everywhere she went, the townspeople would spruce up, sweeping the streets, having litter drives, painting and planting! I thought if we could just keep out on the road we might get the country in good shape.

The press, meantime, was getting a real education in gardening. They soon learned how to spell azalea, and before the five years were over, they had even mastered pyracantha.

Deluged with mail on the subject, Mrs. Johnson insisted that our letter-writers give more than perfunctory answers. So we got the helping hands of two bright young women, Sharon Francis and Cynthia Wilson, who opened an office near mine in the East Wing. Their office became a clearinghouse of ideas for citizens, officials and journalists to spread the beautification gospel.

Mrs. Johnson adored every minute of this segment of her life and cherished every letter. She read and answered a great many of them personally.

And she would go to great lengths to help the individual citizen.

One day a letter arrived from a man in Dayton, Ohio, who wrote:

> Dear Mrs. Johnson:
> You are always talking about automobile junkyards. But the worst eyesore and worst junkyard here is a government airplane graveyard at Wright-Patterson

Air Force Base. It is located on the highway and everyone passing sees four airplane hulks just sitting there ruining the landscape.

As it happened, Secretary of Defense Robert McNamara came to dinner that evening, and Mrs. Johnson showed him the letter and expressed the hope something could be done about this eyesore at a defense installation.

Two days later, I was startled to have a phone call from Secretary McNamara himself. I was startled because, as we say in the government, "our areas of competency didn't frequently cross."

"Liz, you tell Mrs. Johnson that the man out in Dayton was absolutely right," McNamara said. "I have checked it out. They use those old airplane hulks to train firefighters, but they don't need four. It only takes one. And they don't have to have it right on the highway. They have now pulled the old plane back several hundred yards behind a tree where it is screened from view."

I thought this was a wonderful positive story of government in action meshing its mighty gears and moving forward with efficiency. I put in a call to our complainer in Dayton to tell him. He was flabbergasted to hear directly from the White House. I told him we had taken care of his complaint, and I thought it would be a good story to tell the press. Did he mind if I released his letter?

"For God's sake, don't use my name!" he pleaded. "I have the *pie* concession at the Air Force Base."

Sometimes the public gets more action than it expects.

All good works are fraught with peril. In our daily battle for beauty, we had sturdy allies in Secretary of Interior Udall and Secretary of Agriculture Freeman. But a full-scale war broke out between them in what became known to us as the

Great Japanese Cherry Tree Crisis. It took a third high ranking official, the Chief of Protocol, to effect an armistice.

What happened is best explained in a memo to McGeorge Bundy from one of his assistants on the National Security Council:

*Subject: The Cherry Tree Crisis April 12, 1965*

I herewith report a cherry tree crisis. You should be informed but you need not act—as yet.

In the euphoria of the tree lighting ceremony last week, Ambassador Takeuchi offered a large gift of additional cherry trees as Prime Minister Sato's contribution to Mrs. Johnson's beautification program. Mrs. Johnson and beautifier Udall both accepted with alacrity, and Udall has sent us two draft letters of thanks to Sato and spouse.

It appears, however, that Sato's gift is a Trojan horse. Since 1912, when the Japanese first sent us some cherry trees, the Department of Agriculture has been battling to see that it never happens again. Japanese cherry trees, you see, carry a virus that causes harm to other types of fruit-bearing trees. So Sato's gift will be refused admission to the U.S.

All this was news to the State Department when I called up to check on the proposed letters of thanks. They are now engaged in a delicate salvage operation. This involves getting Freeman (Secretary of Agriculture) to break the news to Udall (Secretary of the Interior), then Department of State to inform Takeuchi. One possible solution: The fulfillment of Sato's commitment with what might be called Nisei cherry

> trees; i.e., U.S. grown Japanese cherry trees. We can fuzz up the question of origin and make the action look quite respectable.

Getting Udall and Freeman to see eye-to-eye on this matter was like bringing Ho and Ky to the peace table. The two Secretaries exchanged verbal blows and wound up not speaking to each other directly for several weeks. Their views were exchanged through me.

My telephone was red hot with the ringing denunciations of one Cabinet member for another with the White House in the middle. I kept thinking how great it would be to offer this entertainment for a Democratic fund-raising event.

"Orville Freeman is just being sticky," Secretary Udall told me. "It's embarrassing to turn down a gift from the Prime Minister of Japan. The Agriculture Department can certainly make an exception of those trees and let them come in. That's a $35,000 gift to the City of Washington, and it's not to be sneezed at!"

Well, only in hay fever season, I thought.

I called Freeman and asked if it were possible to bend the rules.

"Those trees aren't coming into this country, Liz," Freeman declared. "Stew Udall is just being pigheaded. We haven't let any fruit trees in for years, and the Japanese knew the quarantine provisions full well when they offered the gift."

Our problem at the White House was to try to hold onto the gift, persuade the Japanese to buy some trees from an American nursery, but help find some way to save face for them. There were many phone calls, all painfully lengthy and through highly diplomatic channels. The ambassador's press officer spoke only to me, the ambassador spoke only to the Chief of Protocol, and poor Nash Castro, our Park Service procurer, spoke to no one. He simply got busy and located an American nursery with $35,000 worth of cherry trees, all descended originally from Japanese roots.

I had the definite impression that over at the Japanese embassy they hadn't had so much fun since Pearl Harbor.

A luncheon at Blair House, set up by Lloyd Hand, then Chief of Protocol, with Ambassador Takeuchi, his press officer, Nash Castro and me, finally sealed the arrangement.

We bowed through the first two courses and "most honorabled" each other clear through dessert. Finally, over coffee, Ambassador Takeuchi gave approval to a press release we had prepared and we agreed on a planting ceremony on the Washington Monument grounds.

Mrs. Johnson and Mrs. Takeuchi did the honors with the shovels. The Ambassador and Secretary Udall smiled. Photographs were made. There was a White House party following the ceremony. And 3800 cherry trees grew happily ever after in Washington. Seldom before has a foreign country received so much publicity from a $35,000 expenditure.

Usually, if there is one thing in Washington that isn't hard to give away, it is money. This is the city which undoubtedly inspired the famous liquor advertisement, "While you are up, get me a grant."

But there was a week in 1968 after the April riots when we literally tried and couldn't give away $50,000.

The spring had been exhausting and nerve-racking for Washington and its official inhabitants. The assassination of Martin Luther King in Memphis set off riots and fires in cities across the country. For nearly a week, there was looting, burning, arrests and drunkenness in Washington. For the city officials, it was a nightmare. The President, the First Lady and all thinking people were desperately searching for a constructive answer to an ugly problem.

Washington was blessed with a black mayor. We were truly blessed with Walter Washington. Mrs. Johnson had urged her husband to appoint Walter Washington as the city's first mayor. And both of them were proud that, in him, they had an effective, responsible public servant. The new mayor never rested. He was out in the streets trying to calm the angry voices. He was on television trying to reassure a worried capital.

While the smoke was still clearing, Laurance Rockefeller's bright assistant, Henry Diamond, called with this message. "Mrs. Astor and Laurance have been talking, and they think it would be well if Mrs. Johnson's beautification committee makes an immediate gesture to help rebuild the burned-out areas in the riot section. Why don't you see what could be done? They'll give $50,000—maybe more."

The First Lady dispatched me to the mayor and half a dozen agencies and experts to see if out of the ashes a phoenix could rise—with our help. We explored everything: a swimming pool, a park in the ghetto with sprinklers, scholarships to Negro architects. But the Negro community in Washington was angry and wanted to do their own thing.

After exhausting all possibilities in looking for a meaningful way to use the $50,000, Mayor Washington called one evening and asked to come by and see the First Lady. He arrived about 9 P.M. Poor, harassed mayor! He looked exhausted from days of anxiety, and nights of sitting in the command post to direct the city's defense against riots. Fortunately, he was often able to foresee the trouble ahead of time, not only because of his own perception, but also because he had once headed Washington's public housing authority and knew the city intimately. There were literally thousands of friends of the mayor who, sensing trouble in a neighborhood, would call and tip him off. The mayor could then put into action whatever means of lessening the tensions he could muster. If a jazz band helped at a street corner, he'd get it there. If a soda pop and a boat ride cooled tempers, he would arrange it. The difficult weeks had been exhausting and perilous, and every line on his face showed the strain.

The First Lady offered him her sympathetic understanding and a drink, which he welcomed even more. But he brought a disappointing message. Hard as it was to believe, there was no way to give $50,000 away in the riot area and make it count.

"At this stage, all we can do is hold the pieces together. Right now, the militants want no help from anyone. Right now, they don't even want the Jewish merchants to rebuild their stores. In another six weeks or so, the situation might ease," the mayor said, "but right now they think they can do it themselves and want no assistance."

He spared us the word "honky" assistance.

That was the message we had also gotten from many lesser sources. But it is the first time, I suspect, in the history of this giveaway city that a giveaway was turned down. How ironic and sad it was that in an hour of great human need, a helping hand was rejected.

The record of Mrs. Johnson's beautification efforts in the social welfare field was a good one from the start. For four years, she prowled the alleys of Washington in an unmarked car. On most any afternoon if she felt a need to get out of the White House for a while, the First Lady would gather up some of us—maybe Mayor Washington, maybe Secretary Udall, or some members of her staff, and we would go to the slums. In front of a barren, institution-like public school, she would count the number of broken windows and wonder aloud "if a little bit of well-placed greenery, perhaps some slides and swings, wouldn't make those children have more pride in their neighborhood." Through gifts from a variety of people, initiated by the queenlike philanthropist, Mrs. Marjorie Merriweather Post, twenty schools were landscaped and in most cases the number of broken windows was sharply reduced. Many schools and parks were given new playground equipment, and school principals were persuaded to keep their playgrounds open after school hours.

Mrs. Katharine Graham, publisher of *The Washington Post* and a member of Mrs. Johnson's committee, was a prime booster of school improvement. Her family foundation financed the renovation of two school playgrounds in poor areas. The newspaper supported the program enthusiastically, as did the other two Washington newspapers, the *Star* and the *Daily News*.

Another benefactor to the schools was Mrs. Vincent Astor, whose foundation had given imaginative "outdoor living rooms" to ghetto areas in New York City. Recreation for all ages was offered in these playgrounds—indestructible stone igloos and blockhouses for climbing, summertime sprinklers for the young, benches and tables for checkers and other games for the old, sometimes a stage for outdoor concerts and plays.

"A rock through a window is an opinion," explained her architect, Simon Breines. "You have to give people ways to express themselves without being destructive."

Mrs. Johnson went to New York to dedicate the Astor playground at Jacob Riis Plaza in the heart of the Puerto Rican section. Thousands turned out to cheer it. I was impressed with the little children from that neighborhood who ran up to say hello to Mrs. Astor or grab her hand. They didn't know who she was except the friendly lady who had been coming there each day while the project was under construction. Lady Bountifuls have changed. They don't just send the check as they used to. They supervise each brick and bush. I felt that to Mrs. Astor, the greatest gratification of all must be seeing the lives she had changed through her handiwork.

There was a party after the ceremony at the Colony Club. As we sped down Park Avenue in her long black limousine, Mrs. Astor powdered her nose and giggled, "Who would have ever thought I would be riding down Park Avenue with the First Lady of the land!"

To which Mrs. Johnson countered with a laugh, "And who would have ever thought I would be riding down Park Avenue with Mrs. Astor!"

Park Avenue was one of many streets they traveled together. In Washington, they found that Buchanan School in the low-income southeast neighborhood was badly in need of help. So Mrs. Astor gave another "outdoor living room."

Mrs. Johnson telephoned her frequently with progress reports, and whenever Mrs. Astor could, she came down from New York to see the new concept in playgrounds in the making. Once she came to Washington despite a cold and fever.

"I feel terrible," she told me. "I've been sick all week."

"Well, you look like a million dollars!" I said cheerily.

"Well, I should!" she countered quickly and promptly forgot about her ailments.

Buchanan playground became another safety valve to keep things cool. The Astor Foundation had given $400,000 for it, but as Mrs. Johnson said when anticipating what this playground would do to relieve the long, hot summer in Washington, "Who can put a price tag on boredom? Who can add up the cost of unchallenged energies? Schoolyards simply cannot be locked at 3 P.M. each day. They must be transformed into round-the-clock community playgrounds as an answer to urban problems."

Laurance Rockefeller was another beautification committee

member who was deeply concerned about the ghetto. He gave $75,000 to transform a junk-filled ravine in a low-income neighborhood into an attractive park and another $75,000 for a work-education-recreation summer program for ghetto teenagers.

In light of far-reaching projects like these, the word "beautification" increasingly plagued us as too dainty and inadequate to describe all the facets of the program. We had lots of suggestions, some of them ridiculous such as "plutonic space-a-fi-cation" and "bonnification," but the words "conservation" and "environmental improvement" were too worn-out for what was happening. We stuck to "beautification" even though we were constantly reminded how misleading it could be.

Once when Mrs. Orville Freeman was in Alaska, she visited a salmon fishing village out on the straits near Juneau. She was introduced to the women who worked in the canneries as "Mrs. Freeman from Washington, a member of Mrs. Johnson's beautification program." A woman raised her hand to ask a question. "Could you tell us some of the latest hair styles from the States?" This was what beautification meant to a group of cannery workers whose hair was tied up in hairnets.

Even in Washington, some people were confused. One of Mrs. Johnson's staff members was introduced at a party to another girl as "Mrs. Johnson's beautification assistant." In complete sincerity, the girl said, "Tell me, do you just do Mrs. Johnson's hair, or do you do Lynda's and Luci's too?"

Beautification was a word which would quickly offend those considered unbeautiful, too—like the hog industry.

Keep America Beautiful, Inc., an anti-litter organization, sponsored some TV spots urging Americans to leave their picnic tables clean and not just "fit for pigs." Their advertisement showed baby pigs rooting around the mess of litter left by careless campers.

The pork industry squealed like stuck pigs!

They protested to their Congressmen who in turn forwarded to Mrs. Johnson their letters extolling the virtues and cleanliness of pigs and protesting this slander against them. The industry had spent years improving the image of pigs, and now we were ruining it.

Try as we might, we found that you can't satisfy everyone. When I first came to the White House, Tish Baldridge, who had been Jackie Kennedy's Social Secretary, warned me: "Clare Luce once gave me great advice for public life: No good deed goes unpunished."

I learned this was often true. One of our many planting projects was an impressive display of yellow tulips around the U. S. Army's 1st Infantry Division Memorial in Washington. To our amazement, a veterans' organization wrote to Mrs. Johnson protesting that the yellow streak of tulips reflected on the valor of the World War I division. So, the next year, red tulips were planted instead.

Another time, castor bean plants were placed along the approach to the busy 14th Street Bridge, near the Jefferson Memorial, to make the roadside more attractive. When the U. S. Department of Agriculture's Research Service announced that the seeds of these plants were poisonous, the press had a heyday. But the way I looked at it, anone who was stupid enough to cross that busy eight-lane highway to get near the plants and eat the seeds deserved to be poisoned. To keep everyone happy and alive, Park Service maintenance men removed the deadly pods.

Despite periodic protests like this, beautification grew in Washington and around the country, more through inspiration than legislation. Try as hard as we could, no really adequate billboard control act was ever passed. The Highway Beautification Act squeaked through Congress, weak compared to what was needed. But it was a first step, the first one Congress ever took on billboards. The President did everything he could to win friends for it. He summoned a meeting in the East Room of conservationists and told them in no uncertain terms the purpose of highways is "not just to get people from one place to another; the purpose is to enrich the journey."

Mrs. Johnson was an active champion for highway beautification, and she had learned how to lobby for it from an expert, her husband. She telephoned Congressmen to urge their support and called on conservation-minded friends throughout the country to do the same. White House guest lists were filled with key Congressmen and conservation leaders. She even had their kinfolks in for tea to rally their support. In a speech to the managing editors of the Associated Press, she urged them to write editorials on this issue. When any did, he received a personally signed letter of gratitude from the First Lady.

I put on my best perfume and went to Capitol Hill to call on members of Congress I knew. We needed every vote we could get, for the billboard lobby was active and well-heeled. One evening at a dinner party, I sat next to a Republican Congressman, Republican Chester L. Mize of Kansas. Naturally I turned the conversation to the pending highway bill. He sounded interested and favorable.

Suddenly he interrupted my treatise, "You know, I don't really know anyone down at the White House I can call whenever I have a problem. May I call you when I do?"

"Absolutely," I replied, willing to be his problem solver if this would help get the bill through.

I didn't have long to wait. Next morning, he called to say that he had three constituents in town—three Catholic nuns from Kansas—and he hoped they could have a special tour at the White House. It was the peak visitors season—which means that about 12,000 people are tromping through the White

House every morning. Our tours had long been filled for that day, but I made the arrangements.

"See that the Holy Sisters see everything," I told the guide, "from the doghouse to Lincoln's bedroom."

Flushed with a sense of power, I called the Congressman and told him of the arrangements. He was pleased. The three nuns came, saw and wrote glowing thank you notes. Soon, our highway bill came on the floor of the House. I called my good Republican friend and reminded him how much I hoped we would have his support. He said he would do his best to vote for the bill.

But when the roll was called, Congressman Mize voted a resounding, "No."

The bill passed anyway, and the President signed it into law on October 22. Slowly and painfully, the billboards began to come down; many junkyards were screened; thousands of scenic overlooks and landscaping projects were undertaken to make the highways more attractive. Some states, like Vermont, even passed stronger laws banning billboards. Interestingly, the junkyard dealers were real statesmen about the new regulations concerning their industry. Rather than continue to lobby to weaken the Act, as the billboard companies did, they voluntarily started a program to screen their property with landscaping.

The impact of Mrs. Johnson's interest in improving the environment is a lasting one. Perhaps her greatest accomplishment was creating a new climate of opinion and a new awareness of how we were desecrating our country. As Republican Bob Gray remarked, "Mrs. Johnson has done so much for beautification that I feel guilty every time I plant a geranium."

He needn't have. She wanted everyone's support and would never let beautification be a partisan issue. She was determined to use her position as First Lady to help solve the problems of blight and ugliness. And she worked at it. She was willing to make the White House the forum and travel across the country applauding citizens who were doing something to improve their hometowns. But she never took credit for her own efforts. Whenever anyone heaped praise on her, she would say, "I only stepped on a moving train."

But she was at the throttle of that moving train for five years.

Her faith was in her countrymen—that once alerted, they would act. She threw out the challenge to them in strong words.

"Many of the great works of beauty in the world are the result of autocratic societies," she pointed out. "The Caesars built Rome. Paris represents the will of the Kings of France and the Empire. Vienna is the handiwork of the Hapsburgs, and Florence of the Medici.

"There are no autocrats in this land," she continued, "our challenge is to fight ugliness in a nation where there is great freedom of action or inaction for every individual and interest, and where there is virtually no artistic control."

Here, she pointed out, "all action must originate with the individual citizen."

Together, she was convinced, a committed citizenry could make things happen.

The President was behind her 100 percent, even though he liked to kid her. "I go upstairs and try to grab a nap in the afternoon," he told a group of friends, "but Lady Bird and Laurance Rockefeller have a whole group of people in the next room talking about planting daffodils."

No one knows better than the President that long after the problems of the 1960s are history, the Johnson years will be remembered for the gentle and gifted hand that a lady gave to improve the landscape of America.

## *The Care and Feeding of Speechwriters*

With Huey Long, it was "Every man a king." With Lyndon Johnson, it was "Every man a speechwriter." No one within range of his Long Arm or telephone service could escape being drafted to turn out prose for the thousands of speeches he made—not to mention the ones he ordered written and didn't make.

One scene explains it the way it was:

One August day in 1965, the President decided to go to the National Institutes of Health on the following day to sign some health legislation and deliver a major speech. The occasion was also to mark the resignation of the U. S. Surgeon General, Luther Terry, best remembered as the man who took the fun out of smoking. So LBJ asked Douglass Cater, his special assistant on health and education, to write the speech. Cater, one of the better wordsmiths, enlisted the help of a young aide, Ervin Duggan, a former reporter who was also an excellent man of prose. They worked all night and turned out a draft which was delivered to the President on his breakfast tray the day of the speech. The President read it and liked it. That is, he liked it until 10:30 A.M. when he decided he wanted it rewritten. He was due to leave the White House at 11:30 A.M. and go by helicopter to NIH in suburban Maryland, where he would address a large assemblage of Public Health Service doctors and nurses and Congressional leaders who handled health legislation. The President ordered Bill Moyers to get the speech rewritten before he left—a matter of a mere hour. The helicopter had already perched itself on the lawn, in readiness for the six minute flight.

Moyers dashed from the President's bedroom to Cater's office and told Cater and Duggan to start a rewrite—and fast. For the next hour they worked frantically. Cater and Duggan were at different tables racing their pencils longhand across the pages, which were then handed to Moyers to edit into a single speech. Two secretaries stood by to type it for delivery. Also standing by nervously was the Signal Corps' majordomo, who must somehow get the speech typed on a Teleprompter and on the podium twelve miles away by the time the President arrived at NIH. Farsighted, he had a military truck parked nearby with a secretary and a Teleprompter typewriter on board all poised for action. A driver would race the truck across town while the courageous secretary typed the words. Two Signal Corpsmen were already at the speaker's stand at NIH ready to grab the copy and put it into place.

The sound of the helicopter rotors warming up in the distance increased the momentum of the Cater-Duggan-Moyers team and also their nerves. A sharp telephone ring on the direct line to the President informed them that the President was on board the chopper waiting. The speeches were yanked out of the typewriters, and Moyers dashed one way to the chopper with one copy to thrust into the President's hands. The Signal Corpsman grabbed another copy and dashed to the truck, and they were off—one by air and one by land, in a dead heat—to NIH. Meanwhile, Cater, Duggan and Moyers collapsed in a state of shock, awaiting the moment they could watch the President deliver their latest brainchild in living color on TV. They reflected dolefully that writing *his* health speech had ruined *theirs*.

At last, the President of the United States—the man to whom they had given their ultimate effort—loomed on the screen, and they were relieved to see his Teleprompters in place. Just as they were about to congratulate themselves, the President began a speech they had never heard before in their lives. It encompassed the Holy Bible, the unholy U. S. Congress and Barbara Ward, a British author he admired greatly.

LBJ began with the Bible, quoting verbatim the text he had heard at church the previous Sunday: "And Philip went down to the city of Samaria and proclaimed to them the Christ, and the multitude gave heed with one accord. And when they heard and they saw the signs which He did for some of those that had unclean spirits, they came out crying with a loud voice, and many that were palsied and many were lame. And they were healed."

His listeners at NIH were intrigued with the new, Biblical LBJ. His TV viewers back at the White House were astounded. Moyers-the-Baptist threw one hand to his head and exclaimed: "How in the hell did Philip of Samaria get in there?"

The President continued in fine form: "A staggering era for medicine has begun. You here at NIH are shaping it, and you can be as proud of what you are doing as we are proud of you."

He then began to pass out verbal bouquets to the members of Congress present. At one point, he introduced Arkansas Congressman Oren Harris, who headed the House committee handling health legislation and whom Johnson had recently appointed to a federal judgeship.

"Here we have Congressman Oren Harris, who will soon

leave the legislative to go to the judiciary—but not leave it until he gets those last five health bills passed," the President said, his voice rising, "and Congressman Springer [a Republican] who supports Oren Harris in this very effective work."

Now with the platform guests, as well as the audience firmly within the President's hand, he was off and running with a long list of "The American Goals" in health that included ambitious aims.

"What are our goals?" Johnson said, as the government hierarchy of health waited to hear their new assignments. "The American goal is to eliminate completely the disability and the death among children that is caused by rheumatic fever. The American goal is to reduce substantially the tragic toll of heart disease."

And, then—and certainly no one could ever accuse Lyndon B. Johnson of lacking optimism—the final one: "Malaria and cholera were conquered in America a long time ago. The American goal is the *complete* eradication of malaria and cholera from the *entire* world."

The exhausted speechwriters at the White House, marveling at all they heard were to hear the ultimate personal insult from their do-it-yourself Boss.

"Last night, I was reading from a little book that I have read many, many times, but I get strength from it every time I read it. It is *The Rich Nations and the Poor Nations* by Barbara Ward—Lady Jackson. And one brief passage appealed to me. I tried to get my speechwriters to put it into my speech, but they wouldn't do it. So I am going to put it in myself."

The audience, enjoying the impromptu performance immensely, howled at the President's declaration of independence from his speechwriters. As was always the case when he threw the text away, he was at his best.

"The ancient enemies of mankind are poverty, disease,

ignorance," he said, pleading now for action. "We have more resources at our disposal than any group of nations in the history of man. We have the means to do better. We can do better. And in the allotted time to us, each of us in his own way is going to make his maximum contribution to healing the lame and caring for the palsied, and adding virtue and knowledge and brotherly love to this land."

It was an old theme for Johnson, but he believed it. He could inspire others to believe it, and he was willing to expend all his energy to do so.

I had received the Barbara Ward gospel from LBJ back when I first went to work for him in the Vice Presidential years. He had told me to write a speech, and I pleaded I needed time to do research on the subject.

"No you don't," he said, picking up Barbara Ward's book. "This is what it's all about—this is what the whole government effort is all about. It's right here in one sentence—the mission of our times is to eradicate the three enemies of mankind—poverty, disease and ignorance."

Of course he was right. And certainly that is what the Johnson years are all about, but any self-respecting speechwriter was bound to be obliged to vary the words from time to time.

There were at least a dozen men and women who worked with some regularity on the President's speeches, though four or five of these were the old reliables. The principal speechwriters for the President during his five years were Cater, Harry McPherson, Charles Maguire, Bill Moyers, Dick Goodwin, Horace Busby and Jack Valenti, who was by far, the most gifted editor of speeches. Valenti's training as an advertising man gave him that keen insight into the arresting phrase that would simplify the issue. All of these men were the first string, during their term of service. They got their orders straight from the President. But there were many others, drafted into service as the needs increased, including Cabinet members.

If you think Presidents are hypersensitive and thin-skinned, you should meet the speechwriters. A greater collection of talented prima donnas I have never known. They conceived words in agony, nursed them tenderly through first, second and third drafts, and paced the floor for the delivery. If their word-children had been discarded, they snarled, snapped, complained and sometimes just sulked for days. That is just the way speech-writers are. You have to put up with them and flatter them and occasionally send them off for a rest when they go stale.

At first, the President thought that speechwriters had endless capacity. Like Old Faithful, they should spout forth with regularity. He would find one speechwriter he particularly liked and keep at him until the poor man was flattened, his creative capacity spent. Once he demanded eight rewrites out of the same writer and was surprised that the last one bore no resemblance to the first.

The President's problem in finding good speechwriters is not uncommon. Good writers are the greatest shortage in government, and thus there is an endless search to find the writer who can turn out inspiration, substance, news and possibly humor. Johnson's demands were tremendous. He made 424 speeches in 1964. That was the speech year that was. While campaigning or on a trip that included many stops, it wasn't unusual to make fifteen or twenty speeches a day. Even though the general public hears only a few major speeches each year, there are hundreds of proclamations, remarks and greetings for groups who see the President each day. He awards medals to heroes. He greets the Thanksgiving turkey. He briefs labor leaders. He exhorts businessmen. He preaches to preachers. Occasionally, and most important, he makes policy pronouncements to the world.

On a heavy speech-making day, his aide Jim Jones, would have his pockets bulging with speech cards which he would hand to the President just as he stepped to the podium. There was one occasion when the President rushed into the Cabinet Room to greet new officials of the Department of Transportation. This speech was wedged in just before an appearance he was to make ten minutes later to volunteers for the American Red Cross. The President reached toward Jim for his Transportation speech cards. Jim fumbled and handed him a set which the President proceeded to read, and after a few sentences realized it was an appeal for the Red Cross. It was too late to turn back and even though he recognized the error, and his listeners were beginning to smile, he continued until the end and stated: "That's what I think about the Red Cross. Now let me tell you what I think about the Department of Transportation."

Our stable of speechwriters needed replenishing with this heavy demand. Everyone joined in the talent search for speechwriters, turning them up in unlikely places and confiscating them for White House use. Johnson "borrowed" talent from Henry Ford II, John D. Rockefeller III and Secretary McNamara. He even called in Barbara Ward–and we were off again with poverty, disease and ignorance.

The story of Ben Wattenberg is typical. He was sitting in his Stamford, Connecticut, office one day, counting up the royalties of his recent book, *This USA,* when he received a phone call from Press Secretary Moyers' office. He was told that the President and many staff members had read his book and were impressed by it. "Can you come down to Washington right away?" Astonished but flattered, Wattenberg drove to Washington, met with various staff members, and suddenly found that Bill Moyers was shuttling him into the President's bedroom just as LBJ was finishing a conference with Henry Ford II and getting ready for a nap.

"Suddenly I was standing face-to-face with the President of the United States in his blue robe," Wattenberg recalls. "We chatted briefly and the next thing I knew I was in a strange office with a typewriter in front of me, working on the first speech I had ever written for anybody—and it was for the President of the United States."

The influx of speechwriters stretched the White House walls, and the newest ones were housed in "think tanks," large, spacious offices with high ceilings and lots of room for pacing, in the Executive Office Building next door to the White House. There they wrote, paced, pasted, downed gallons of coffee and pored over numerous reference books long into the night. Next day they rested, waited for word from the top about the President's reaction, and then—if the coast was clear—escaped for a long martini lunch. Or as more often happened, they had to begin the rapid rewrites.

Probably better than anyone, Robert Kintner, the President's longtime friend who had helped in obtaining speechwriters, understood their idiosyncrasies. Kintner, exiled by NBC in one of those network turnovers, was made a special assistant to the President, and he provided the speechwriters' needs: a highly organized, calm and patient secretary, peace and quiet, and constant praise. He also dispatched flattering notes and held weekly staff meetings to hand out writing assignments.

Speechwriters are by nature vain. There was only one occasion when I found a speechwriter who openly admitted he had produced something less than the Gettysburg Address.

Ervin Duggan was long overdue a vacation. For three months he had planned a trip to the Virgin Islands. I had helped him arrange a cottage, a moon and some potential feminine companionship. The night before leaving, he was summoned to the LBJ Ranch—much against his will—to rework a speech draft by the State Department—a notorious factory for dull prose.

In the evening, after Ervin had struggled with the draft throughout the day, the President asked him what the speech would be like.

Ervin replied apologetically, "Mr. President, what I have come up with is a long, dull, unexciting speech."

The President impressed with his honesty, told him to work over it some more. The next day the President asked him what the speech would be like.

Ervin, weary wordsmith that he was, felt he had to be honest. "Sir, I have worked over this thing for two days. Now it's a short, dull, unexciting speech."

Ervin was excused to leave for his vacation.

The speechwriters we borrowed from the corporations and foundations were never returned. The heady atmosphere of the "think tanks" of the White House had much more appeal than the mundane world of commerce or finance.

Although I had written occasional speeches, mostly humorous ones, for the President when he was Vice President, I was busy working on words for Mrs. Johnson, who was in demand on the speaking circuit herself. The workload required assistance, but there were a few able people I could call on for help, such as Mrs. Douglass Cater and Eric Goldman. Barbara Ward, the brilliant British economist, would visit the Johnsons occasionally, and if I could find her free for a brief spell, her rat-a-tat-tat brain would always stimulate ideas—even on subjects other than poverty, disease and ignorance.

But the day did dawn when I found myself on a regular assignment for *him*. The order was out: "Tell Liz to keep providing me with some of her jokes. Tell her to put some sex into my speeches." By sex, he didn't really mean *sex*. He just meant for me to humanize it, warm it up. I was to get together with Ben Wattenberg, who had a gift for wit, and we were to produce humor, and on an assembly line basis for speech openers or light remarks for light occasions.

So the Humor Group was born. The meeting place was my office. The time was every Monday at five. And I invited five or six of the better jokesters around the White House. The meetings were well attended because I served drinks. There is nothing about producing humor that gin doesn't improve. I moved in a small piece of furniture which I called my Marvin Watson Cabinet, in honor of the White House's best known teetotaler, and we stocked it. Ernest Cuneo, round of face and body, smiling and full of chuckles, always arrived with a pungent cigar and a bottle of Chivas Regal Scotch, and two pairs of eyeglasses—one for seeing and the other for gesturing. Ernie had a stock of mellow stories about FDR and Fiorello La Guardia, whom he had served years ago. He had been sugar-cured in the smoke-filled rooms of the New Deal, and he provided a battery of stories which so often illustrated a current political issue.

Cuneo illustrated how essential speechwriters are by frequently telling us of the Negro leader who was introducing Jim Farley. The Negro, speaking of Farley, said, "His skin is white, but his heart is as black as ours." "That shows," Cuneo said, "how disastrous impromptu remarks can be."

My office on Mondays during the Laugh-Along-With-Liz meetings, was a disorderly picture. In the interest of efficiency, I would place my manual typewriter on the coffee table in the center of the room, and the various men who had arrived from the West Side would mix their drinks and find the most comfortable stance for thinking and writing.

We would have an assignment from Charles Maguire, who tried manfully to bring order to the chaos of the speechwriting effort, and away we would go creating funny lines that we hoped the President would use.

It was a relaxed group, each to his own favorite thinking habits. Scholarly and bespectacled Peter Benchley, the grandson of the great humorist Robert Benchley, couldn't think unless he paced. Ben Wattenberg, tie always in disarray, liked to slump horizontal in a lounge chair with his coat off. Wavy-haired Ervin Duggan, cleancut and boyish as a choirboy, sat on the edge of his chair ready to spring forth with a suggestion. Joe Laitin would puff cigarettes incessantly. Elfin in appearance, his eyes would light up mischievously when the well chosen word had hit its target. There were various others who dropped in and out of our group—Hal Pachios, Clark Tyler and Al Spivak.

The air was heavy with smoke. The door would open for one purpose only: to dispatch a secretary down the hall to Bess Abell's refrigerator for more ice cubes. I cut off all phone calls unless they were from LBJ, Mrs. LBJ or a Cabinet member. And we worked. By 6:30 or so, we would dispatch a draft of our better lines to Maguire whose sober, life-is-real, life-is-earnest manner, we well knew, would never fully appreciate our efforts. He would send our draft up to the President, who would use or reject them, or improve them, to our chagrin. The days we really feared were when Maguire decided to turn humorist and rewrite our wit before he sent it up to the President. After this happened, I stopped sending drafts to him and took them right to the President's valet to give to the President before he went to bed.

Female writers can be prima donnas, too!

Humor at the beginning of a speech is vital for it provokes response from the audience. Their laughter sparks the speaker. This especially served LBJ who could sound mechanical before the mechanical props of TV. But once he would get a chuckle or a belly laugh from a live audience at the start, he really warmed up to the crowd. And, on occasion, became as eloquent as an Adlai Stevenson and as persuasive as a Billy Graham. He was never at ease under the soulless eye of a television camera, and he was at his best in small informal groups.

I could certainly sympathize with the President's aversion to public speaking, because I did some myself—mostly to news media groups in various parts of the country. When I had to make a speech and, of course, write it first, I became tense and irritable. My staff tried to stay clear of me as I struggled over my immortal words. Unfortunately, I didn't have a "think tank" to write my speeches, and the constant interruptions of my office work frayed my nerves. My tranquilizer consumption went up, along with my blood pressure and I prayed that the group I was addressing would have at least two cocktails before I spoke—and I would have two afterwards.

I would always confide this weakness to my audience with this confession: "I was so pleased when your president invited me to speak to you tonight. He assured me that he would provide a friendly audience and a potted palm. I told him what I really needed was a friendly palm and a potted audience."

I used this joke so many times that my staff would shriek, "Not the potted palm gag again!" But I kept using it everywhere I went. In fact, once I received a gift from a woodcarver. It was a humorous coat of arms, showing the faces of a drunken audience sheltered by several large potted palms.

I had more inclination and freedom to kid the press and politicians than the President, so despite the anguish I suffered I did have some fun with my speeches. Whenever I could prevail upon outside talents, I called upon everyone within the sound of my voice, at home and abroad.

Most of our group assignments were to write some introductory gags for a speech. The President used them. He won applause. His critics saw a completely different President—one who could occasionally laugh at himself.

The demands increased. Soon we had to meet not once, but twice a week to fulfill our requests. The word spread and the gag group was tapped by the Vice President, several Cabinet members and Betty Furness, the President's adviser for Consumer Affairs. Some of the best gags were rejected by the President and I would then pass them on to the Vice President. I lived in constant fear that LBJ and HHH would end up some night on the same platform with the same lines.

This literally occurred once at the White House Photographers' Association dinner. LBJ had been invited, and a speech had been written for him. That afternoon he decided that he wouldn't go, so Vice President Humphrey was to do the speaking. We took LBJ's speech and reshaped it for HHH, but the gags were the same.

The dinner progressed happily enough for everyone until dessert time, when I suddenly noticed two familiar Secret Service men appear at the door. My heart sank. They were on the President's detail and this surely meant he was on his way. Sitting across the table was Ben Wattenberg frozen in place and staring with horror. We knew that the President's speech cards were almost identical with the Vice President's. No one has ever called on the Lord more imploringly than we did during the next long minutes: "Please, oh, please, let the President speak first!" He answered our prayers. The President spoke and the Vice President wasn't called on to speak. Our jobs were safe again.

The Gridiron Club in Washington, a collection of esteemed newsmen, is the principal humor platform for political figures. A speech for that group requires weeks of worry and writing. One of the most successful was delivered by LBJ in the historic setting of old Williamsburg, Virginia. It occurred during the dump-Johnson movement, when his polls were declining.

"This is an old political town you have chosen for your meeting," LBJ began, "I understand the archaeologist has recently turned up an old plank on which two words were written: 'Dump Jefferson.'"

"It was in Williamsburg," he continued, "that we first saw the classic American blend of pragmatism and idealism. For it was here that a special courier delivered Patrick Henry a private poll from his home district of Richmond: 46 percent for liberty; 39 percent for death; 15 percent, undecided."

The President did not sit idly by and simply deliver our lines. He became something of a gag writer himself, and and sharpened and improved our efforts.

As our demand increased, we tapped new sources. I had met Larry Markes, a Hollywood gag writer, primarily because he had written, *Save Your Confederate Money Boys, The South Will Rise Again,* with my longtime friend, Hank Fort. So we "drafted" Larry by long distance to give us the professional touch. If we were stuck on how to make a line funny, I would telephone Larry in Encino, California, where he was beating out TV scripts for Alan King and such shows as *The Flying Nun.* He welcomed the intrusion.

"Oh, that's all right," he'd say to my apologies. "Glad to escape *The Flying Nun.* I just got her up in midair with the Mother Superior, and she can stay there a few minutes."

LBJ particularly liked some humor with the verbal bouquets he generously handed out when a member of his official family departed for a better job. When director of the Budget Bureau Charles Schultze and director of the Council of Economic Advisers Gardner Ackley left, there was a joint reception for these two monetary experts in the Department of State's large reception room. The President scored high in a two-minute greeting which included a jibe at the pinch-penny chairman of the House Ways and Means Committee, Wilbur Mills.

"I dropped over tonight to join you in saying goodbye to two very good friends—the bag men of the United States Government. There are many reasons I hate to see them go. But one is that I am constantly accused of surrounding myself by 'yes' men and these two—above all others—stand out as the two greatest 'no' men of the Administration. As you all know, Gardner Ackley is headed for Rome where he will be my ambassador; Charlie Schultze is headed for Brookings. In other words, one is going off to an embassy and the other to an institution.

"Charlie did a great job in helping me to squeeze out every last dollar and every last cent from the budget but what we forgot about was the *mills*. In fact, I remember so well the day when you and I, Charlie, unveiled the 1969 budget for Chairman Mills. We had worked so hard to make it lean and perfect. I'll never forget Wilbur Mills' words when he took a look at it. He said, 'It's the ugliest thing I ever saw.'"

When the Humor Group gathered the next afternoon, there was a commendation from LBJ and our taskmaster, Charles Maguire.

MEMORANDUM

THE WHITE HOUSE

Washington

February 6, 1968
5:30 P.M.

MEMORANDUM FOR THE HUMOR GROUP

The President called me this afternoon to reiterate his pleasure with last night's light-hearted speech at the Schultze-Ackley dinner.

He asked that we all 'work at that kind of phrasing in the future—it went over real big.'

He also asked for the names of those responsible, which I gave him. I also took the opportunity to explain again the workings of Liz Carpenter's Monday evening group, noting their successes, such as the Dirksen speech, the fact that they were in session last evening when the speech requirement broke so suddenly, and saying other nice things about y'all.

Now what have you done for the President today?

Charles Maguire

Flattery paid off with greater productivity. That was what was needed as we edged toward the end of the Administration and the President was eager to receive many groups "just one more time."

In late 1968, the National Press Club invited me to make a farewell speech. I accepted and set the date for January 16, 1969—just four days before the inauguration of the new President. Without my knowing it, the Press Club also invited LBJ to make a speech there, but he didn't give an answer. Such a speech had not been scheduled on his writing assignments.

It was my own speech, entitled, "The Swan Song of a Lame Duck," that was occupying my own thoughts. I wanted it to be my best effort—to leave them laughing, and—hopefully—missing me.

I lay awake nights and worried about what I would say, got up at dawn to write it down. I nagged Les for advice and good lines. I browbeat my office staff into stopping their packing long enough to do the typing. I sweet-talked Ervin Duggan, a former newsman and comforting friend, into lending me a hand. On the big day—January 16—I was emotionally spent, and all the sorrow of saying goodbye formally to the press was putting me in tears. Just before the most important speech of my life—the last speech I would make in my White House job—Bess Abell, who had gone into mourning over our departure since the President's decision the previous March, rose to the occasion and came to my aid with a glass of champagne as we left the White House.

"One glass won't hurt you, and you need it," she said with the authority of a physician, pouring it and thrusting it in my hand. I felt better when I reached the Press Club. My husband was near by, and my office staff was seated at a table just in front of the podium, watching lovingly and tearfully. They had tried to cheer me during the luncheon by sending gag notes to the head table saying: *"FYI—The moving men have just removed your desk and typewriter."*

And I began: "It has come to our attention over at the White House that we are leaving. I can't say that I welcomed the topic which brought me here—the Swan Song of a Lame Duck. I don't know whether to honk or quack."

And for twenty minutes, I was able to milk the laughs that threaded all the memories. Most of the audience were old friends and reporters who had covered the White House. They were nostalgic, too, sentimental and gracious.

But as I wound it up with a serious ending, the tears were hard to hold back: "One more word from the heart. It was more than eight years ago that I was called by the newly nominated Vice President candidate and his wife. They asked me if I would share the great adventure of their lives. It has been just that. And every step of the way I have been aware that I was serving two great people."

It was getting very difficult to continue, but I took a deep breath, bit my lip and went on: "You may come to the White House a partisan. You never leave it as one. I only wish the new First Family well. They will do their best as all of those families who have gone before them."

I knew I had to muster a smile for the last lines which I hoped would end with a laugh: "A great many of my colleagues have asked me what I plan to do. Well, there is only one thing for a Washington has-been to do. I'm announcing my candidacy tomorrow for governor of California. And please put one lonely reporter on the trail, because I'm going to miss it terribly when you don't have Liz Carpenter to kick around any more."

My office staff was dissolved, and I was close to it. The audience was wonderful. It gave a standing ovation to a former colleague who was now returning to the profession.

Anyway, it was over, and it hadn't gone too badly. My husband had a cheer-up glass of champagne waiting for me on my way out, and my office staff and Ervin Duggan walked back the two blocks to the White House with me. The White House corridors were already filled with packing boxes labelled to go, and we threaded our way through them. Even though I was emotionally spent, I could hear those phones ringing all the way down the hall. My secretary, Oghda O'Gulian, ran ahead to answer them. It was Charles Maguire, and he was frantic.

"The President has decided to accept the invitation of the National Press Club and speak there tomorrow. He wants a farewell speech by tonight."

Ervin and I collapsed in chairs, and Oghda summoned the only other speechwriter she could find, Peter Benchley, to come over on the double. "I'm working on another speech to the astronauts, but I'll help a while," Peter said.

Bess's half-empty bottle of champagne was sitting there still—tempting us. For the next three hours, we worked and sipped.

"In this speech, why not just let ourselves go?" Ervin asked. "Why not take every Achilles' heel the President ever had with the press and poke fun at them?"

"That's right," I agreed looking at the calendar. "After all, we have nothing to lose but our jobs."

"Let's take the Peter Hurd painting incident, and Walter Lippmann and everything the press has ever said about the President that annoyed him. He can make light of it with good humor," Ervin reasoned, "then, in exit, he'll show he wasn't offended."

"Everything?" I asked in wonder.

"Not the *scar!*" Peter Benchley said incisively.

"Even the scar," Ervin said, feeling no pain. So we wrote.

We sent our speech draft, including jokes about THE SCAR, to the President for his approval, and we all went home to recover and have second thoughts about the wisdom of it all.

Next morning, I ran into Ervin and Peter in the corridor and gave them a guilty look. "He liked it," Ervin said. "He's going to use it. He's even improving it. He called and dictated a short insert of serious points."

We decided to go over to the Press Club at noon and watch the President deliver this speech in person.

Intimates of LBJ had always known he was a great storyteller, a master of mimicry. But it amazed reporters, more than any others that day, that he appeared as a stand-up comedian delivering his oneliners flawlessly; laughing at all the sacred cows.

He began: "I couldn't leave Washington without coming here to acknowledge the close and frank relationship we've always enjoyed.

"You were frank, and I was close.

"You may wonder why I came over here today.

"And I may wonder that when I leave.

"A lot of people have been asking me what I'm going to do with my spare time. Well, I'm going to sit on the front porch—

for about ten minutes. I'm going to write a little and teach a little. And then I'm going out and find Walter Lippmann."

The reporters roared.

"Someone told me the other day that the press had a few complaints about the treatment you had during my Administration," Johnson continued coyly. "This is a fine time to be telling me. Why didn't you mention it sooner? Well, I've got some complaints of my own. And maybe I should have mentioned that sooner to you. Getting misquoted, for instance. Take that Peter Hurd painting. I never said it was ugly. Actually, it was a pretty good likeness, except for one little detail."

He paused a full thirty seconds, and then added: "He left off the halo.

"Again—I was quoted as saying that an ancestor of mine was in a fight at the Alamo. It's true. But you didn't give me a chance to finish the sentence. What I was trying to say was: 'He was in a fight in the Alamo *Hotel*, in Eagle Pass, Texas.'"

The press was rocking with laughter.

The President continued: "On one occasion, you were absolutely accurate—I *did* show my scar. But it was only after a question from Sarah McClendon. She said, 'Mistuh President, you've been in office almost two years. What do you have to show for it?'"

By now the whole room was cheering and clapping for the man they had branded as thin-skinned and hypersensitive.

"Now," the President concluded, "I will take your questions. This is your last chance to roast the lame duck."

But there was no roasting that day. Only surprise. The press was a little startled to find they were saying goodbye to a man they had *never really known.*

# *Never Send to Know for Whom the Wedding Bell Tolls*

Marriages are *not* made in heaven. During my years at the White House they were put together by a Social Secretary, a Press Secretary, months of hard labor—and, as we discovered, it best be Union labor!

The day Luci Baines Johnson married Patrick John Nugent of Waukegan, Illinois—on August 6, 1966—and the day Lynda Bird Johnson married Captain Charles Spittal Robb of the U. S. Marine Corps—on December 9, 1967—climaxed some of the most exhausting, nerve-racking months of my life. I am glad they lived happily ever after. I managed to live through them—but that is all I can say.

The problem of surviving was intensified because we still had business as usual on other East Wing activities, while trying to plan the wedding and satisfy the insatiable appetite of the press for wedding details.

There were still trips, receptions, State visits and correspondence. During the week of Luci's wedding, the crescendo of activity was heightened by a State visit from the President of Israel. While the pastry chef, Ferdinand Louvat, was putting the final touches on the five-foot wedding cake, he was also making the strawberry bombe for the 186 guests at the State dinner. And in the flower room, Elmer Young and James Nelson were arranging facsimile bouquets for the rehearsal for twelve bridesmaids with one hand and with the other, eighteen centerpieces for the State dinner.

The problem is—all the world *does* love a lover. And until Luci, then a brunette sprite of nineteen, became engaged, there hadn't been a White House bride for fifty years. Instantly every hardbitten reporter become a syrupy armchair cupid. Every would-be Washington hostess wanted to entertain the bride. Every commercial firm wanted to supply the necessary ingredients, from flowers to cake to blue satin garters.

There was, as I predicted shortly after the announcement, summertime rioting in the East Wing among five hundred news-hungry reporters who wanted every morsel of information about the wedding, which I kept trying to convince them was to be "a private family event." (I learned quickly not to say "affair.")

The world will remember the Johnson brides as two pretty girls walking down the aisle on the arm of their father, the President of the United States.

I remember the weddings as crises-on-crises. Once, Richard Nixon had campaigned on his experience—"The Six Crises of Richard Nixon." I always wondered how he could possibly feel he was qualified with only six. I had 6666 just working on weddings.

The reporters who came to cover the Nugent-Johnson wedding from the groom's hometown must have felt as I did. After the ceremony, they dispatched a wire to the "next" White House daughter, Lynda, saying, FOR GOD'S SAKE, DON'T MARRY A BOY FROM WAUKEGAN, ILLINOIS. Signed, SEVERAL WAUKEGAN REPORTERS. But we saw them again on the second round when Lynda's husband was from Milwaukee. She didn't marry a

Waukegan boy, but she did pick one in the same greater Chicago circulation area.

My crises are the untold stories of the weddings. It is only now that I can laugh at them.

Crisis Number 1: *'Twas the Night Before Christmas*

The whole problem started with a call to my Washington home from Luci and her mother, who were at the ranch in Texas.

"Guess what?" said the breathless Luci. "Patrick has given me an engagement ring, and we want to announce it right away."

"Now?" I replied, looking at the clock which said 11:30 P.M., Christmas Eve.

"Well, we are going to Midnight Mass in Stonewall soon. There may be reporters there. I'm not going to take off my ring. And I don't want the story to leak. I want to announce it like any other girl."

This seemed like a reasonable request.

I concocted a brief announcement "like any other girl would have" whose father didn't happen to be President of the United States: "The President and Mrs. Lyndon Baines Johnson tonight announced the engagement of their daughter, Luci Baines, to Patrick John Nugent of Waukegan, Illinois. A late summer wedding is planned. Mr. Nugent's gift to Miss Johnson was a white gold engagement ring with three diamonds—a large center diamond and two smaller baguette diamonds on either side. Before placing the ring on Luci's finger, Mr. Nugent showed it to the President and received his approval to present it."

It was now nearing midnight and I knew that the White House press would be celebrating the Eve of this religious holiday in an non-religious manner. They operated out of a press room in Austin, Texas, during holidays when the LBJ's went home to the ranch.

With announcement in hand, I telephoned Joe Laitin, an assistant to Bill Moyers, then the President's press secretary. Joe was dining with a large group of reporters, including Helen Thomas of UPI, one of the most romantic-minded newswomen in the entire world. In fact, Helen had scored the beat on Luci's becoming a Catholic, and was determined she would have the story of Luci's engagement. She had written periodic rumor stories over the past weeks, much to the annoyance of LBJ who kept reading the news before Pat had even asked for his daughter's hand.

"I need to talk to you, Joe. Can you talk?" I asked.

Joe, an old-time Hollywood reporter who had gone straight—and into government—caught on immediately. "I'll phone you back."

With Helen Thomas eavesdropping, he decided it was best to find another phone. He went across the street, found a pay phone in an old deserted warehouse and called me.

I told him the big news, and Luci's desire for a midnight announcement and asked him to call the press together then and inform them. This seemed to be the quickest way to get it done, and also the way to be fair to all reporters spending their holidays and their newspapers' money covering LBJ in Texas.

"Look, Liz," argued Joe who was totally unmoved by the glad tidings. "I wish this story could wait until morning. In the first place, it's going to be hard to lay our hands on all the reporters at this hour, particularly those being laid. For another thing, there are so many rumors going around about a cease-fire in Vietnam, that a press call will make them think something is underway."

"Tell them it's a tryst, not a truce!" I demanded and continued to dictate the release. When I got to the "baguette" diamonds, I had to spell that word three times.

Suddenly both of us were convulsed with the humor of the situation.

Neither of us in all our days of journalism ever foresaw that our jobs would lead us to a Christmas Eve midnight announcement of the first White House wedding in fifty years. But the announcement was only the beginning, and Luci's story was page one on Christmas Day.

Crisis Number 2: *Beware of Gifts*

Soon after the announcement, it became apparent that we needed to set some rules to discourage gifts for the bride. Phone calls from foreign embassies wanting "advice" on what their Heads of State should give, letters from commercial firms wanting to bestow a whole electric kitchen on the bride and then advertise it, and an array of sweet hand-crocheted doilies —made by sweet little ladies with romantic hearts—began coming in by the dozens.

Bess Abell, the social secretary, and I were getting most of the heat in letters and phone calls; and we needed guidelines, what could be accepted and what couldn't. The press seemed to envision Kings and Queens arriving for the nuptials preceded by footmen bearing golden chalices and jewel-encrusted wedding plates. Part of the reason was the published reports of Alice Roosevelt's gifts when she married Nicholas Longworth in 1906.

I called Mrs. Longworth for advice. *There* was a credibility gap for you. "I only wish I'd gotten all those things they said I got," she said tartly.

We corralled Clark Clifford, prominent Washington attorney and a friend of the Johnson family, and went into a series of summit meetings that produced the guidelines which I was to discreetly leak to a "trustworthy source."

The Chief of Protocol was to discourage foreign governments from giving gifts and to advise their governments that it was a family, not a State, event. (There went that word "affair" again.) No gifts or visits were expected.

Gifts from strangers which had intrinsic value would be returned with a polite note. Gifts from close friends would be accepted. All gifts from commercial firms would be returned. The doilies and potholders made by little old ladies would be accepted and answered personally. (Mrs. Johnson had a weakness for not hurting any of the little ladies.)

Crisis Number 3: *My War with* Women's Wear Daily

Press interest began building to a crescendo! Hard as we tried to keep from saturating newspapers with advance stories, there was frenzy among wedding-minded reporters at the White House, long before the wedding date.

Magazines wanted layouts in January for their June bridal issues. Why couldn't Luci dash out, select her china and silver and wedding dress to suit their deadlines? This way they could carry the pictures of the bride in her gown in their June issues.

Even *The New York Times* chose to remind me of the important fashion news the wedding provided. Charlotte Curtis, women's editor, wrote me two months before the wedding: "I do hope you know we can hardly wait to report who designed all the clothes and what they will look like. This is a major fashion event, as well as a social event of the most historic sort."

Not to be outdone, I wrote her back a sarcastic note: "Isn't it funny? All this time I've been thinking of Luci's wedding, not as a major fashion event, but a major romantic event.

Oh well, it just goes to show how corny you can get here in the provinces."

Networks wanted to televise the whole thing. Even without consulting us, they made surveys of the National Shrine of the Immaculate Conception, the church Luci selected for the wedding, to check camera positions and lighting.

Reporters tried to interview bridesmaids, potential bridesmaids, groomsmen and the best man—and their families—and members of the clergy.

Speculation on all wedding clothes was the daily fare of the fashion houses in New York. And *Women's Wear Daily,* with its network of informants, both good and bad, could have given a few tips to the CIA.

Luci began to wonder whose wedding it was. While she had always been sympathetic to my problem of satisfying press needs, there were just some things a girl believes she should call her own. Being a traditionalist, young and the most sentimental of brides, she wanted to keep her wedding gown a secret from her groom. And I was determined to defend her right to observe the old admonition that a groom must not see his bride's gown until the wedding day.

Meanwhile the newspaper girls were demanding to know when they would know details.

Monsignor Thomas J. Grady, director of the National Shrine of the Immaculate Conception, called in amazement to say that Isabelle Shelton, one of the most able and knowledgeable reporters for *The Washington Star,* had invaded the Shrine, scene of the wedding, armed with a pad and pencil and hundreds of questions on the wedding plans.

"I think," the Monsignor said to me placidly, "you should design the wedding dress with a large hoop skirt so that Mrs. Shelton can run down the aisle under it making notes all the way." I adored the Monsignor—if that's permissible. He had the problems and the patience of Job. If we had let Isabelle run down the aisle as the Monsignor jokingly suggested, she might not have been alone. We also had a request from a German newspaper correspondent who wanted to interview the President during the wedding march. I wrote a memo to Bob Fleming, the President's assistant press secretary: "Gladly do I pass along this request. Now I have heard everything. He wants to interview him walking down the aisle." The request was not granted.

Obviously, order had to be brought into this free-for-all. Bess Abell was coordinating the bridal party's clothes, and so I worked out a press release schedule in conjunction with the clothes delivery dates. At the press's request, we put a penalty on anyone breaking the release date: no pass to the wedding area. This, the press said, would stop the bootleg reporting.

On June 20, I summoned the reporters together and put out the release schedule in an effort to say, "Relax girls, you're going to be treated fairly." It read in part as follows:

NOT FOR PUBLICATION
FOR GUIDELINE PURPOSES ONLY

In answer to inquiries and to accommodate your summer planning, the following dates are earmarked for stories in connection with the wedding of Luci Baines Johnson and Patrick John Nugent.

July 17, Sunday: Bridesmaids dresses and flowers. (Sketches and detailed descriptions will be available on Wednesday, July 13 to accommodate Sunday layouts.) Any publication breaking the release date on either the sketch or the description will automatically be excluded from working press area and denied credentials for wedding coverage.

The action brought instant relief to my assistants who had been performing like switchboard operators on twenty-four-hour duty. It brought instant irritation to *Women's Wear Daily*. Most of the press were happy. They could begin to see the light at the end of the tunnel. And no one would be scooped in the interim.

*Women's Wear Daily* was off like a tiger in heat, stalking the clothing houses of the East Coast in search of the scoop on style, color, designer and price. They purposely skipped my July 13 press conference when I gave advance details of the bridesmaids' dresses for July 17 release—and according to their code of ethics—thus freed themselves from my promise to ban any violators from the wedding. And possibly, guillotine them on the Mall!

That night several newswomen who were covering the story—and staying with the rules—phoned to tell me that they had been called by *Women's Wear Daily* to glean the details. Small surprise that *Women's Wear Daily* came out with a near description two days before the story was scheduled for release.

Hell hath no fury like a press secretary scorned! To my mind, a hold-for-release is a hold-for-release, whether or not the reporter is in attendance. I banned them from the wedding—publicly spanking them and stating there is no reason to throw chaos into Sunday newspaper layouts all over the country because of the "unethical behavior of one small publication."

The war had begun! The battle lines were drawn.

*Women's Wear Daily* editor Jim Brady, who must be descended from early shareholders in Western Union, started sending voluminous telegrams blasting me and the White House, and graciously made copies of his messages available to the wire service and networks.

*Women's Wear Daily* even quizzed the President about the decision to exclude their reporters.

Some newspapers, eagerly looking for copy to break the summertime pace, jumped on me. *The Washington Post* worried that I had "bridal jitters."

Bless the President, the First Lady and Luci! They never uttered one word to me, despite the furor, and simply left the matter to my judgment.

Much of the mail berated me for making such a fuss over a small thing "when our boys are fighting in Vietnam."

I have no regrets . . . only a few saddle sores from riding it out. Certainly nations weren't going to rise or fall over Luci's "pink-pink" bridesmaids' dresses.

I am not good at holding grudges, and my blood pressure no longer soars when *Women's Wear Daily* shows up. But this incident did introduce me to a new brand of mischief-making reporting—a brand I have seen reappear on some of the women's pages of major newspapers. I only hope it doesn't close the doors which have been opened by many hardworking newswomen throughout the years.

With all our energies and time devoted to the wedding, the bride's dress, and the pink-pink bridesmaids gowns, Bess Abell and I had no time to think of what we would wear on that day.

"Don't even give it a thought," said Adele Simpson, the pint-sized, soft-spoken designer who was frequently in the White House planning Mrs. Johnson's dress.

Keeping her word, she appeared a few days before the wedding and while we had our ears on the phone, she pinned and fitted our wedding day dresses, hats and shoes. They were perfect.

Crisis Number 4: *I Was Martyred for St. Agatha*

The closest I may ever get to Heaven are the two frantic weeks I spent in search of a saint. Not just any old saint! Luci, alas, selected an obscure saint, whom we ultimately established to be St. Agatha, the patron saint of nursing.

At the time of her engagement, Luci was studying nursing at Georgetown University. One of her teachers, who had a flair for public relations, suggested that it would be very nice if Luci left her bridal bouquet at the feet of the patron saint of nursing, instead of the Virgin Mary. To an old psalm-singing Methodist like me, the idea of a bouquet gift to a saint was an education anyway. In my church, brides take their bouquets with them and toss them to the most conspicuous old maid in the family. But Catholics, I learned, have a traditional moment when the bride and groom are departing the church. The bride leaves her bouquet at the foot of the nearest Virgin Mary and then departs with the groom. If she wants to toss another bouquet, she has a surplus bouquet handy for this purpose.

Luci's wish presented difficulties for a variety of reasons: establishing who was the patron saint of nursing, finding the replica, getting enough bouquets to satisfy both Luci and Dorothy Territo, the string-saver of LBJ papers and memorabilia. Mrs. Territo also had her eye on Luci's bouquet to preserve for the LBJ Library.

We ended up with several saints and three bouquets.

Searching for the patron saint of nursing was, if you'll forgive the expression, like looking for the Holy Grail. But I had as my ally Monsignor Grady.

"Monsignor," I said, for we were on very chummy terms by now, "how can we find out who is the patron saint of nursing?"

"That's no problem at all, Liz," he said. "I'll just look in my 'Who's Who of Saints'—I've got one in my library—and call you back."

In ten minutes, he was back on the phone. "Well, there is a slight problem," he said. "There are seven patron saints of nursing, four of whom are men."

"Pick a woman and tell me about her," I replied.

He did, and a more ghoulish biography I had never heard. In ancient Sicily, Agatha, a girl of noble birth who was sworn to chastity, refused to yield to a lecherous Roman official. So he had her tortured, using the Emperor's edict against Christianity as an excuse.

Even after being mutilated, Agatha refused to give in. To top it all off, she was rolled in hot coals, but she still would not die. Then, according to one version of the story, a well-timed earthquake put an end to these indignities, and eventually she went on to her reward.

I could see why she had become the patron saint of nursing, for if ever a girl needed a Band-Aid, she was it.

Bess Abell and I were both convinced that seventeen centuries later Agatha really deserved some attention, so we set about to find her statue for the big day.

I made phone calls to every church in town. Nowhere in Washington was St. Agatha to be found. I also enlisted the help of Monsignor Grady who had a lot more pipelines in this direction than I did. He finally gave up and asked me to come out to the Shrine and take a look at their craft shop where they sold all sorts of saints.

"Most saints are really just symbolic," the Monsignor told me, waving toward the shelves of male and female statues with beatific expressions. "As a matter of fact, we have a lot of pretty nondescript saints here. Just pick one and we can place it on the altar."

I was shocked. "Why, Monsignor," I replied, "you are contributing to the credibility gap!"

The *Catholic Standard*'s reporter, Sheila Nelson, had located a rehabilitated St. Agatha at the Franciscan Monastery in Washington.

Their statue of St. Agatha had originally been St. Philomena, but had been repainted into Agatha when Philomena was stricken from the list of saints.

I could just imagine what would happen if we used this Agatha and the story leaked out. The headlines would be: "Saint Whitewashed for Wedding." So the search continued.

Meanwhile, back at the White House, the President's barber, Steve Martini, told me he had found St. Agatha in Brooklyn at a relative's church. "She stands five feet high and we can quietly borrow her if we can return her by Sunday," Martini said.

I started checking shipping charges on saints, and was secretly hoping this would work out because it would be the first time in history that a saint had been produced from a Martini.

Bess was much more practical in her search. She dismissed my Brooklyn Agatha "because she's the wrong size saint."

Meanwhile, she had given up locating an appropriate Agatha and simply decided to have one made to her own specifications.

Two sculpture artisans at the National Gallery of Art were busy shaping up two saints, one in bronze and one in plaster. In addition, the *National Geographic* had located a picture of St. Agatha which they were reproducing in beautiful color tints. The picture would be framed and Luci would choose between sculpture and painting.

In reproducing St. Agatha, her lurid past kept posing a problem. She is most frequently portrayed with pincers in her hand and two bosoms lying on a tray. Bess thought this highly inappropriate for a wedding; so she just left the pincers in hand and skipped the bosoms.

Luci finally selected the picture of St. Agatha for the altar but Bess found the new bronze replica so aesthetic she slipped it on the altar, too.

Some day in the Great Beyond, I hope I meet the real St. Agatha and tell her about our sacrifice.

Crisis Number 5: *In Union There Is Strength*

Maybe Republicans in office don't have much trouble with their nuptials. But the Democratic Party, the workingman's friend, has so many ties of heart and tradition to organized labor, that it is hard to turn your back on them.

Take Jacob Potofsky, the president of the Amalgamated Clothing Workers of America, and the only labor leader I know who looks like an ad for Colonel Sanders' Kentucky Fried Chicken.

Once, back in our Vice Presidential days, Mrs. Johnson was seated at dinner next to Mr. Potofsky. She found him absolutely delightful and was enchanted when he told her, "You have no idea how much you ladies in the news influence fashion and affect our economy."

He pointed out that it was—alas—a hatless era, that none of the Kennedy women were wearing hats, and it had a telling effect on jobs among the milliners.

Hats were out of fashion at the time due to the popular Jackie bouffant hairdos, but Mrs. Johnson never forgot Mr. Potofsky and about every third event, she would say, "I'll wear a hat today for Mr. Potofsky."

That was the thinking that lay behind our dilemma in the Great Luci Wedding Dress Crisis. Through Stanley Marcus of Dallas, we had obtained Priscilla of Boston to design and produce Luci's wedding dress. And, after looking over many designs, Luci picked *the one*. Now, to get it made!

Priscilla had been designing wedding dresses, I suspected, since John Alden and the original Priscilla. She is a pretty, prim New Englander—and was the match for the AFL-CIO organizer who started riding, like Paul Revere, all over Boston sounding the alarm: "Priscilla is a nonunion shop." The echoes reverberated through the trade press and clear back to the ears of David Dubinsky of International Ladies' Garment

Workers Union fame, in New York. Mr. Dubinsky is an emotional man who literally wept over the phone when confronted with the thought that his good friend, the President of the United States, would let his daughter marry in a gown without a union label.

Poor President! Poor Luci! Poor nimble-fingered nonunion ladies who were sewing on pearls!

We leaned on the wise and able James Reynolds, Assistant Secretary of Labor. He welcomed this happy problem as an escape from the meat-cutters negotiations, now in the cleaver-for-cleaver stage.

One solution was a suggestion that Priscilla yield and join the Union. "Absolutely not," said Priscilla. "I pay higher than Union wages."

The next solution suggested was that we should choose another dress! This put Bess Abell on the couch reaching for tranquilizers. She could not bear to think she would have to go through the long tedious selection process again. Besides, Luci *liked* the dress.

The third solution was to hang Stanley Marcus from the nearest tree for not warning us about this problem. But he was too likeable for that, and besides we all had handy charge accounts at his store.

So, we negotiated a compromise. Priscilla allowed the dress to be "assembled" at a nearby Union shop, and her own talented artisans did the beadwork which Union machines cannot do. This didn't please anyone completely, but Dave Dubinsky stopped crying, Priscilla kept her employees happy, Luci got a gown, and Bess and I survived.

We posted a poem of the week: *The bride wore something borrowed, something blue—and a label from ILGWU.*

This was not to be the end of the union problem.

August 6—the wedding day—loomed on the weatherman's

calendar as a day when the Washington temperature would top 90 degrees. A sweltering Saturday was in store, and, as Marie Smith pointed out in *The Washington Post,* "There is no air conditioning in the Shrine."

Out of the blue, and in the middle of an airline strike, a United Airlines representative called to say, "We've read in the papers about the temperature problem at the church. We should be glad to help. Our blowers, which air-condition the planes on the ground, are just idling out there at the airport during the strike. We could turn the blowers into the doors of the Shrine the night before and have it nice and cool for the ceremony."

This sounded like a good offer, but I asked for time to check it out with our bridal consultant, Clark Clifford, to see if we could accept such assistance.

Clark thought the suggestion was acceptable, and I proceeded to map out the invasion of air-conditioning units to arrive at 6 P.M. Friday, August 5, the night before the wedding. At that hour the last Mass would be over. We would be moving telephone equipment into the crypt—our makeshift press room for the five hundred reporters covering the event. And the mobile blowers could be driven from United's hangars to the church and go to blowing.

Marcia Maddox, a member of my staff, headed for the Shrine, walkie-talkie in hand, to get these complicated operations underway. I was still answering queries and trying to go home and dress and get back to handle Luci's rehearsal dinner.

The phone rang and it was James Reynolds of the Labor Department. There was a note of alarm in his voice.

"I have a tip that United Airlines is lending you blowers to air-condition the church."

I confirmed this, and he—as politely as a man who has just

left the meat-cutters for the airline negotiations could—let me know this was a terrible idea.

"I'm going to check with Bill Wirtz," I told him and promptly put in a call to his superior, the Secretary of Labor.

About this time my alarm button—three rings if it's the President—sounded, and You-Know-Who was on the phone.

The President asked me if the rumor about the blowers was true. "Yes," I replied. "Did it ever occur to you to check with someone?" His voice implied I was the dumbest woman in the world.

I confidently told him that I had checked with Clark Clifford.

"That's not enough, you should have checked with Bill Wirtz," he said.

"I'm trying," I replied. "But it's going to be hot in that church."

"Well, check it out," he said, "and if we have to sit there and sweat, that's just what we'll have to do."

I frantically tried again to reach Secretary Wirtz, who was still in his limousine en route home. Meanwhile I could visualize the airline trucks descending on the Shrine where TV cameras were already in place. I called on the Lord please not to let those cameras be hooked up or we would be all over the networks with our "struck" airline trucks showing.

When Secretary Wirtz and I finally got together, he was immovable.

"No! No! I know it's tough, but this strike affects 35,000 men. Feelings are high. Negotiations are difficult. All we need is a struck airline truck photographed at the President's daughter's wedding. Call them off!"

I let out a very unbride-like oath and grabbed a walkie-talkie.

"Shrine, Shrine, come in Shrine," I yelled. "Do you read me Shrine?" I was calling my assistant, Marcia Maddox.

"This is Marcia at the Shrine," came the welcome voice. Marcia was in the crypt of the Shrine directing the electricians.

"Are the air-conditioning men there yet?" I asked.

"No, but they are on their way, somewhere in Rock Creek Park," she replied.

"You aren't going to believe what I am about to tell you, Marcia, but just don't ask any questions and follow instructions exactly," I said. "Get the Park Police and turn those trucks around and send them back to the airport."

"You've got to be kidding," she replied.

"Do it and don't argue—and then go to a phone and call me so we can talk privately," I said.

To her eternal credit she did just that. She countered the whole invasion of United trucks with Park Police, turned them around, and they never reached the Shrine. That girl will go to Heaven for sure!

Back at my office, I could just visualize how confused the drivers of the mobile blowers must have been to see the fleet of Park Service police cars converging on them.

I dictated a terse message to the President: "Mission accomplished. We'll just sit there and sweat."

Then, I headed for home, ankles swollen, nerves frayed, limp with the accumulation of eight months of pre-nuptial torture. I had grown to hate love. But I only had eighteen more hours to go until Luci walked down the aisle. I couldn't believe it when the car radio came on, "Is Springtime in car 17?" Springtime, bah! That was my Secret Service code name, but at this moment I felt like dead winter.

"Ask her to call the President's office on her arrival."

I did, and would you believe that this was the message: "Liz, the President says for you to find an airline that isn't struck that has blowers. Try to get them to air condition the Shrine."

Down with labor! Down with Presidents!

So I phoned Warren Woodward, our longtime friend and the American Airlines representative. "Look, Woody," I said, "you've always been known as a can-do man, and this is the test."

I outlined the problem.

"Liz," said Woody, as though he were talking to an idiot child. "*We* are not struck and we are *using* our blowers. Does that answer your question?"

Well, that's the way we didn't blow the wedding.

Even LBJ had to take that for an answer. But wouldn't you know that Bill Wirtz, who made me go through this whole routine, came *late* to the wedding? He knew that church would be hot!

*Miscellaneous Luci Crises*

I don't want any one to get the idea that those were the only crises in Luci's wedding. The others were just smaller and more easily solved. For instance, a James Nugent was arrested for disorderly conduct two days before the wedding by the Florida police. Luckily, he was not one of "our" Nugents, but for a few hours the press was sure he was.

For instance, even the wedding date, August 6, provided a crisis. Hardly had it been announced before a group of Japanese pacifists protested because it was the anniversary of the day the atom bomb had been dropped on Hiroshima. The American Embassy in Japan notified the White House Situation Room (home of the Hot Line). Bromley Smith of the National Security staff called me, nervously wondering if we could change the date.

"Yes," I replied hotly. "We'll change it to December 7, the day the Japanese bombed us."

In a calmer voice I argued, "Don't you know that a girl

sets her wedding date for reasons quite apart from politics. And you tell our ambassador that!"

"That's not a bad answer," Bromley said. "I'll let Tokyo know."

But this was not the end of the problem. American pickets, encouraged by their Japanese brethren, showed up at the Shrine to protest the bride, the date and the father of the bride. But there was too much action elsewhere for them to get much attention.

For instance, Speaker of the House, John W. McCormack, tried to solve the recurrent press question, "What is the Congress going to give Luci?" by letting any member who wished to do so contribute $5 toward a gift for her. Even this voluntary effort drew rage and public rebuke from H. R. Gross, Iowa Republican and self-appointed critic of expenditure. The flap appeared in print—our first inkling of any Congressional gift. Luci respectfully asked the Speaker to withdraw the gift. H. R. Gross scored again! He managed to embarrass a young girl, hurt the President's feelings, infuriate 435 members of Congress and still not save one cent of the taxpayers' money.

There were many other sidelights the public never heard about—for instance, our walkie-talkie network. Walkie-talkies were essential to run a wedding held in the sixth largest church in the United States. It was possible to coordinate the choir's first note, the bell tower's first peal, and the temperamental organist by having members of Bess Abell's staff stationed in each place with a walkie-talkie. As the wedding bells gave their last peal at high noon, the walkie-talkie in the bell tower notified the organ walkie-talkie which notified the choir to begin.

For instance, Marie Antoinette may have said, "Let them eat cake." I certainly never will utter those words about a wedding cake without realizing what is involved. For Luci's wedding, we planned to have a nosegay of fresh lilies-of-the-valley on top of the cake. But a hardworking government employee read this in the newspaper and frantically called me at the White House.

"Not fresh lily-of-the-valley," she said. "Don't you know that fresh lily-of-the-valley is poisonous. If its juices should drop on the cake, they can cause hallucinations, coma, staggering, loss of memory, and the partaker is apt to wander about in a strange manner." This concerned bureaucrat documented her worry by citing a recent government bulletin with this information.

So we solved this problem by spraying the lily-of-the-valley with plastic. If any of the wedding guests had hallucinations, it wasn't due to the dripping lily-of-the-valley.

Another ridiculous thing I remember is the sight of two well-known TV commentators, Martin Agronsky and Herb Kaplow, crawling on hands and knees to interview pint-sized ring bearer, Corky Hand.

For instance, the last-minute discovery that the wedding invitations read: "The Shrine of the Immaculate Conception," instead of "the National Shrine . . ." A quick re-engraving job had to be done.

For instance, our hurried press release on the wedding day with a typographical error. "Priscilla of Boston taught the bridesmaid how to *sin* in the car" when all she taught them was how to *sit* in the car.

A summer of rioting reporters came to an end in a matter of forty-two minutes before the altar of the Shrine. A timetable given by NBC's Ray Scherer to the eagerly waiting press is not much to show for eight months of hard labor in the Hell Department. Mr. Scherer summed it up like this:

12 noon The choir sang "Alleluia."
12:04 Mrs. Nugent was escorted up the aisle.

12:05 Hale Boggs, Archbishop O'Boyle and clergymen enter at the right of church.

12:08 The groomsmen came up the aisle by two's, 20 feet apart. The organ was fortissimo.

12:09 The bridesmaids came down the aisle singly. Phyllis Nugent leading.

12:13 and 15 seconds—Corky Hand came up the aisle with a bemused expression on his face.

12:14 Bedar Howar, the tiny flower girl, came up the aisle.

12:15 Luci came up the aisle very slowly. Luci nodded to friends as she walked by. The President was walking very straight. He nodded to the Vice-President on the left on the way in.

12:18 All the wedding party was in.

12:19 The President delivered Luci to Pat at the altar, both kneel.

12:20 The Mass began.

12:25 Hale Boggs read the Epistle.

12:34 The Gospel was read.

12:35 The Exhortation.

12:40 The Sacrament began.

12:41 The vows "I do." Luci and Pat were inaudible.

12:42 The priest said "I join you to sacred wedlock."

After the wedding everyone returned to the White House for the reception. There was dancing in the East Room until 6 P.M. Every crumb of cake was devoured. And Luci—ecstatic—was dressed in her going-away outfit. She called me into her room where she was packing. "Thanks, Liz," she said and hugged me and handed me a box. In it was a gold bracelet with a single jeweled charm, engraved on the back, with these words: "For immediate release, I'm grateful to Liz. LJN 8/6/66"

One daughter down, one to go!

Lynda didn't get married until almost a year and a half later—thank God for small favors. And, compared to Luci's wedding, Lynda's was a breeze. Bess and I had learned with one White House wedding and could foresee the problems. Also the press had felt fairly well treated, and they weren't as restless. They knew there would be certain announcements, a pool, and we'd all live through it.

For several months after Luci's wedding, the George Hamilton story brought lots of questions to the office. Lynda and George popped in and out of the better showplaces—Hollywood openings, Acapulco, the LBJ Ranch and the White House. They made a handsome couple—tall, dark and glamorous.

The press gave George a hard time, chiding him first, because his movies got more attention than they had in his pre-Lynda days. Then they began heckling him about his military service record. They also darkly hinted that the President was anti-George.

The treatment was wretchedly unfair to George Hamilton. He always behaved as a gentleman and, to my knowledge, avoided every opportunity to exploit his friendship with the President and his daughter. He called me on several occasions when reporters were clamoring for interviews, and asked my counsel on how to subdue them. I, of course, was not in the business of guiding George Hamilton's press relations, but it illustrates his courtesy—and the lengths he went not to "use" his friendship with Lynda to foster his own career.

The President never interfered in George's and Lynda's friendship, and months later when columnists insinuated that the President was delighted that Lynda had not married George, LBJ was indignant.

"The press is trying to hurt George," the President said. "Call him and tell him that I never tried to direct Lynda's marriage in any way whatsoever. She's the one who has to spend a lifetime with her choice. Not me. And tell him that I have always liked him and respected him." I was touched that the President would take the time to do this, but he had been treated unfairly before and he was sympathetic.

I made the call. It was deeply appreciated by a young man who had been a glamorous and considerate escort in Lynda's life.

Meanwhile, the Marines had landed at the White House. One new addition was tall, good-looking, twenty-eight-year-old Captain "Chuck" Robb who led the White House Color Guard. He caught the eye and the interest of the President's daughter and vice versa. Bridge playing, dancing and weekends at nearby Rehoboth Beach, Delaware, increased. The press got wind of it, which created traffic jams and more attention than this sleepy beachside resort had ever received.

The Rehoboth Beach city fathers were delighted. The President's daughter was *not.* She wanted her own privacy and plotted at length with the Secret Service to keep her dates with Chuck top secret. Some of Chuck's colleagues among the White House social aides were less cooperative! They loved being included in the publicity, and leaked each excursion to the Washington papers.

I took a know-nothing attitude about the whole romance because I thought it was Lynda's own business, and, also, because romances of young couples just don't grab a forty-seven-year-old press secretary who is more interested in social welfare than social events. In my subconscious mind, I may have been trying to fend off what romance might lead to—another White House wedding, and all the work and headaches it entailed.

But one weekend, the Labor Day weekend, when Newport society opens its door and its wine cellars for the America's Cup Regatta, my husband and I were ready to live it up as houseguests of the James Van Alens in Newport, Rhode Island.

*Enter Crisis Number 6—Another White House Bride!*

The phone call from the ranch caught me just as I was between bath and evening gown, preparing to attend a party for the King of Greece in Newport.

"Liz," said Mrs. Johnson on the phone, "are you ready for another wedding?"

"No," I replied, ungraciously but honestly.

"Well, take a firm grip on both sides of your chair," continued Mrs. Johnson cheerfully, "and I'll put Lynda and Chuck on the phone."

So we were at it again! Lynda and Chuck wanted the engagement announced promptly because they were going to San Antonio to see Lynda's great friend, Warrie Lynn Smith. The press might get wind of the rumor instead of the firm announcement.

I got the meager details and remember asking two questions of Chuck, whom I knew only slightly.

"Are you a Catholic?" I asked.

"No, I'm an Episcopalian," he said.

"That's a relief," I said.

It's not that I'm a bigot, but frankly, a complicated Church in the midst of ecumenical indecisions, just plays havoc with an inquisitive press.

I searched my mind for any questions reporters would ask when I broke the news to the world—and quickly recalled there had been stories that Chuck would go to Vietnam.

"Does this in any way alter your plans to go to Vietnam?" I asked him.

"Absolutely not!" he replied. "I asked for duty in Vietnam, and I intend to serve in Vietnam."

They proposed to marry in December, and Chuck would be headed into combat in the spring. This sounded a poignant note in an otherwise happy announcement, but I wanted the situation made clear from the outset, so no mischief-making reporter could write or even hint that this marriage was motivated to change Chuck's assignment.

The news was followed by the frantic business of trying to reach the wire services simultaneously for a conference call announcement. Again, I was glad to be married to a newsman who zipped up my dress, and placed the phone calls for me. An added dividend was that Candy Van Alen, our hostess, is a former newswoman with the New York *Herald Tribune*, who helped me locate members of the national press corps down in Newport for the weekend.

The news was on the air within an hour, and I set off for the Wiley Buchanans' dinner dance for King Constantine and Queen Anne-Marie. Lynda had attended their wedding in Greece, so they were happy to hear the glad tidings.

Lynda's wedding plans and the crises involved were much less trying than Luci's. The time span was shorter. Lynda was engaged three months, Luci eight, so there was a briefer period to build up hysteria.

None of us was nearly as uptight as we had been before. Bess now *knew* it was necessary to locate a union-shop dressmaker from the start. So it was Geoffrey Beane and Cyril Magnin who performed the honors. The White House was air-conditioned, and besides, the wedding was in December so we had no repeat of the "church blower" problem. And Lynda and Chuck, several years older than Luci and Pat, were not easy prey for exploitation by enthusiastic hostesses.

The press was just as plentiful, however.

The week before the wedding, five hundred reporters descended on the White House to cover the event. We had a briefing each day at 9:15 A.M. and 4:30 P.M. alternately, and tried to make them as pleasant as possible by calling them "Love-ins." I wore various buttons each day reading "Marine Power," "Love," "I'll Never Tell," and usually opened the briefing with long-range weather forecasts for the wedding day, including wind velocity, temperature range and chance of rain and snow.

Our chef, Henry Haller, and housekeeper, Mary Kaltman, would arrive at the briefings with samples of the hot dishes of Quiche Lorraine, miniature shish kebab, country ham with biscuits and other delicacies slated for the wedding reception table.

Our object was to keep everyone smiling until the big day. Some of the briefings prompted hilarious questions like the day I announced the recipe for the wedding cake, a 250-pound old-fashioned pound cake. "The top tier will include raisins soaked in fruit juice," I explained. Norma Milligan of *Newsweek* spoke up. "How many raisins in the wedding cake?"

"I don't know," I said, "but I'll find out."

At the next briefing, I was prepared. I produced a cellophane bag containing 1 and 1/4 pounds of raisins—the amount used in the cake. To get even, I named Norma head of a "pool" to count the raisins, and invited everyone to join a ten cent lottery and guess how many. It took Norma two days to count the raisins, but she came back with the answer: 1511 raisins. The winner of the pool was Malvina Stevenson of *Editor and Publisher*, who guessed 1600. She went home from that love-in richer by $3.90.

A few days before the wedding, Captain Robb agreed to see the press. Everyone who had asked to interview him was notified of the hour and place—2 P.M. in the bachelor quarters of the Marine Barracks, where he lived. One of the biggest blizzards in history hit Washington that afternoon, but it didn't deter more than a hundred zealous reporters from trudging to the Marine Barracks to meet the captain.

He sat there straight, tall and handsome, surrounded by females of varying ages who wanted to know: What are the requirements of being a good Marine wife? What do you think of George Hamilton? What do you think about a Marine's wife working? Can Lynda cook? Why do you want to go to Vietnam? How do you really feel about Lynda?

He must have thought about using his Marine saber at least once before the afternoon was over, but he won the battle hands down. Smooth, genuine, a real man!

Unfailingly polite, most of his answers to the barrage of female questioners were: "Yes, ma'm," "No, ma'm," and "Oh, boy!"

But there was a duty-officer decisiveness about him, too.

"I haven't given Lynda any instructions on being a good Marine wife. I am marrying a girl who is well qualified to be a wife under any circumstances. I don't feel any specific instructions are necessary."

"I think George Hamilton is a very, very fine gentleman. If you are looking for something adverse, I certainly have nothing adverse."

"I wouldn't object if Lynda continued working after our marriage. In a lot of cases and in Lynda's case, she has a very keen mind and a flair for writing and creativity."

"Lynda's cooking ability is progressing nicely. We both understood that neither of us was marrying a gourmet cook."

"I am a Marine officer. That is our stock-in-trade. I feel I have an obligation to go, and I will take whatever duty is assigned me and try to do it to the best of my ability."

"I was first attracted to Lynda by her physical beauty and

her very keen mind. She is very perceptive and just a delightful person to be with, who has a good sense of humor and is always interesting."

The captain got A-plus from his inquisitors—and his future father-in-law who read the transcript with new admiration.

The week before the wedding was threaded with announcements about the bridesmaids, the parties, the sixpence for the shoe, the decorations of topiary trees filled with hundreds of twinkling white lights.

The pressure increased for invitations. Bess Abell would receive perfume, flowers, notes with the *hint,* "You know I haven't seen you in so long . . ." from friends and strangers who wanted an invitation. Then, one well-known Washington hostess called tearfully to demand an invitation and even reminded us how much money she had contributed to the beautification program in Washington. Bess stood firm.

There were more last minute details. Bess obtained twenty sets of smelling salts in case someone standing at the crowded ceremony fainted. And we borrowed several tiny walkie-talkies—about the size of a cigarette lighter—like the ones used by the CIA, so the spell of the wedding wouldn't be ruined by the larger equipment we usually employed on trips. They were so small that when we spoke into them an observer thought the whole event had gone to our brain and we were talking to ourselves.

We assigned our fifteen-man pool to strategic locations and designated various reporters for the Crossed Swords Pool, the Wedding Cake Pool, the East Room Pool and the Foot-of-the-Stairs Pool. Closed circuit television made it possible for all five hundred reporters gathered in the East Wing press room, complete with champagne, to cover the ceremony.

There was room for one small reporter behind the altar, so Bonnie Angelo of *Time* magazine, size 5 and weight 97 lbs., 5 feet tall, was selected.

"I've worked hard all my life to be a brainy, capable journalist," Bonnie wailed, "and I owe my selection for this important position to my mini-size."

The pool reports were full of delicious tidbits for history. Phyllis Battelle of the King Features Syndicate, who was part of the Crossed Swords Pool, gave this report.

PHYLLIS: I don't think my crossed swords coverage is very good.

QUESTION: Did they go over them or under them?

PHYLLIS: They went under them. That part I do know. I was so busy watching George Hamilton . . . if anyone is interested in George.

QUESTION: Yes, George, baby.

PHYLLIS: He was located on the right side of the hall as the bridal couple came out. It seemed all the movie people were out in the hall. Carol Channing, Merle Oberon, George and the Ford girls. It appeared to me the Fords were trying to cheer him up. He looked quite grim throughout. Maybe he just looks grim ordinarily, but he looked extremely grim to me. On the way out, Luci looked at him, smiled and winked.

Joe Garagiola, who claimed he came to cover the wedding because marriage is a sport, asked: "Which eye?"

QUESTION: How about the swords?

PHYLLIS: They are lovely. They shine.

Among the great American public there are always the pack-rats, even at White House weddings, and Lynda's was no exception. When the time came to give out the favors—tiny heartshaped boxes containing a piece of the cake—one member of Congress who had had too much champagne simply packed his coat with about fifteen boxes.

An adroit White House secretary, Margaret Deeb, helped him slip into his coat with one hand while filching the boxes back with the other. He never knew until he got home.

The couple was off for a honeymoon. Two daughters down, none to go.

Western Union called me to say that on the wedding day alone, 25,300 words were filed over their wires; UPI sent 5500 words and 38 pictures; AP sent 3750 words and 60 pictures; *National Geographic* transmitted 350 prints to news agencies from Moscow to Tokyo.

Of such details are White House weddings made!

# *Memo-Rabilia*

The average citizen probably thinks that White House interoffice memos are full of weighty information, succinct prose, perfectly typed in quadruplicate and marked *EYES ONLY*. Well, some of them are, but in the Johnson Administration, the day's mail was often brightened by memos from some of the humorous people on the staff.

We did things by memo, in addition to or instead of by telephone, because it was safer to have something in writing in case the subject arose later. Of course, occasionally, a subject arose later to haunt you and make you wish you'd never put your name to that piece of paper.

Memoranda gave us a chance to let off steam, vent our wrath or display our sense of humor. Memos were also the way to reach the President. He devoured his night reading file, and you could be sure you got the attention of the man at the top if you made your message interesting enough. Sometimes, I would shortcut his secretaries and simply leave a memo on his pillow. My access to the family quarters made this easy and surer.

Here are some samples from my files which illustrate the variety of immortal activities that crossed my desk:

THE WHITE HOUSE

MEMORANDUM March 4, 1965

To: The President
From: Liz

Anna Rosenberg called today to suggest you might like to have Walter Lippmann in for a talk alone.

"He's too modest to ask to see the President," Anna said, "but I saw him the other night and he said he hadn't seen you alone in a long time."

Do you want to see him?

Yes____ No_X_ (checked by LBJ)

When we were preparing for a trip to rugged Big Bend National Park, I noticed that the more I talked about panthers and other wild animals to be found there, the more reporters signed up for the trip. The President teased me about my panther stories and said they were contributing to the credibility gap. After the trip, I wrote to the President:

THE WHITE HOUSE

MEMORANDUM

To: The President
From: Liz

Don't tell me those panther stories don't pay off. Buck Newsom, who runs the horse riding concession at Big Bend National Park, was in town recently and said that since the First Lady's visit there, his business has gone up 35 per cent over last year. And she didn't even ride a horse!

In reply, I got a handwritten note from LBJ. He said, "I agree. I'm strong for both of you as well as the panther."

The following memo is the type that rises up to haunt you!

THE WHITE HOUSE

MEMORANDUM October 20, 1964

To: The President
From: Liz

Did you know that Peter Hurd got his beginning as a WPA artist? One of his paintings has been stored in a government warehouse. Nash Castro found it and wondered if you would like to see it?

Yes__X__ No____ (checked by LBJ)

Newswomen insisted on following Mrs. Johnson everywhere, including the Virgin Islands where she planned to make a thirty-minute speech to the College of the Virgin Islands and then disappear for a well-earned vacation into the cottage of Laurance and Mary Rockefeller at Caneel Bay. Under these circumstances, the role of the First Lady's press secretary was to set up the trip in such a way that the press would be on one island and the First Lady on another. Any other obstacles or accommodations handed out in good humor were generally helpful and diversionary.

THE WHITE HOUSE

MEMORANDUM

To: Reporters following the First Lady to the Virgin Islands
From: Liz

Notice:

You have just been chosen to advance Liz Carpenter's fall vacation. Anything you can "lay on" that's legal and enjoyable during your forays around the islands will be appreciated.

In case you have to call Bess Abell, her number is 774-9218. This telephone extension is located several fathoms below the surface of the Caribbean where she will be skin-diving, but happy to answer all questions except, "Who designed the bathing suit?"

Have fun, and if the joy juice that Mack Mitchell serves you just as you have filed the last word of the commencement speech seems a little strong, it is only because that's the way the Voodoo Queen and I worked it up.

Much later, when the President flew around the world, winding up at the Vatican where he presented the Pope with a gift, it caused quite a stir. Those of us who had been reading a series of memos between the military and the President's assistant, James Jones, knew that another present had been contemplated which would have been much worse.

The exact memoranda on this event are as follows:

THE WHITE HOUSE

MEMORANDUM

To: Jim Jones
From: Haywood Smith (Marine Aide to the President)

A suggestion has been made that the President might like to forward to the Pope a container of melted snow that fell during the lifetime of Christ. As you may recall, this snow was recently discovered by the Antarctic Expeditionary Force, has been melted, and is being held by the Navy Department.

I think this is something the President might like to do. Would you please give me your thoughts on the feasibility of this recommendation?

THE WHITE HOUSE

MEMORANDUM July 19, 1965

To: Harry McPherson
From: Jim Jones

Seriously, what is your recommendation on this?
Attachment

THE WHITE HOUSE

MEMORANDUM

To: Jim Jones
From: Harry McPherson

I think Protestants might object to this. It would suggest that the Protestants believe the Papacy to be the sole repository of Christ's heritage. There are plenty of Christian relices in the Vatican, but they are associated with the development of the early Church. Snow from Antarctica isn't in that category. You might as well send the Pope a box of dirt from an ancient Indian mound.

Besides, imagine the *Daily News* headline: PRESIDENT SNOWS POPE.

THE WHITE HOUSE

MEMORANDUM

To: Colonel Haywood Smith
From: Jim Jones

I think this answers your inquiry.
Attachment.

Often the battles behind the White House doors revolve around expense money. In an economy move, it is the East Wing that suffers first. Marvin Watson was the economy devil in the Johnson Administration. Short and Rotarian in his good looks, he had an unorthodox trait. He treated the taxpayers' money as though it were his own—demanding efficiency, thrift and other unheard of virtues in Washington. It was his task to cut down on all possible expenses, and he started by cancelling multiple newspaper subscriptions for my office. My violent threats met, however, with a surrender from Marvin, for reasons obvious in the memo.

THE WHITE HOUSE

MEMORANDUM July 19, 1965

To: Marvin
From: Liz

I returned from Texas to discover what I am sure is an oversight. You have cut off our newspapers. To cut off the newspapers of a press office is so ridiculous, it must be a mistake.

We read them for our link with the world—to know how the First Family is faring in print—and to clip them for three sets of scrapbooks: (1) for Mrs. Johnson, (2) for Lynda and (3) for Luci.

As you may not be aware, First Ladies get very little consideration. They have no salary. They have no military transportation. They still must fulfill commitments in a demanding way to help the President.

We have some 50 hungry, eager reporters who cover this side of the house on a daily basis and write about it. We think we do a pretty good job in keeping the ship of state steady on this side.

We need all three Washington papers, *The New York Times,* the *Chicago Tribune* on a prompt daily basis to do it.

Do you put this press office back on the list—or do I take up whoring to pay for it?

Next morning the papers were there!

THE WHITE HOUSE

MEMORANDUM

To: Marvin
From: Liz

To be greeted by those newspapers when I walked in the office this morning was sheer heaven.

Thank you for saving a middle-aged woman from a life of sin.

Coordinating statements between the East and West Wings of the White House was always somewhat difficult, but it was almost impossible when Bill Moyers was press secretary to the President. Most often, he was unavailable by phone to everyone except the President, so memos became essential and I tried not to waste any words.

THE WHITE HOUSE

MEMORANDUM

To: Bill Moyers
From: Liz

You are no longer just my Bill!

Why didn't you let me have a look at the President's Head Start remarks as promised? Only by being my usual alert self was I able to find out five minutes before the President spoke and be able to get in a one-line commercial for the national chairman, his wife.

What goes on over there in the West Wing that

is so worthwhile you can't tend to these little details?

In reply Bill wrote in red ink, "My face is as red as my ink! I'm sorry. I goofed."

Another example of poor communication between the East and West Wings occurred over the dinner for Princess Margaret—one of the most elegant parties of the Johnson Administration.

THE WHITE HOUSE

MEMORANDUM

To: Bill Moyers
From: Liz

Gad! It is really embarrassing—and probably costs us the cover of *Life* magazine—that your office released party pictures of the President and Princess Margaret to the wire services.

My office had arranged for ALL media to have a picture made in the Queen's Room. We left the other shots (dining room, etc.) for *Life*'s exclusive coverage.

So, for the future, to keep things coordinated could ALL members of your staff please check with us before releasing any pictures having to do with social events, the coverage of which, by pencil and picture, is the responsibility of THIS office.

Our occasional differences notwithstanding, I sent up a plea for help when Luci's wedding came around and sought to borrow Tom Johnson, Bill Moyer's assistant.

THE WHITE HOUSE

MEMORANDUM

To: Bill Moyers
From: Liz

I would like to ask for Tom Johnson's hand for the week beginning August first through the sixth. This is not a scandal, but I need him because at this point we've got to be "managing" photographers and press at some of the events concerning Pat Nugent. Up to now I have treated Pat as a suitor and, therefore, all questions about him are off bounds. But beginning then, to prevent a melee, I think we had better have someone on hand to arrange for the picture at the bachelor dinner or the rehearsal dinner.

So, if I could borrow him to help with all the "bodies" it would be a great help to me.

Yes, he's yours X
No, he's mine ____

Tom was lent to the East Wing for the duration, and he quickly became our pin-up boy. But Bill reconfiscated him as soon as the last grain of rice was thrown.

Security at the White House is always a concern, and our file cabinets and desks were checked each night to see that no confidential papers were left out, or secret file drawers left unlocked. If they were, you received a sharp reprimand and, on occasion, secretaries have been banished from the White House. One classic exchange on the subject occurred between Marvin Watson and Dick Goodwin, a speechwriter for President Johnson. In a memo, Marvin noted that Goodwin's file cabinet had been found open after midnight for the third time, and asked him and his secretary to please remember to lock the safe. Goodwin's reply, which was widely circulated among the staff as the laugh for the day, is as follows:

THE WHITE HOUSE

ABSOLUTELY CONFIDENTIAL

MEMORANDUM May 19, 1965

To: Marvin Watson
From: Dick Goodwin

Perhaps due to inexperience, you have rather clumsily spoiled one of the most skillful espionage operations in the history of the American government. Every few weeks a number of documents classified top secret are placed in my file cabinet. These documents contain information which is deliberately misleading. Then I usually invite someone from the Russian Embassy over for a nightcap. At an appropriate moment (around 12:45 A.M.) I say I have to go over to the Mansion and leave. The result of this has been a series of Soviet and Chinese diplomatic blunders of the first magnitude. However I am afraid you have—inadvertently, I am sure—destroyed this ingenious offensive against the communists. Don't feel badly, however, we'll find another trick.

In addition it is very rare that I am not here at 12 midnight and later. Your security officer insists on coming in when I am in the bathroom. In fact, I think they use that peephole over the second floor washbasin just so they can sneak in and find a security violation.

However, even though we are completely blameless, I have informed my secretaries of your wishes. They said, "If Marvin wants it, we will do it." But don't worry, I won't tell your wife—it'll stay a secret between the boys.

NEVER AGAIN!

Dogs prompted occasional memoranda. During the lifetime of Him, the President's beagle, we received steady mail about the dog which Luci had made famous. On one occasion the dog was invited to make a personal appearance, and I had to go to the President about it.

THE WHITE HOUSE

MEMORANDUM

To: The President
From: Liz

If you need a laugh, this is it. Senator Ross Bass wants you to lend him "Him" to parade at the halftime of the football game between Tennessee and South Carolina. The student body of the University of Tennessee made this request of the Senator. They want "Him" to parade down the football field with their mascot, a hound dog.

THE WHITE HOUSE

MEMORANDUM

To: Liz
From: Bill Moyers

The President says no. He was amused, but "Him" has a full schedule.

One of the regular duties of my office was to release occasional White House recipes to the press, or to anyone who wrote in and requested one. If the recipes didn't turn out (which frequently happened), we would hear about it. I was always suspicious that Zephyr Wright, a cook of the "just a pinch of this and a handful of that" school, was holding out on us. Zephyr remains one of the great cooks of the world by *not* divulging her recipes entirely.

But we couldn't blame the Big Pound Cake Failure on Zephyr, since it was not her recipe. According to our infuriated housekeeper, Mary Kaltman, the great failure was caused by the stupidity of housewives. It was prompted when we released the ingredients of Lynda's wedding cake—a pound cake.

THE WHITE HOUSE

MEMORANDUM January 23, 1968

To: Liz Carpenter
From: Mary Kaltman

The correspondence office tells me they are receiving many complaints on pound cakes which have fallen. I have now given them a mimeographed sheet suggesting that the size of the pan may be the reason. Actually, most of these women can't cook and that is the biggest basic reason why the cakes are failures. Everybody in the whole world who knows anything about cooking knows you bake pound cake in a loaf pan or a small square pan.

How basic do you have to get with the recipe? Do you begin with "Open the cupboard door and remove a pan. If there are other pans on top of the pan you want, remove those pans before you try to remove the pan you need, otherwise there will be a great crash of pans and your cupboard will become disarranged?"

I seriously recommend and plead with the press office to make a new policy wherein we do not—repeat not—release any more recipes. Especially in an election year. I have the feeling that tapioca recipe, coupled with this pound cake recipe, have cost the Democrats plenty of votes.

THE WHITE HOUSE

MEMORANDUM January 23, 1968

To: Mary Kaltman
From: Liz

I loved your note, but I disagree with the conclusion. The way to a voter's heart *is* through his stomach, and we have to reach for those gaping food pages each Thursday like Nancy Reagan, Lenore Romney and—hold your breath—Happy Rockefeller are doing.

I have some suggestions: (1) Write (because you are so clever) an amusing disclaimer for the results of some wedding cake attempts—i.e., cook at your own risk because the temperature and sea level in Washington differ from town to town.

(2) Let's test the accuracy of the recipes and be absolutely sure of what we are using; i.e. don't tell a lay cook like me to use powdered sugar if you mean super fine granulated sugar.

(3) Let's get some recipes that are both elegant and buffet type—leave out the Western—and make

them fit for the global American, as the London Economist says the President is.

We could make some good points and now is the time. You could even go down in history, Mary, as the Kook of the Kitchen.

Thanking people for various kindnesses—gifts, favorable new stories, parties and luncheons became a time-consuming task. So I devised an all-purpose checklist which would fit almost any situation, including a few mythical ones. Once after Merriman Smith had written some very funny gags for a speech I was making, I sent him such a checklist:

THE WHITE HOUSE

MEMORANDUM

To: Merriman Smith
From: Liz Carpenter

You are an angel and I want to thank you for

____ The lifetime subscription to Women's Wear Daily.
____ The favorable clippings.
____ The libelous clippings.
____ Picking up the check.
____ The brilliant broadcast.
____ Voting Democratic.
____ The bottle of My Sin.
____ Your perceptive reporting.
_X_ The absolutely hilarious gags.
____ The foreign aid.
____ Letting me steal your ideas.
____ A Miracle Morning at Elizabeth Arden's.

____ The favorable mention.
____ The bottle of champagne.
____ The autographed picture of Stokley Carmichael.
____ The Peter Hurd original.
____ The quote.
__X__ Your kind words.
____ The beagle pup.
____ Keeping your mouth shut.
____ The wilted azaleas.
____ The tree.
____ The memories.
__X__ Being you.
____ Your wretched complaint.
____ An enchanted evening, an enchanted morning.
____ Nothing.

But he replied with a torrid memo that put my checklist to shame:

THE OFFICE

To: Liz
From: Merriman Smith
Re: Yours of the 18th

____ I didn't say a word about your being frigid. All I said was that you yawn a lot.
____ WHAT husband?
__X__ Make it in small denomination bills.
____ All mail and phone calls to the office. Otherwise, letters get all mixed up at home with the bills and garden club notices and we wouldn't want that to happen, would we?
____ Tell him it's your bowling night.

____ If you got the pills mixed up with the aspirin, I'd say in all fairness that's YOUR problem.

_X_ The Lotus Restaurant closed years ago. Think of another place.

____ I'm no prude but damned if I think Shirley Highway at 5 P.M. is the place or time for *anything.*

____ Deny it.

____ Admit it, but chuckle while you do it.

____ Let Hubert march with them.

_X_ Let Dr. Hornig explain it. Then nobody'll ever know.

____ Send him to Rostow. It can't *hurt.*

____ This definitely is not a matter for George Christian. He's taken to answering questions lately.

_X_ You're kind to think of it.

____ Only if Rusk is in town, which sort of rules it out.

Perhaps it was this kind of activity which prompted one of the more straight-laced staff members, secretary to Marvin Watson who was an ardent Baptist, to decide that the White House needed religion. A mimeographed notice went around to all White House staff members:

> A prayer group for both men and women will be meeting in the Fish Room every Thursday morning at 7:30 A.M. You are most welcome to join us any morning that your schedule will allow. The session will begin with a Scripture reading and/or comments by the reader and others in the group who so desire. This will be followed by a quiet time and spoken prayers according to the wishes of the participants.

> There will be no further notices unless there is a change in the meeting date or hour.

There was no further notice, but the early morning prayer meeting was never standing room only.

For some strange reason, I was the channel for peculiar requests to the President:

> THE WHITE HOUSE
>
> MEMORANDUM
>
> To: The President
> From: Liz
>
> Drew Pearson invites you to come out on June 8 or 9 to his farm where he will be entertaining 2,000 Holstein dairy raisers from all over the U.S. He thinks it would be terrific if you would make a speech on a bale of hay–a la LBJ Ranch–and let these men meet a real cattleman. He'll have it either date for you.

The message came back with this tart reply: "No. Tell him not to count on me. (signed) LBJ"

I have an old college friend, Maury Maverick Jr., one of the more unorthodox Democrats, who was a frequent letter writer, and unsolicited advice-giver. He took this liberty because our ancestors had known each other in the early days of Texas and as he said, "We have been close friends for 135 years." My widely publicized war with *Women's Wear Daily* in the middle of Luci's wedding plans prompted this brief note: "Don't lose your cool over that dress. Your great-great-grandfather at the Alamo had it worse."

Naturally this provoked a response from me:

THE WHITE HOUSE

MEMORANDUM July 22, 1966

To: Maury
From: Liz

The Alamo was a mere skirmish compared to what I've been through. In the words of the immortal Travis:

"I am beseiged by a thousand or more—I have sustained continual bombardment and cannonade for 24 hours and have not lost a man. The enemy has demanded a surrender—I have answered the demand with a cannon shot and our flag still waves proudly from the walls. I shall never surrender or retreat.

"The enemy is receiving reinforcements daily and will no doubt increase to 3 or 4,000 in four or five days. If this call is neglected, I am determined to sustain myself for as long as possible and die like a soldier who never forgets what is due to his own honor and that of his country—victory or death."

The world is full of people who want desperately to work at the White House. One of the most persistent was a nice, cleancut young man who helped us on the Whistlestop trip through the South. So I tried to give him a boost.

THE WHITE HOUSE

MEMORANDUM

To: Jack Valenti
From: Liz

Jim Jones, an attractive young man with real ability at orderly office work would like to work at the White House. He ranks along with Marvin Watson for talent.

Steady, calm, able, he's the kind of man you're proud to have around.

THE WHITE HOUSE

MEMORANDUM

To: Liz
From: Jack Valenti

Marvin Watson is giving your friend, Jim Jones, a job beginning next week.

But, as I had learned, "No good deed goes unpunished." It took only a few brief weeks in the White House before Mr. Jones was in charge of approving my "per diems." Many of them were returned with a crisp, "No."

When we were planning a trip through Texas, our advance woman, Cynthia Wilson, called in from Gonzales, Texas, and dictated a memo to my secretary.

To: Liz April 1, 1968
From: Cynthia

Everything is going well here. We don't need to worry about the covered-dish lunch. We'll have enough food to feed an army. (In fact, I've gained five pounds in the three days I've been here. Your sister, Alice, is giving me room and *too much* board—two desserts every night.) All the local groups are going to bring their best home-grown, home-cooked dishes, including five kinds of potato salad. The Thompsonville Wolf Hunters Association is going to provide picnic tables. Believe it or not, that's the name of the club.

I explored Palmetto State Park, after I went to J. C. Penney's and bought a pair of sneakers. I think Mrs. Johnson will enjoy a walk through it, but tell her to bring old shoes because it's soggy. The park rangers are going to walk through the paths just before we do, and scare away all the rattlesnakes.

The Western Union lines were put in, but we had a hard rain and the river rose 14 feet and washed them out. However, I have been assured that they will be fixed in time. I hope so, since there are no phones in the park.

Some ranchers (ardent Democrats) who live outside of town want us to drive by and see their prize cattle—which are named Lynda, Luci and Lady Bird. The prize bull is named LBJ. They have a nice field of bluebonnets too, but I think we'll skip that stop. Note: Better warn the press that this is a DRY—repeat—DRY county. Everything else is okay. The

> whole town is excited that the First Lady is coming, and everyone in the county will be at our little ceremony in the courthouse square.

One time I wrote the following memo to Cliff Carter, who was in Atlantic City advancing the Democratic National Convention of 1964.

> THE WHITE HOUSE
>
> MEMORANDUM
>
> To: Cliff Carter
> From: Liz Carpenter
>
> Don't just sit there. Think funny! Apparently most of the press is going to be housed in the most depressing kind of rooms—some you can only see at low tide. How about drafting a memo of welcome to them, getting humorous about the beastly situation? Something like, "If your accommodations don't suit you, at least you have the pleasure of associating with Democrats."

Apparently the memo never reached Cliff, because the press was very *unfunny* about their accommodations.

Offers of gifts to beautify Washington often crossed my desk:

THE WHITE HOUSE

MEMORANDUM

To: Mrs. Johnson
From: Liz

Polly and Jack Logan want to give some crepe myrtle trees to your beautification program because Polly thinks "they are a Southern tree and they are being ignored." Shall we tell her, "As far as this President and his wife are concerned we value the Southern crepe myrtle"—a la Whistlestop?

In reply, Mrs. Johnson wrote back on my memo, "Set up an appointment. Sounds good."

Returning from a trip always creates confusion with baggage, and when we came back from Central America I wound up at home with a strange walkie-talkie.

THE WHITE HOUSE

MEMORANDUM

To: Charles Maguire
From: Liz

When I woke up this morning and found your walkie-talkie in my bedroom, it came as a big shock to me and a greater one to my husband.

My humor group labored long and hard to produce jokes that the President might incorporate into his speeches. If he didn't use our jokes, naturally we, being prima donnas, blamed someone else.

THE WHITE HOUSE

MEMORANDUM

To: The President
From: Liz

Mr. President, I have the feeling someone is coming between us.

For instance, did you read those glorious, sure-fire gags I wrote for you for the Governors' meeting?

He never replied.

Luci's romance, marriage and then her potential motherhood prompted constant inquiries and the need for frequent checking.

THE WHITE HOUSE

MEMORANDUM

To: Helene Lindow

From: Liz

Helen Thomas of the UPI keeps insisting that Pat and Luci are expecting. Can you ask her and let me settle this?

THE WHITE HOUSE

MEMORANDUM

To: Liz
From: Helene

Luci is NOT with child!

This is the word as of September 23, 1966, 5:45 Eastern Standard Time.

Perhaps this just points up that the accuracy of memoranda was a fleeting thing.

# *Exit Smiling*

There I was, five years later, still minding *everybody's* business and thoroughly enjoying it. The date was March 31, 1968, and I was at home watching the President's televised speech. Like the rest of the country, I couldn't believe what I was hearing: "Accordingly, I will not seek, and I will not accept the nomination of my party for another term as your President."

I grabbed the phone, punched the White House button, and asked the operator for Mrs. Johnson. By now the speech was over, and I reached her in the small sitting room just off the President's office.

Her voice was quiet, unemotional, and I could sense a desire to reassure those who questioned the decision: "Oh, Liz, you were so much on my mind, and I knew you would be one of the most disappointed, but we have done a lot. There is still time to do a lot more, and maybe this is the only way to do it." She went on reassuring me. "These have been five marvelous years, especially because of the wonderful people we worked with. They have been grinding and soaring years, rugged and exciting."

I asked her if she had known of the decision before, and she replied, "I had not really known for sure until he read it, though I have lived with it for weeks. He earned a right to this decision, Liz, and, in the end, it was his."

For the next few hours I ran the whole gamut of emotion: shock, then overwhelming admiration for the President, and then, blind fury. I was ready to strangle the speechwriter, or whoever was around who might have talked him out of this decision but didn't.

Next morning when I got to my office, the first thing I saw was a stack of newly framed pictures of the Johnson family I had ordered, which were to be sent to the 1968 Johnson campaign headquarters. For weeks, I had been urging Mrs. Johnson to let us get organized. She had listened, and once agreed. "I don't mind losing, and I don't mind not running, but I do mind losing by not doing anything," she had said.

I was determined we were going to start doing something, and so were many others who kept phoning and urging us to get to work. On March 29—three nights before the announcement—I had gathered a small group of friends and White House staff at my home to talk about organizing women, Whistlestops and any campaign efforts to get the show on the road. Mrs. Johnson had dropped by and listened attentively.

Political organization for the forthcoming election had been muffled, but it had certainly existed. In early March the President had brought three of his most competent political lieutenants up from Texas to Washington: Cecil Burney, John Ben Shepperd and Culp Kruger. All were veterans of Johnson campaigns. They were already at work in the Watergate Hotel, and Marvin Watson was pulling the organization together from the Executive Office Building.

No one knows all the reasons for the President's decision, and historians will mull them over for years. Certainly, it had been an ugly winter for the President. Two Senators from his own party—Gene McCarthy and Bobby Kennedy—were running against him and denouncing him almost daily. The war in Vietnam dragged on, with only a flicker of light at the end of the tunnel.

Lynda had come back from California early on the morning of March 31 after a tearful goodbye to her husband—a Marine Captain en route to Vietnam. Luci and her husband, Pat, were spending their last days together in the White House before he, too, left for Vietnam.

Each day there was a fresh hurt in the news stories and political advertisements with the names of members of his old club—the U. S. Senate—who had deserted the President for one of his opponents. Certainly he must have asked himself when he came upon the Vance Hartkes, the Steve Youngs, Joe Clarks and Bill Fulbrights—men he had gone to the well with so often—why they couldn't do the same for him.

The temptation to resign was not new. Even in Senate days, he would occasionally talk about going back to Texas. As Vice President, he had wondered out loud with friends if he wouldn't be happier living at the ranch, perhaps lending a hand to better education in Texas, helping the small colleges he believed in so strongly. But those within his hearing, friends or aides, discouraged him, and really dismissed this line of conversation as "just talk," for, after all, didn't Lyndon Johnson just love politics?

He toyed with quitting even before the 1964 convention in Atlantic City. Again in 1965 when an operation gave him time to brood, he wanted to draw up papers of resignation. Aides talked him out of it, and chalked it up to post-operative depression. With each month, the problems and the abuse of the President mushroomed.

But retirement was never out of his mind. The President

had occasionally hinted at this desire to Vice President Humphrey. "You ought to be getting around the country and getting people to know you better," he said. He mentioned it to Secretary of State Dean Rusk, who also suggested to Humphrey that he get busy. "He just may not run, you know," Rusk told the Vice President long before the announcement was made.

"But I didn't take it seriously," Humphrey related to me later. "All of us in public office get kicked around and say to ourselves 'What the hell, I don't have to take that!'"

When election year of 1968 rolled around and the President went to Capitol Hill to make his State of the Union speech at the opening of Congress, he carried in his pocket a declaration of his plans to retire at the end of his term. Marvin Watson, standing on the House floor, knew about it and shook his head vigorously "no" when the President looked his way.

Even on the day of the announcement, there had been labored soul-searching. Sunday morning—March 31—the President summoned Horace Busby once more to come to the White House from his Maryland home. Busby had worked for Johnson many times in the past. He was a talented writer, particularly on statements of a philosophical nature. The President knew, too, that Busby's thinking coincided with his own, that, perhaps, the only way to make himself believed, to regain some control of public opinion, was to remove himself from the political arena.

Busby went to work on the second floor of the White House, again consulting with a file of drafts that had been written "in case," including one by Mrs. Johnson. Over in Harry McPherson's office in the West Wing, the final words were being put into the major part of the speech—a call for an end of the bombing in North Vietnam.

The President left them working, and went to church with

Luci and Pat Nugent, stopping by the apartment of the Vice President on his way back to the White House. There, he drew the Vice President aside and showed him the two pieces of paper.

"He showed me two endings for his speech," the Vice President recalls. "Ending number one was a very fine statement on the desire for peace and a call for unity. Ending number two, which he said he had considered for a long time, was his decision to retire at the end of his term."

The Vice President told him, "I hope you're not serious."

"It's the only way to make these skeptics believe I am serious about peace," the President said. "They are so bitter and willing to believe the worst about me."

The President warned Humphrey not to mention it to anyone, "not even to Muriel."

"I hope it will be ending number one," the Vice President said. "All of us take abuse from time to time."

"This is a necessity," the President replied. "It is the price we have to pay for those critics to make them believe in the seriousness of my purpose."

On his way out, the President hugged Muriel with such special fervor that she immediately sensed something was different. "What's wrong with the President?" she asked her husband the minute he had left.

The Vice President tried to dismiss it. "It's a very important speech he has tonight on Vietnam. There's nothing wrong."

"No," she said thoughtfully. "It is something more than that."

At the White House, there was a Sunday lunch and afterward, in the West Hall, the best conversation spot in the house, the President gathered his family, Busby, and the Arthur Krims, who were houseguests and close friends. He wanted to let them know what he had in mind. The statement was read aloud.

Arthur and Matilda Krim, shocked to learn such a decision was seriously under consideration, kept shaking their heads. Both girls, their husbands bound for Vietman, argued against it, perhaps because they felt there were many who, like their husbands, would still go to the well with him. Mrs. Johnson listened, and the gathering ended without anyone really certain how the speech would finally develop.

Five minutes before the speech began, Vice President Humphrey, now in Mexico City, and every Cabinet member received a phone call from Marvin Watson or one of his assistants: "The President wants you to know that tonight he will be announcing his retirement at the end of his term." After the phone call, the Vice President turned to his dinner companions—Ambassador Fulton Freeman and Mexico's President Diaz Ordaz—and said, "The President is going to make an important announcement. Let's watch it all."

But for those in the Oval Office with him, there was still uncertainty.

"I thought for a moment he wouldn't do it, even when he got to it," Luci said later that night. "You noticed he paused several moments before he started reading it."

After the President's detailed announcement about the bombing halt, television viewers saw him take a deep breath, wet his lips, and continue: "Fifty-two months and ten days ago in a moment of tragedy and trauma, the duties of this office fell upon me. I asked for your help and God's that we might continue America on its course, moving forward in new unity. Our reward will come in the life of freedom and peace and hope that our children will enjoy through the ages ahead.

"What we won when all our people united must not now be lost," he continued, "in suspicion, distrust and selfishness or politics among any of our people. Believing this as I do, I have concluded I should not permit the Presidency to become involved in the partisan divisions that are developing in this political year. With America's sons in the field far away, with America's future under challenge here at home, with our hopes and the world's hopes for peace in the balance every day, I do not believe that I should devote an hour or a day of my time to any personal partisan causes or any duties other than the awesome duties of this office, the Presidency of your country. Accordingly, I will not seek . . ."

The announcement caught everyone by surprise. Most of the country, like me, were in pajamas. Senator Eugene McCarthy learned about it after he finished a campaign speech in a small auditorium in Wisconsin; Senator Robert F. Kennedy, flying back from campaign speeches in New Mexico and Arizona, heard the news on landing in New York.

Perhaps the most stunned of all was a group of 56 Young Democrats for Johnson who had just landed in Milwaukee and headed by bus to the Johnson headquarters. They were going to make a two-day crash effort to help the President defeat McCarthy in Tuesday's Wisconsin primary. Someone rushed out from headquarters and shouted, "The President is not running! The President has just announced he is not running!" For a minute there was total silence, then a mass rush to get to the TV sets inside and see the replay.

"We decided that no matter what had happened in Washington, we were going to go on out and campaign anyway," Stuart Ross, one of the Young Democratic leaders, recalls. "So at 5 A.M. next morning, we were out at plant entrances, asking people to help persuade the President to stay in. There was tremendous sympathy for him. Everyone was asking, 'Might he change his mind?' And, even though the announcement had been made, 34 percent of the vote was cast for Johnson that day."

Why did he do it? There were those who said he quit

because Bobby Kennedy ran him out of the race. There were those who said it was the only way he could make his efforts for peace in Vietnam credible. There were those who said he did not believe the country could endure the bitterness of a vicious campaign and make any headway along the precipice of peace. So he—like his sons-in-law—was willing to go the ultimate and lay down his political life for his country. There were even those who said that the joys of being a grandfather, which he had recently discovered with little Lyn, were a factor. He had given thirty-four years of life to public service, burdens, deadlines and decisions and, as Mrs. Johnson said, he earned a right to retire.

Whatever the reason, or mixture of them, certainly the President had gone to the well to regain a united public opinion, without which, even Presidents are helpless.

In the months that followed, each time Mrs. Johnson passed the gaunt portrait of Woodrow Wilson which hangs in the Red Room, her faith in the rightness of his decision was confirmed. "When I see that picture, I see what a toll the Presidency takes on a man," she told me.

All the rest of us looked back—it was only human—on how it might have been different. Much had been done in those five years. There was irony in the evidence.

Wasn't it ironic that the man who engineered and delivered the first Civil Rights Act in a hundred years had been the man with the drawl whose closest political allies were the Southern bloc of Senators?

Wasn't it ironic that the man who launched an education revolution that was producing a new college every week, who stepped up education at every level, was the graduate of a little teachers' college in San Marcos, Texas?

Wasn't it ironic that the President who made Uncle Sam the angel of the arts for the first time in history was the man who probably never saw a great painting—except on the front of a Masterpiece school tablet—until long after he was an adult?

Wasn't it ironic that it was the "rich Texan with the fat-cat friends," as the critics loved to say, who fought the war on poverty on the front lines of the ghetto with Head Start and the Job Corps?

Wasn't it ironic that the press, the freest press in the world and, therefore, surely the most perceptive, never really covered the whole story?

Perhaps if he had been cut of a different cloth—another more stylish (wasn't that what they always clamored for?), less open in his likes and dislikes, a man who was more orderly about his daily schedules, a man who operated in smaller terms easily understood—

Perhaps if there had been no Vietnam—

And, finally, the thought kept recurring: maybe the man with "The Long Arm" occasionally needed a hand extended to *him.*

Perhaps if there had been some public words of encouragement from the bereaved family after the assassination . . . He never mentioned it, but being a woman and a partisan, I was conscious of the silence.

Lyndon Johnson had come on stage before a black curtain, and the Kennedys made no move to lift the darkness for him, or for the country. He had gone to the well for them so many times. "Lyndon would like to take all the stars in the sky and string them on a necklace for Mrs. Kennedy," his wife said softly in the dreadful days that followed Dallas.

But the Kennedys looked at the living and wished for the dead and made no move to comfort the country.

From the morning of April first on until January 20, the momentum of the White House was high pitched. Within sixty hours after the announcement, there was just the hint of hope—the first small break in the long diplomatic stalemate as Hanoi agreed to establish contact to see what else might be arranged.

Telegrams and letters and phone calls of goodwill and best wishes for the President came by the truckload. The public wanted one more of everything—one more autographed picture, one more invitation to the White House, one more chance to see the President while he was in office, one more tree-planting, one more bill for education, one more speech at every sort of gathering.

And the White House staff began its slow exodus to other jobs—in business, in the Humphrey, McCarthy or Kennedy campaign camps.

"Not since the girls' weddings, not since Eartha Kitt's performance have we had such a heavy workload," I groaned.

And, it seemed as the summer came, that everyone on the staff had become pregnant.

"Right after your speech on March 31," I told the President, "half the women in this house went off The Pill."

He burst into laughter and repeated it everytime he saw one of them. But it was true. Many of the young married women had delayed starting their families because for four years they had been too busy and they wanted to be a part of the campaign in 1968. Now, there was no campaign, so why not?

The President, in typical fashion, decided he wanted to hold a "few" more gatherings, too. He held small farewell parties for staff who were leaving, and began a heavy schedule of receptions.

"I just don't want to go back to Texas without having people like Ray Dwiggins in this house while I'm President," he said. And so, at the most sentimental gathering of his Administration, all the Texans who had been so much a part of his early career came to Washington for a dinner on the White House lawn.

We threw ourselves into planning one more trip for Mrs. Johnson, from coast to coast, with stops at Cape Kennedy in Florida, New Orleans and Denver, and winding up in the Redwood National Park in California. It was one more "last hurrah," and the trip ended with the press serenading the First Lady with a tearful "Auld Lang Syne."

Events toppled on top of one another—an emergency appendectomy for me, Christmas planning for the White House, more Christmas gifts than ever from the Johnsons to the staff, and holiday open houses from December 1 until January. Then came conferences with the new Nixon staff, helping our replacements get acquainted.

Inevitably, the men with the empty cardboard cartons came, the family pictures on the walls came down, leaving those ugly discolored squares where each had hung. The sorting began—five years of papers, notes, memos, souvenirs. There were clippings and press releases scattered untidily, a half-empty box of Metrecal cookies. (*That* was certainly a lost cause.) A broken hourglass with all the sand, every grain of it, gone, my favorite picture of Mrs. Johnson—smiling and waving to the crowd as the Whistlestop train pulled out of Raleigh, North Carolina.

We packed and packed, laughed a lot and cried a little. Down in Bess's office, she opened the wine supply—a little earlier each day. One of the Nixon people, an immaculately dressed, stiff-necked, efficient military aide on the transition staff, looked at the wine-sipping secretaries, drew one aside and asked in disbelief, "Do they drink like this all the time?"

She replied gravely and, of course, it was a lie: "Yes, everyday. It has been just like this for five years."

He beat a hasty retreat to his office and never looked up again.

On January 19, the President and Mrs. Johnson asked sixty of us for a "last supper" very much "family" with the two girls and their babies—little Lyn and Lucinda almost three months old. We danced, ate and talked, telling our favorite stories. No one wanted to leave that evening. Finally, it was almost midnight, and one by one we left, but Les and I walked out on the Truman Balcony to feast our eyes once more on that magnificent view—the glistening white dome of the Jefferson Memorial and the Washington Monument, standing like an exclamation mark, both lighted through the night.

Next morning, the Nixons and the Agnews and their families arrived at 11 A.M. The President was still signing letters on his pale green stationery. He would chat a while with the Nixons in the Red Room, then dash into the Blue Room where Jim Jones had a stack of letters waiting and sign a few. There were a few more honorary appointments to be made, nothing monumental, but he was still President. I walked into the Blue Room just as he was in the middle of issuing some orders. He caught a glimpse of me, and I heard him say to Jim Jones, "And put Les Carpenter on the Board of Visitors of the Naval Academy."

"Les was in the Navy, wasn't he?" the President rattled on to me.

"Yes, sir, and I'm sure he would be very honored to serve," I replied.

I could hardly wait to tell Les, and I laughed all the way back to my office. Pure Johnson, I thought. So like him—and I loved it. Les was in my office waiting to watch the Inauguration on my TV set. We had wanted to be together.

"Guess what?" I said. "The President of the United States has just named you to the Board of Visitors of the Naval Academy."

"The hell he has!" Les said.

"Yes, and when you are officially notified, accept!"

"But I don't want to be on the Board of Visitors," he said. "I didn't really like the Navy at all. I could hardly wait to get out of it."

"That's good," I said. "You will make an excellent member of the Board of Visitors."

I raced back to the steps of the North Portico to help set up the pictures of the departure of the two families.

First the two Presidents came out, then the two Vice Presidents, then the two First Ladies and Tricia and Julie and David Eisenhower, Luci and Lynda. They got into the long line of black limousines for the ride to the Capitol where the oath of office would be administered and the 37th President would be sworn in.

The President shook hands, gave several of us a hug and was off. As we watched the back of Mrs. Johnson's car, with Pat Nixon riding beside her, pull out of the driveway, Mrs. Johnson looked back and blew us a kiss.

Finally all the cars were gone, and we were left for one more hour. Just as I started back to my office, I noticed the familiar figure that made the transition complete. There stood Mr. Bryant, with *their* dogs. Yuki had gone out of office.

# *Meanwhile, Back to the Ranch*

A bitter January wind whipped across the airstrip at Andrews Air Force Base. The President waved one last time. The First Lady blew a kiss. The door of Air Force One closed snug. With a scream of the engines, the great plane swept down the runway and into the gray sky.

I watched, eyes fastened hungrily to savor every last minute of that day. Higher and higher—then only a speck. Finally, nothing but one last bit of jet trail blowing apart, and then nothing more. From this day on, they would always be known as the "former" President and the "former" First Lady, except to me.

All around me, people were in tears. There were familiar faces from across the years—friends from Capitol Hill (Republicans and Democrats), the Johnson Cabinet and staff—and hundreds of ordinary citizens who had come to say goodbye to the President.

Only then did I realize I was still clutching a placard which read, "Culpeper says, 'Thank you, Mr. President.'"

This was almost a private joke between the President, me and Culpeper, Virginia. Nine years before, as we whistlestopped through Culpeper, that tiny town turned out 6000 strong at the depot. Lyndon Johnson, campaigning for the Kennedy-Johnson ticket, stood on the back platform, brimming over with enthusiasm to the applause of those Virginia farmers who had come to town to cheer on the Democratic candidate.

As the train pulled out, he kept talking and he shouted over the loud speaker with boyish enthusiasm, "What did Dick Nixon ever do for Culpeper?"

There was a roar of laughter, and then an old farmer joined in the joke and shouted back, "Hell, what did anyone ever do for Culpeper?"

So on that January 20 when Lyndon Johnson was saying goodbye at the airport to the Presidency and thirty-four years in public office, while down on Pennsylvania Avenue Dick Nixon was leading the Inaugural Parade to the White House, the memory of Culpeper was about all I could muster up to make us laugh. The First Lady had glanced at my sign as she boarded and laughed, "You would, Liz!"

Not that there is anything wrong with Dick Nixon, if you can overlook the fact that he is a Republican. But it was the end of an exciting time in my life, and I was saying more than goodbye to a President. I was saying goodbye to the excitement of working in the White House.

My husband handed me a handkerchief and pulled me toward the black government Mercury, and we began the last ride home in it.

God bless him! He had stashed away a bottle of chilled Dom Perignon and two glasses for the occasion.

"Well, here's to the Great Society," I toasted.

"Here's to a girl from Salado, Texas," he replied, and added: "Think of all the good things about it. No more pressures, no more worrying if you've said the wrong thing. No more telephones ringing all night long. No more flying in bad weather. No more worrying about what *he* thinks."

No more fun, I thought dismally.

We pulled into the driveway of our home. I kissed the startled driver, a red-haired Army sergeant, goodbye.

"Miss me, dammit!" I said.

Les followed me into the house with the champagne.

My eyes lighted on the telephone and that White House button on it.

"I'm going to make one last call before they cut it off," I said, picking up the phone.

Too late. The umbilical cord had been cut. No more White House for me.

My home seemed strangely cold.

"The furnace doesn't work any more," my maid said. "Everything's broken down."

I wondered if the Republicans had turned them off, too.

Sure enough, all of our appliances which had held up so stoically through my time in the White House had quit. I dialed the electrician and prepared for a week of hand-to-hand combat and repairing.

Meanwhile, back at the ranch, Lyndon B. Johnson and his family—now private citizens—were landing. They had been met at a brief stop in Austin by 10,000 cheering people. Then they transferred to the smaller Jetstar for the flight to the LBJ Ranch, and there they found the most sentimental welcome of all. Strangers, old friends and kinfolk from up and down the Pedernales River had piled into their cars and come out to welcome Lyndon and Lady Bird home. He took his time now in greetings, stopping for a hug and a word with each of them. There was plenty of time now.

For the military, the "Operation: Deliver Ex-President" was almost completed. All the luggage was dumped in a big heap—

garment bags, hat boxes, suitcases tumbled together by the kitchen door. The steward checked the plane. Nothing more. The plane and its crew roared off.

It was dark and drizzly by the time Mrs. Johnson got to the big house. There, amid the piles of suitcases and boxes, she found her older daughter. Lynda, after considerable difficulty, had located two of her own bags and was struggling into the house with them!

Mrs. Johnson sat down on a suitcase, threw back her head and laughed, "The chariot has turned into a pumpkin, and all the mice have run away!"

Next day the President slept late. There was no ringing phone to stir him into action. In Washington, it rained all week, as it can only rain there–sideways, up and down, chilling to the bone.

The people who had shared those years with the First Family began sorting out their own lives. Some joined law firms and promptly sent out engraved announcements about it. Some canvassed the job markets in New York and Washington. Others went to universities, or back to their old jobs in business. Those who stayed on in government watched for the pink slips.

For all of them, when they met occasionally, the pain of withdrawal became a family joke.

"There ought to be a de-briefing period for the Cabinet," Willard Wirtz, the former Secretary of Labor, said. "It's too cruel to have that black limousine taken away all at once. Perhaps we could be given a pool car, and each of us share it at least twice a week until we got slowly used to being without it."

The former Secretary of Agriculture had a tale of woe. "The first time I drove myself to the airport," said Orville Freeman, "I couldn't find it. I rode all over Washington and Virginia. And when I did get there, I had missed my plane."

All through February and March, it rained. All those weeks, I sat in my upstairs study and wrote, trying to recapture and relive every minute. And then, quite suddenly, the sun was out. Spring was here. Along the Potomac, drifts of Mrs. Johnson's daffodils began to show their golden heads. The parks throughout the great city were ablaze with red and yellow tulips.

The busloads of children came, from all across the country—now and then a Head Start group, now and then a cluster of well-scrubbed students from a small community college.

One late afternoon, a taxi driver bringing me home was cheerfully unfolding the story of his life. "Two years ago they opened these adult education classes, and I signed up. Tonight, I get my high school diploma. This is my last run, lady. Tomorrow I'm gettin' a better job."

The Johnsons had left their mark.

*Notice to Congress,*
*members of the Great Society, the press*
*and all Americans everywhere:*

Due to the intense desire of the author to sell every book possible, no index has been included. You will have to buy and hunt for your name.

Good luck!